THE FIRST LOVE STORY

THE
FIRST
LOVE
STORY

Adam, Eve, and Us

BRUCE FEILER

R A N D O M   H O U S E
LARGE PRINT

Published in the United States of America by Random House Large Print in association with Penguin Press, an imprint of Penguin Random House LLC, New York.

COVER DESIGN BY CHRISTOPHER BRIAN KING

COVER IMAGES: (FRONT) BORCHEE/GETTY IMAGES; (SPINE, TOP) MAKS NARODENKO/SHUTTERSTOCK; (SPINE, BOTTOM) IAN 2010/SHUTTERSTOCK

The Library of Congress has established a Cataloging-in-Publication record for this title.

ISBN: 978-1-5247-5621-5

www.randomhouse.com/largeprint

FIRST LARGE PRINT EDITION

Printed in the United States of America

10 9 8 7 6 5 4 3 2 1

This Large Print edition published in accord with the standards of the N.A.V.H.

For Andrew and Laura

Love is our true destiny.
We do not find the meaning of life
by ourselves alone—we find it
with another.

—THOMAS MERTON

CONTENTS

THE FIRST LOVE STORY

INTRODUCTION

THE FIRST COUPLE

Why Adam and Eve Still Matter

W E HEAR A LOT of stories about individuals these days. One person. One hero. One genius. One gunman.

This is not one of those stories.

This is the story about two people. Learning to be together. Learning to live as one.

And it's the story, it seems, we were meant to hear first. Because if you go back to the very beginning—we're talking Garden of Eden beginning—the story you'll find there doesn't begin with one person. It begins with two.

Yet that story of togetherness is not what we usually remember. Because of all the things we're told were present in that garden—man, woman, serpent, sex, temptation, deception, sin, death—the thing that's most important usually doesn't make the list.

Yet it's the thing that's most critical for us to survive. It's the antidote to all the suffering the story says plagued us then—loneliness, isolation, anxiety, fear—and that plagues us even more today. It's the essence, the story insists, of what it means to be human.

It's love.

Yes, love—mysterious, lustful, painful, beautiful, exhausted, strained, resilient, triumphant.

That's the real story of the Garden of Eden, yet it's the story we somehow neglect to hear.

This book is the story of how we forgot that message, and the story of how we can reclaim it again.

This is the story of Adam and Eve.

The first love story.

The story we never tell.

WHEN MY IDENTICAL TWIN DAUGHTERS were a few years old, I went to a nursery to buy some plants for the front stoop of our home in Brooklyn. The attendant was a man with driftwood-coarse skin, white stubble, a widow's peak, and a black hole where his canine tooth was supposed to be, out of which stuck a gnawed toothpick. He had once been a groundskeeper at

Yankee Stadium. When I described the blustery conditions of our neighborhood, he perked up.

"What you need is a holly!" he said, and began wending me through the thicket.

Remembering my grandfather leading me through similar underbrush in Pin Point, Georgia, when I was a boy, looking for sexually compatible wisteria, I said, "But with hollies, don't you need a male and a female to berry?"

"Oh, don't worry," he said. "One male can take care of seven females."

"That's perfect," I said. "I have two daughters, a wife, a sister, a sitter, a mother, and a mother-in-law. I'm a holly!"

For more than a decade, I have lived largely in the company of women. At least in my house, that means certain conversations come up over and over again: girls and math, girls and coding, girls and body image, girls and bullying. (I'm ignoring the conversations about the deficiencies of dads.) In many ways, these topics reflect the larger conversations that my wife and I have every night and that most couples I know have in one way or another—men, women, and work; men, women, and power; men, women, and sex. But there's one conversation that I rarely hear about.

Men, women, and God.

As a father—especially one who cares about such old-fashioned things as values, service, and spirituality—the subject of faith is particularly fraught. On one hand, I would love nothing more than for my daughters to grow up with a healthy interest in spirituality, the freedom to explore what they really believe, and the sensitivity to live alongside others with whom they might disagree. On the other hand, given how organized religion has systematically, deliberately, often violently discriminated against women for centuries, can I rightly encourage them to find their voice in a world that has long tried to blot them out? Even more radical, can I possibly suggest to them—or to myself, for that matter—that something as staunchly lopsided toward the sexes as religion has anything to say about relationships today?

And yet we need all the help we can get. It's hardly daring to suggest that we live in a time of great confusion over how we relate to others. We're all so busy looking at our screens 24-7 that we've forgotten how to look at the people directly in front of us. Instead of being drawn closer together by the advances of modern life, we seem to be being pulled further apart. Our most basic bonds of community, family, even civility appear to be fraying. In our hyperconnected world we have a crisis of connection.

Add to that, the last generation has seen breathtaking shifts in what it means to be in a long-term relationship with another human being. The simplest rules of who we pair up with, who does what within our relationships, and how long we agree to stay together are being rewritten every day. That includes more women working outside the home, more men helping out inside the home, and more of everyone grappling with the definitions of togetherness, happiness, and a meaningful life. Marriage rates have plummeted; divorce rates have become entrenched; nothing seems fixed anymore.

The Internet has made a complicated situation even more unsettled, with whole new ways to hook up, break up, or simply hole up by yourself. With sexting, infidelity apps, and online porn, once taboo subjects like polyamory, open relationships, and other types of "consensual nonmonogamy" are exploding. Sexuality has become so ubiquitous and nakedness so commonplace that even **Playboy** stopped publishing nudes.

As a grown-up, I find these changes baffling

enough. As a parent, I'm downright afraid. And like many, I can't help wondering: Is there any wisdom from the past that can help us today? Has everything from the old days become outmoded? Or are there any values, lessons, or stories worth preserving?

In my own family, I struggle with these issues every day. My wife, Linda, has a fabulous but demanding career, which means I'm proud of her and the example she sets for our daughters, but I don't get to see her as much as I'd like. When we do get together, either by phone or at the end of a long day, we spend much of our time deciding who's supervising homework, who's taking the kids to their flu shots, and who's making plans to get away for the weekend when we'll all stare into devices in far more interesting places. And while I may be a statistical outlier in a world where women show greater interest in religion than men and take more responsibility for teaching values to their children, in my home I'm often the one who's insisting we reenact some bygone ritual or discuss some dated text. Especially in an era of neuroscience and nanotechnology, I still believe there's insight in timeworn truths. I tweet, but I Talmud, too.

All these issues came to a head unexpectedly

Michelangelo's Creation of Adam
in the Sistine Chapel.

one day when our eight-year-old girls and I tagged along with Linda on a business trip to Rome. On our first day, I had the brilliant idea to take our sleep-deprived daughters to the Vatican. See some art! Learn some culture! It didn't go well. As I tugged the girls through the tapestry-lined hallways of the museum, filled with stunning Greek nudes and Raphael frescoes, they were in full-on rebellion. "We hate carpets! My feet hurt. This is booooooring."

Finally we made it to the Sistine Chapel. I insisted they look down, led them to the center of the room, and finally said, "Look up." One of my daughters took one glance at the magisterial image of God, flying superherolike through the air, reaching his index finger toward a listless Adam, and said, "Why is there only a man? Where am I in that picture?" Her sister, meanwhile, not to be undone, pointed out something I had never seen before. "Who's that woman under God's arm? Is that Eve?"

And that's when it hit me.

At every stage of Western civilization for the last three thousand years, one story has stood at the center of every conversation about men and women. One story has served as the battleground for human relationships and sexual identity. One story has been both the ultimate source of division and a potential source of harmony in the history of the family. For some that story is a fantasy; for others it is a fact. But for everyone, it has enduring impact on how we live today.

It's the story of Adam and Eve.

Created fully grown, Adam and Eve have no history; they create history. Born without precedent, they become precedent for generations of their descendants. Married with little road map, they generate the road map that nearly every couple in the West has wrestled with in one way or another ever since.

And though few people acknowledge it, that wrestling continues. Many of today's most enduring social tensions—from equal pay to diaper duty, from sexual assent to same-sex marriage—have their roots in the Garden of Eden. No matter if you're a believer, a nonbeliever, a seeker, a meditator, an I-go-to-services-two-times-a-year-otherwise-leave-me-aloner, every part of your interaction with the opposite (or even the same) sex is shaped to an astonishing degree by a three-thousand-year-old story that has fewer than two thousand words.

If you're in a relationship with another person, you're in a relationship with Adam and Eve.

Even today you can't understand your love life, your home life, your spiritual life, or your sex life without understanding what happened in that garden "in the east" among Adam, Eve, the serpent, and God. And then what happened when centuries of religious leaders—99 percent of them men—manipulated the tale to further their own perversions and preserve their own power. Followed by the revelation of how new generations of leaders—many of them women—reinterpreted the story to highlight its more egalitarian themes.

I decided at that moment in the Sistine Chapel to revisit the tangled story of Adam and Eve. I would travel in the footsteps of the most famous couple in history—from the rivers of Mesopotamia to the birthplace of the women's movement, from John Milton's paradise to Mae West's Hollywood—and try to answer the question: Are Adam and Eve merely the cause of sin, degradation, and distrust between the sexes or might they be a source of unity, resilience, and, dare I say it, inspiration?

Can Adam and Eve be role models for relationships today?

. . . .

AT FIRST GLANCE, the idea that Adam and Eve are still relevant today seems absurd. For starters, many people simply dismiss the story. It's made up! It's a fairy tale! We're smarter now. We know better. And who can blame them? The story seems to take place in a fog of history. Despite centuries of searching, there is no evidence that any of the events in the Garden of Eden—or the rest of Genesis, for that matter— took place. And despite centuries of denial, there is overwhelming evidence that humans evolved in a way contrary to how Genesis describes. We know a lot more today about how the world was created, the origins of humanity, and the biological roots of being male and female. Who needs Adam and Eve anymore? We've moved on.

Even in the world of deeply religious believers, where I've spent a lot of time in recent decades, many view the story as allegorical. No less an authority than the fourth-century bishop St. Augustine, who built an entire theology around Adam and Eve, said that to view the story as verbatim was "childish." While he may have been ahead of his peers, the world eventually caught up. Over time, Adam and Eve became the forgotten patriarch and matriarch, having ceded the stage to their upstart descendants Abraham, Moses, David, and Jesus. They are civilization's doddering grandparents, taxidermied in some old-age home in Boca, rolled out a few times a year for family occasions, where they sit in the corner, ignored.

And it gets worse. Even those stalwarts who still acknowledge Adam and Eve have never forgiven them for ruining life for the rest of us. Adam and Eve are the opposite of role models; they're the first antiheroes. For thousands of years, they've been almost universally blamed for being selfish, unfaithful, lustful, disgraceful, and for single-handedly bringing shame, sin, immorality, even death into the world. Theirs was the original trial of the century, and the court of public opinion has been brutal. It's been conviction by sermon; death by a thousand midrash.

Actually, it's the biggest case of character assassination in the history of the world. As the modern plaint goes, "Where do I go to get my reputation back?"

Well, let's start here.

There are three principal reasons why Adam and Eve still matter and why they deserve our respect, even accolades.

First, they're part of who we are. The same

modern learning that has taught us about biology, psychology, and the power of the human mind has taught us that certain ideas, tropes, and symbols, what Jung called "anima," live deep within cultures and express themselves in powerful and unexpected ways. Stories are the chief ingredient of this shared tradition. Told and retold, stories are our social glue, our means of understanding the world, and our way of changing the world when we reinterpret them. Woven together, these shared stories become memes that form our cultural DNA.

Adam and Eve are the ultimate meme. For as long as our species has left traces, our most enduring stories have revolved around births, weddings, journeys, deaths—events associated with the beginnings and endings of social bonds. We are irredeemably connected to Adam and Eve because they constitute our earliest bond. Our family tree begins with them. They are the big bang of humanity. And that's true even if we don't happen to believe they existed exactly as the Bible says. We don't have to believe in Greek myths, for example, to believe they teach us something vital.

Certainly in the arena of relationships, thirty centuries of humanity have grappled with this story—that's a hundred and fifty generations. Think of nearly any major creative or intellectual figure in the last two thousand years; odds are good that they interacted with Adam and Eve in a meaningful way. That includes Michelangelo, Raphael, Rembrandt, Shakespeare, Milton, Mary Shelley, John Keats, William Wordsworth, Sigmund Freud, Mark Twain, Zora Neale Hurston, Ernest Hemingway, Bob Dylan, Beyoncé. The list goes on and on and on. It would take nothing less than complete arrogance to believe that our generation could simply erase this story from our mind like a massive cultural lobotomy.

As the dean of biblical archaeologists, Avraham Biran, once told me about Abraham, "I don't know if he existed then, but I know he exists now." The same applies to Adam and Eve. I don't know if they were alive in the Garden of Eden, but I know they've been alive outside of there for the last three millennia. To ignore them—to confine them to the curio closet or Creation Museum—is to ignore something vital about who we are.

Second, Adam and Eve still matter because they capture what remains a fundamental truth about being alive: Our biggest threat as individuals is feeling left out, isolated, fearful, alone;

our biggest threat as a society is succumbing to similar forces of disunion, disharmony, fear, hate. Look around, and by any measure our daily conversations are dominated by anxiety and confusion about the risk of disconnection and drifting apart, about the challenge of maintaining strong societal bonds; about concerns over the decay of our social fabric. Is our communal whole dissolving? Are we forgetting who we are?

The deep-seated human need for connectedness is the theme—maybe even the dominant theme—that runs throughout the story of Adam and Eve: from the very beginning, when God looks at Adam and says, "It's not right for humans to be alone"; to Eve's decision to share the fruit with Adam rather than risk living without him; to the first couple's painful choice about how to react to the unimaginable pain of having one of their children die at the hand of the other. Adam and Eve are constantly wrestling with whether they should remain together or break apart. God clearly wants them to find refuge in each other. The aching question of their story is whether they can find a way.

It took the rest of society three thousand years to catch up with this insight into being human.

In contemporary thought, Freud was among the first to write about the perils of feeling isolated and alone. Half a century later, pioneering psychologist Erich Fromm made it the centerpiece of his work. "We are social creatures, made anxious by our separateness," he wrote. Being separate means being cut off, he said; it means losing our capacity to be human.

Today, these simmering fears have become an outright plague. We are awash in divisive rhetoric and overwhelmed by the collapse of familiar institutions. The percentage of Americans living alone is higher than at any time in history. The number of seniors living alone has grown; the number of parents going it alone has soared; even the number of young people who say they feel alone has spiked. We have fewer friends, studies have shown, fewer people we can confide in, fewer people we can turn to in times of trouble. Depression rates have surged; unhappiness is rampant; suicide is at an all-time high.

A key question of modern life has become how to overcome this separateness, how to achieve union, how to transcend one's individual life and live in concert with another. How to connect. It's the same question Adam and Eve faced, and I believe their answer still holds.

That answer is the third and final reason
Adam and Eve still matter. They were the first
to contend—sometimes successfully, other times
not—with the central mystery of being un-
alone: being in love. Their lives are a testament
to the power of relationships and to the idea that
the greatest bulwark to the forces of isolation
and division that threaten us every day is the
even stronger force of relatedness. Confronted
with chaos, God answers with connection. His
message: The only thing more powerful than
separateness is togetherness. The only thing
more forceful than hate is love.

Over the last century, during the time that
Adam and Eve and other biblical luminaries were
losing favor, a new way of engaging the world
was gaining popularity. It involved using social
science, DNA, and big data to explain human
behavior. Whereas once we quoted preachers or
theologians, now we quote TED Talks or Nobel
laureates. That God-shaped hole in the universe?
It's been filled with brain scans.

While our instinct is to believe that this
cutting-edge knowledge has rendered moot insights from the past, in the arena of relationships, at least, the inverse is true. The two show
remarkable convergence. Social scientists are

now saying what the Bible's been saying all along. A central finding of modern psychology, for instance, is that our well-being depends on our interactions with others. To be happy is to be connected. And that includes the most central connection of all: a romantic attachment to another person.

One of the most effective things you can do to improve your quality of life is to succeed in the one aspect of life that's most difficult to pull off—love. Viktor Frankl, in his postwar classic **Man's Search for Meaning**, called love "the ultimate and the highest goal to which man can aspire." Even in a Holocaust camp, Frankl said, love was the only thing that could bring peace. "I understood how a man who has nothing left in this world still may know bliss, be it only for a brief moment, in the contemplation of his beloved."

Erich Fromm, in **The Art of Loving**, published in 1956, linked the drive for love directly with the drive to overcome aloneness. "The desire for interpersonal fusion is the most powerful striving in man," he said. "It is the force which keeps the human race together." Famed twentieth-century mystic Thomas Merton went even further. He said love is so powerful that even those who claim not to be interested in it are bound up in its tentacles from the moment they're born. "Because love is not just something that happens to you: **it is a certain special way of being alive**." Love, he continues, is "an intensification of life, a completeness, a fullness, a wholeness of life."

This line of thinking is hardly new, of course. It emerged out of a centuries-long tradition of trying to fathom what Joseph Campbell called the "universal mystery" of human bonding. Across history, our deepest thinkers have explored the notion that life is built around the merging of two souls. That life is lived more deeply and experienced more fully if it's a narrative of shared identity. Being alive is too overwhelming to be done by yourself; we can only fully be ourselves when we are with another. Philosopher Robert Solomon summed it up well: "Love is fundamentally the experience of redefining one's self in terms of the other."

In recent years, as romantic love has once more become a fashionable thing to discuss, any number of sources in the West have been credited with giving birth to the idea: European Romantics, Enlightenment thinkers, medieval courtiers, Roman poets, Greek philosophers, the Gospels. I believe all these are wrong and that they overlook the real source of this insight. Conditioned to think that any enduring idea must have its roots in the cradle of Western thinking, we have failed to see that **this** enduring idea actually came from the cradle of Western belief.

The Greeks did not invent love as we know it, nor did the Romans, the Persians, the Europeans, or the Americans. The Israelites did. The earliest model of a robust, resilient, long-lasting relationship appears in the Hebrew Bible.

It is the fundamental premise of this book that the greatest chronicle of human life in the ancient Near East introduced the idea of love into the world. And not in the psalms, the prophets, or even the patriarchs, as is sometimes claimed. But in the first story of human interaction.

It is my further conviction that this story speaks in profound and unexpected ways to the deepest yearnings of human beings today. How we lost sight of this achievement is a remarkable, rarely told story. How we can revive it is a vital challenge. I believe we can and we must meet this challenge, because to restore the idea of cocreation to the heart of our lives is to create the strongest bulwark we know against the forces of alienation and self-indulgence that risk tearing us apart.

"O tell me the truth about love," Auden wrote. The truth is it began with Adam and Eve. They are our civilization's first couple. Their story is the one we need to reclaim.

FIRST COMES LOVE

How Adam and Eve Invented Love

IN THE WINTER OF 2004, less than a year
after the fall of Saddam Hussein, I drove
south of Baghdad, deep into the Mesopotamian
valley of southern Iraq, toward the tribal town
of Qurnah, at the juncture of the Tigris and Euphrates rivers. The jubilation that followed the
toppling of one of the region's bloodiest dicta-
tors had been replaced by a feeling of chaos and
fear. Roadside bombings were on the rise; a wave
of kidnappings of American journalists and con-
tract workers had shattered any sense of order. I
was accompanied by a driver, a security guard,
and a fixer named Hikmat, a jocular English
professor with a dense, Saddam-like moustache.
Our intention was to fulfill a decadelong
dream of mine and visit the confluence of the

two rivers at the northern arc of the Fertile Crescent. It was in this vicinity, the Bible suggests, that God, after creating the world, planted a garden filled with flora and placed within it his triumphal creation, man and woman. The Bible says Eden is located at the crossroads of four rivers. Two are unknown; but two are the Tigris and Euphrates. For as long as these stories have been told, Eden has been linked with this watery terrain.

The highway was filled with the aftereffects of war: bombed-out bridges, scorched tanks, looted oil tankers. Every few feet was a fruit vendor hawking the spoils of lifted sanctions: apples, oranges, and bunches and bunches of bananas. Once embargoed, bananas were a status symbol of freedom.

Another side effect of that freedom was the complete absence of law and order. I was wearing Kejo Level III Rapid Response body armor, made with Kevlar HT 1100 and containing two ceramic plates capable of stopping 7.62x39mm ammunition from an AK-47 assault rifle. I was also wearing a scarf wrapped around my head and black pants. Everyone disagreed about proper precautions—drive an SUV, don't drive an SUV; tint your windows, don't tint your windows—but everyone agreed on one thing: Don't wear blue jeans. Only Americans wear blue jeans.

An hour south of Baghdad the scenery changed, from dusty, open plains to greener, more watery marshland. Date palms projected from the ground in a hundred different directions; rivulets and tributaries lapped at the road. More like a desert oasis than an English garden, the landscape reminded me how much our vision of the Garden of Eden is filtered through European art. But it's this marshy reality that is reflected in the opening passages of Genesis, with God creating an expanse in the midst of the watery morass, separating the waters above from the waters below, then drawing land from the water. Water is the one thing God doesn't create; it's just there, at the beginning, as it's here, where that beginning was inspired.

Qurnah was a parking lot. A long, dense traffic jam of cars was waiting in line for petrol. We maneuvered around the congestion and arrived at the spot where the rivers merged—two wide boulevards of silver that converged on the horizon. It would be easy to romanticize this confluence as the birthplace of Mesopotamia, but the truth is Saddam diverted the rivers slightly and they've only met in this specific location since 1993.

Still, that didn't stop the locals. A few blocks away was a small public park about the size of a basketball court. Residents call it **Janat Adan**, the Garden of Eden. It contained two living olive trees and one dead one, and was covered in concrete. Joni Mitchell was right. They paved paradise. A few children were playing when I arrived, and soon more hurried over. They tugged on my coat and asked for coins. The scene was joyful and full of life.

But minutes later Hikmat came rushing to my side. "Mr. Bruce," he said, "do you see those men over there?" He pointed to a small band of what looked like hooligans, dressed in dark pants and leather jackets. They certainly weren't wearing blue jeans. "They want to rob you," he said. "They even offered to give me ten percent of everything they stole off you."

We hurried to the car, and I tossed my backpack into the trunk. The men stepped forward, flashing guns. My mind was racing, and I barely had time to register the irony of the moment. **We're being kicked out of the Garden of Eden. Not since Adam and Eve . . .** I was just about to hop into the backseat when suddenly a little girl pushed through the crowd of men and offered me a small token of my visit.

An olive branch.

Humans might spoil the garden, but Eden never dies.

BEFORE WE TALK about what Adam and Eve might mean for today, we have to talk about what Adam and Eve meant in the ancient world. Though we tend to imagine the story as taking place in the fog of prehistory, it actually grew out of a distinct time and place at the dawn of human civilization in the Fertile Crescent. And more than just growing out of that era, the story of Adam and Eve represents a radical break from that era in a number of critical ways.

First, the story has one god.

Second, the story has two people.

Third, those two people are in a relationship built on love.

In order to unpack those coded messages hiding in plain sight, I decided to begin my journey in a place that we don't often associate with Adam and Eve but that is central to their legacy, Jerusalem. A little more than a decade after my visit to Iraq, I flew to Israel in early fall, during the week when the opening chapters of Genesis are read in synagogues around the world. In Hebrew, this portion of the Torah is known as **Bereshit,** from the opening word of the Bible, which was indelibly rendered into English by the King James translators as "In the beginning."

And what a beginning it is.

The man and woman who become known as Adam and Eve make their first appearance in history in the first chapter of Genesis and almost from the outset a peculiarity surrounds their lives: There's not one story about their origins in the Bible; there's two. The second story is both longer and more famous. It begins in Genesis 2 and continues all the way into Genesis 5. This more detailed narrative contains many of the iconic episodes in Adam and Eve's life. God forms Adam from the earth and places him in the Garden of Eden. Adam feels lonely, so God creates Eve from part of his torso. Adam is besotted with Eve, declares her "bone of my bones and flesh of my flesh," and the two are united.

These joyful scenes are followed by the drama surrounding the tree of the knowledge of good and evil. A discontented Eve leaves Adam and

ventures into the garden alone. She meets a
talking serpent, who persuades her to eat a piece
of fruit from the tree, which God has expressly
forbidden. Eve offers the fruit to Adam, who
also eats. The two open their eyes and discover
they are naked.

In the final act, God visits the couple, doles
out consequences for their behavior, then ban-
ishes Adam and Eve from Eden. The couple
heads into exile and quickly have two sons, Cain
and Abel, one of whom murders the other. Adam
and Eve then reunite to have a third son, Seth,
who finally fulfills his parents' destiny to be
fruitful and populate the earth.

One reason this second story is better known
is that it contains many of the flash points that
have caused such epic debate over the years:
Who is superior, man or woman? Who is guilt-
ier, Eve or Adam? In essence, which is God's
chosen sex, male or female? But when you consider the second story in light of the first, these
questions take on starkly different meaning.

The first story occupies the second half of
Genesis 1 and is both shorter and less plot driven.
More important, its message about the relationship between man and woman is almost the opposite of the second story. If the second story is

about the shifting hierarchies between man and woman, the first is about their fundamental equality.

On the sixth day of creation, God creates humanity in his image. This human creation has no identifiable gender or personality. God then divides this creation into male and female, gives these humans dominion over the animals, and enjoins them to have lots of children. The story ends with God declaring his new creations "very good."

Many explanations have been offered over the years as to why there are two stories that in key details are quite different. Traditional commentators stressed that the first account was more general and the second more specific. True, but not entirely satisfying. Beginning in the nineteenth century, historical criticism linked the first account with the more formal, priestly biblical author, known as P, and the second with the more narrative source, J. Also true, yet that doesn't explain why the editor of the final text chose to include both versions.

There's another explanation that seems to grow out of the stories themselves. The narrative of Adam and Eve at its core is about the power of two. There are two people, two points of view, and, yes, two sides to the story. The fact that there are two versions of the narrative reinforces this notion that life is fundamentally about creative tension. Creation is cocreation. And this message is not accidental or ancillary. It is central to the entire Bible. Abraham has two wives who duel for his legacy and two sons who do the same; Isaac has twin sons who are also rivals; Jacob has two wives from the same family. Later, there are two tablets of law, two kingdoms, two exiles, and two temples. For Christians there are two testaments, old and new. In the biblical worldview, unity is the rarity; duality is the norm.

There's one more prominent duality at the heart of the Adam and Eve story and that may be the most radical of all: There's only one God but there are two people. There's a partnership between the divine and humans. In this detail alone, the biblical account is unlike any origin story that came before it. To understand the significance of that, I left Jerusalem one morning and headed south toward the city of Beer Sheva to meet one of the premier excavators in the ancient world.

Yossi Garfinkel holds a chair of archaeology at Hebrew University and is an authority on the Neolithic world, the period that extended from around 12,000 B.C.E. until 2,000 B.C.E. This was the period when civilizations first emerged in the Fertile Crescent; it's also the period when the Adam and Eve story was first told. Yossi is in his early sixties and nearly bald, with skin darkened from years in the sun. On this morning he was digging at a site believed to be connected to King David. He left a group of students, and we settled under a tree. He began by putting Adam and Eve into historical context.

Scholars largely agree that the book of Genesis emerged through a series of oral stories that were passed down for centuries and written down beginning in the first millennium B.C.E. Robust city-states thrived in the Tigris-Euphrates Valley as early as 5000 B.C.E. These civilizations, among them Akkadian, Sumerian, and Babylonian, all used storytelling to explain their origins.

"The earliest humans were hunter-gatherers," Yossi said. Beginning around seventy thousand years ago, humans lived in small, tight-knit bands that moved around a lot. As anthropologist Yuval Harari said of these communities, "Members of a band knew each other very intimately, and were surrounded throughout their lives by friends and relatives. Loneliness and privacy were rare." Men and women in these societies divided responsibilities more or less equally. Men did the hunting, while women did the gathering. Their gods reflected this diversification.

"In hunter-gatherer societies, there were no central powers so there were no central deities," Yossi said. "People had a god of the rain, a god of the wind, and so on." Some of those gods had male characteristics; others female; many had both.

Next came the period that Yossi studies closely, the birth of farming. "Around 12,000 B.C.E., people began to settle in permanent villages," he said. "They started agriculture; they domesticated plants and animals; they began cultivating their own food. This is really when humans started raising themselves from nature."

"Some say this is the biggest revolution in history," I said.

"Exactly. And it's perfectly reflected in the Adam and Eve story." When Adam and Eve were in paradise, he explained, they got food from nature without having to work hard. Once they were expelled, they faced what everyone else faced after the agricultural revolution. They had to work a lot more. "God even says they'll have to live 'from the sweat of their brow,'" Yossi said.

"Are you suggesting that transition is captured in the biblical story?"

"Absolutely. Adam and Eve symbolize the movement from hunter-gatherers to village life."

This transition was also reflected in the way these societies understood their gods. Whereas before there had been a wide variety of deities, now the number winnowed. "When people started to live in villages, they began to have a single leader, so they created gods with more concentrated power," Yossi said.

Also, as societies became more complex, the number of male deities increased and the number of female deities decreased. There's disagreement about why this happened, but certain facts are not in dispute. Female gods predominated in the preagrarian world. Of the tens of thousands of miniature sculptures found across the Mediterranean in the Neolithic age, Yossi said, 95 percent have been female.

It became popular in recent decades to conclude that all these figurines meant early human societies worshipped goddesses. "In the beginning, people prayed to the Creatress of Life, the Mistress of Heaven," the artist Merlin Stone wrote in her influential 1976 book **When God Was a Woman**. More recently this view has come into question. Historian Gerda Lerner, writing a decade after Stone, found that women were held in high esteem in agrarian culture, as were female gods. But they still weren't in charge. "I would conclude that no matriarchal society has ever existed," she wrote.

Still, female gods were plentiful, especially in private spheres like weaving, brewing, and fertility.

So what happened to all those female deities? The answer, Yossi said, is that around 2500 B.C.E. the prominent role women played in society began to slacken. The transition to agriculture put more pressure on resources, which increased the need for war, which elevated men. Agrarian societies made some people wealthier, which allowed elite males to have multiple wives. Kinship was slowly replaced by class as the organizing principle of societies. Women as preeminent voices started to wane; women as supportive players started to rise.

These changes were eventually reflected in the stories of the gods. Roles once assigned to female deities were gradually transferred to male ones. In Sumer, the goddess of pot making morphed into a god; the powers of incantation, once controlled by a female god, were given to a male; the goddess of healing was demoted and forced to share powers with a male. "By the end of the second millennium," writes Assyriologist Tikva Frymer-Kensky, "the ancient goddesses have all but disappeared."

The significance of this for the Bible is that the period during which this shift was taking place, the second millennium B.C.E., is exactly the period in which the major events of Genesis take place. Not surprisingly, these events revolve around men—the patriarchs!—with women assigned a secondary role. This tension is also reflected in the story of Adam and Eve.

Humanity makes its debut in the Bible in Genesis 1:26. It's the sixth day, and God has so far created light, sky, the earth, the seas, the stars, and the animals. Already the God of the Bible shares similarities with Mesopotamian gods—water plays a crucial role in both traditions, as does the chaotic void that exists before creation.

But the differences are greater. The God of Genesis has no appearance or shape; God uses words to create the world, not physical powers; and, most important of all, God is solo. Gone are the elaborate rituals that characterized the mating of gods and goddesses; gone are the sexual partnerships between male and female deities; gone is the whole idea that god has female characteristics at all. The God of the Hebrew Bible is almost exclusively male.

There are several history-shaping consequences to this change. First, a lonely God needs a human partner to keep him company and fulfill his mission. Second, a solitary God needs a man and woman to carry out the sexual function he no longer can perform by himself. But how does a singular God create two human beings with enough diversity to populate the earth but without too much rivalry that might hobble their effort?

The way the story solves this dilemma is electrifying. God becomes plural. After starting off masculine at the beginning of the story, the singular, male God suddenly declares in Genesis 1:26, "Let us create a human after our likeness." This use of plural is shocking, and it's followed by an even more startling elaboration: God creates a single human entity that mirrors this plurality. Genesis 1:27 says, "God created humankind." The Hebrew word the text uses for God's creation, **ha-adam**, literally "the adam" or "the human," is not the proper name for Adam or even the word for "man." It's a more generic, gender-neutral term for all humanity. The text is clearly suggesting that all of humankind is the reflection of God.

This choice of language has many implications for Adam and Eve, but what was most relevant for my visit with Yossi is that the birth of humanity as described in the Hebrew Bible contains a moment of parity between a singular/plural God and a singular/plural humanity. Long before the hierarchies that have burdened male-female relations for millennia, at the start of the story there is pure equality. God contains both male and female; humanity, created in God's image, also contains both male and female. To drive that point home, the text goes on to say that God then divides this human entity into two parallel sexes. "Male and female he created them."

So what's being communicated here? Some commentators have suggested God is speaking in a majestic plural (the "royal we") or perhaps referring to angels in his heavenly court. Some Christian interpreters said this plural implies God is speaking to other members of the Holy Trinity. But the more I learned about the history of gods and goddesses, the more I wondered whether Genesis might contain an echo of the not-too-distant past when divinity was shared between male and female. In that case, maybe Adam and Eve were the heirs of an era when men and women, like their gods, divided responsibilities more equally.

I asked Yossi what he thought. "Look, do I think it's possible that the biblical story contains an echo of the female gods of Mesopotamia?" he said. "Absolutely. We have references to female gods later in the Bible, in the book of Kings, so we know the Israelites were aware of them."

"But why have this echo so prominently in the opening verses of Genesis?"

"Because Adam and Eve are designed to represent the entire human species," he said. "Since they reflect this broader shift of humans from the paradise of hunter-gatherers to the difficult life of agrarians, it would be logical that they represent the broader shift from male-female gods to a single male god and from male-female cooperation to patriarchy."

"But here's what I don't understand," I said. The morning had turned to midday by now and some excitement had been generated by the dig.

"The people who wrote down this story had no way of knowing all this. They didn't know about the history of hunter-gatherers or the battle over the sexual identity of gods. How were they able to capture this transition?"

"That's what we call the **longue durée**, the long memory," he said. "At some point there were people in the Neolithic period who remembered that their grandfather was a hunter-gatherer. They were able to tell their children about that transition. And slowly, slowly, as the stories were passed down, some details were forgotten and others were added, until you get to the biblical narrative."

"I would have thought with all your studies that you would dismiss this story as being a plaything," I said. "Yet the opposite is true. You respect the story even more."

"I respect all these stories because if they didn't have these wonderful cultural lessons in them they wouldn't have survived. At one point there were millions of stories, but in the Bible you have twenty or so. Think what it means to be twenty out of a million. Even very, very good stories were forgotten. The ones that have been preserved must have been jewels in the crown."

. . .

JERUSALEM isn't commonly associated with hills but it still has some of the most famous in the world, including Mount Zion and the Mount of Corruption. Mount Scopus is located in the northeast corner of the city, part of the ridge that includes the Mount of Olives. Look north from Scopus and you can nearly spot the Sea of Galilee; look south you can see Bethlehem; look east you can eye the Dead Sea. But look west and you have one of the most iconic views of the Old City, the Temple Mount (originally Mount Moriah), and the Dome of the Rock.

It was on that mountaintop, in the first millennium B.C.E., where the Israelites built their Temple, using stones and wood carvings to re-create a home for humans and God that was modeled explicitly on the Garden of Eden. And it was here, tradition said, after Adam died, that the angels washed his corpse, wrapped it in a garment, and buried it under the rock that all three monotheistic religions continue to hold sacred. Adam and Eve are not just at the center of every relationship; they're at the center of the fiercest religious conflicts of our time.

I came to Mount Scopus after leaving Yossi

because it's home to the premier academic institution in Israel, Hebrew University. I was hoping to explore the second big breakthrough that Adam and Eve represent. If the first milestone is that their story has only one God but two people, the second milestone is that the story features two characters who aren't just generic placeholders for all humanity. They're real individuals, with real personalities, and real feelings.

To help piece together the meaning of all this, I came to meet the fastest rising star of Mesopotamia studies. Uri Gabbay is tall, thin, with a boyish shock of black hair. A few days after his fortieth birthday, he still looked young enough to play with superheroes. Actually he plays with gods and goddesses. His résumé lists a mastery of nine languages, including Sumerian, Akkadian, Ugaritic, and Syriac. I began by asking him to explain the significance of having a man and woman, with clear romantic, even erotic feelings for each other, at the start of the human line.

"In Mesopotamia, the creation of the world and the creation of humans are not in the same story, so right there you have a difference with the Bible," Uri said. There are three main stories about human origins, he went on, and all three contain a different combination of two key details: Humans are created from clay and they're given life by the blood of a dead god. In the story of Enki and Ninmah, there is clay but no blood. In **Atrahasis**, there is clay and blood. In **Enuma Elish**, there is blood but no clay.

The creation of Adam and Eve has similar details, especially the version in Genesis 2 in which Adam is formed from earth and animated with the breath of God. But the differences between the biblical story and the earlier ones are even greater, Uri said. In the Mesopotamian stories, humans are an afterthought. The gods are center stage. In the Bible, humans are center stage. God creates all the natural elements—sun, moon, land, et cetera—so humans don't have to bother. Then he assigns humans dominion over all the animals. Humanity is clearly the pinnacle of God's world.

"Mesopotamian stories don't care about the people," Uri went on. "There are seven pairs of males and females created in these stories. None have names. They're completely anonymous. The stories are not about individuals."

"And in the Bible?"

"The first thing I notice is that Adam and Eve are characters. They eventually have real names. They have real feelings. There's clearly a narrative there, and that's unusual. I would say the Bible is trying to deliver a message. Most stories in the ancient Near East were about kings or elites. The people who write these stories are elites, so they don't care about everyday people."

"The Bible clearly does care," I said. "The story of Adam and Eve is all about their personal lives, their relationship, their children."

"Exactly."

"So might that be the message?" I said. "That we should focus on these things? That we should care about our relationships, our marriages, our families?"

He nodded.

"This is what I really want to ask you," I said. "Is Adam and Eve the first love story?"

He thought for a second, then a second more. "There's love poetry going back—I mean way back—into the second millennium B.C.E. There's some in Mesopotamia, in Egypt. So there's certainly writing about love. But that writing is not about couples. And it's not really in narrative form.

"It's possible a love story was written down that hasn't come to light," he continued. "Or that there's something in Africa or India or

China that wasn't known in this part of the world. But if you're talking about the cradle of Western civilization, I'd say the story of Adam and Eve is unique in that way."

"And what's the significance of that?"

"What stands out to me is that the Bible is not simply interested in the lives of the rich and powerful. It's interested in everybody. The king may not be interested in how we love, but the people are. And Adam and Eve are not royalty; they're everybody. And in that way, they're a revelation."

BUT ARE THEY IN LOVE?

On the surface, the notion that Adam and Eve represent a love story is dubious. Most couples begin separate and come together; Adam and Eve begin together and move apart. Most couples start clothed and later get unclothed; Adam and Eve start naked and later get dressed. Most couples flirt, coo, tease, banter, and otherwise exchange words of affection; Adam and Eve barely say a word to each other.

But in other ways, Adam and Eve are the ur-love story. Love is fundamentally about looking forward, not backward. It's a commitment to becoming, not merely being. It's an enlistment in togetherness, not aloneness. In that way, Adam and Eve are an ideal couple. They don't have a past, they have only a future. They have no ancestors, they have only descendants. Also, they don't have antecedents who've been in love before, so they can't mimic the experience of anyone else. They can't steal someone else's pickup lines or dance to anyone else's love songs. They must write their own story. They must invent what it means to be in a relationship.

One thing we've learned from social science in the last half century is that the feeling of romantic love is universal. In a detailed examination of 166 cultures around the world, anthropologists found evidence of romantic love in 151 of them, or 91 percent. In the remaining 15 cultures, researchers simply failed to study this aspect of people's lives. Helen Fisher, the prominent anthropologist of love, has found that the ways we experience love also differ little across age, race, gender, religion, and sexual preference. People of all types can be just as passionate, tender, aroused, angry, and committed toward their loved ones as anyone else.

Yet while the underlying feelings are similar, the ways people understand and express those feelings vary widely according to time and place. In recent decades, a consensus has emerged about what we might call the standard history of romantic love in the West. That history has three large phases, and though they overlap and are not exactly linear, the changes they represent are critical to understanding the way relationships have evolved. That includes the relationship between Adam and Eve. The three phases are:

1. Love is rooted in the divine.
2. Love is rooted in humanity.
3. Love is rooted in the individual.

The first phase begins in the ancient world with the idea that love, like most things, is a gift from the gods. Many cultures identified a specific deity of love, who took responsibility for beauty, pleasure, and relationships. In Greece it was Aphrodite; in Rome, Venus; in Egypt, Hathor. Plato, writing in the fourth century B.C.E., said the purpose of love was to convey messages back and forth between humans and the gods. Through love we become immortal.

The New Testament picked up this idea and carried it even further. The First Epistle of John contains the ultimate expression that love is bequeathed from the Lord. "God is love," it says. "Let us love one another, because love is from God; everyone who loves is born of God and knows God. Whoever does not love does not know God." Over time, this Christian notion merged with the Platonic ideal to become the prevailing view of human relationships for the next thousand years.

Beginning around the eleventh century, the grip that the Church had on relationships began to wane and a new view of love started to appear. What was once the unique provenance of the divine becomes the shared provenance of the human imagination. No longer simply top down, love becomes more bottom up, shaped by our actions, our choices, our minds. Humans become cocreators of love alongside the Creator. This view is seen in the "art of courtly love" in France, with its elaborate wooing of mistresses; in the popular but adulterous stories of Heloise and Abelard or Tristan and Isolde; and in the romantic plays of Shakespeare, with their starcrossed lovers and cross-dressing shenanigans.

Beginning in the eighteenth century, love becomes even more profane. It breaks away from religion and class to become the full creation of the individual. No longer a gift from above or even natural law, love becomes the domain of each person's heart, mind, and soul. Love is private, internal, ecstatic—the chief route to personal fulfillment (or despair). This type of romantic love grows from a world in which people break away from their families and cultural roots and see romance as a path to self-actualization. This is the love of romantic novels, Italian operas, and half the Hollywood films ever made.

While this overarching consensus narrative contains a lot of truth, it overlooks a critical detail: When exactly does the story of love begin? Most accounts start in classical Greece, but Plato and his contemporaries were writing in the fourth century B.C.E. The principal stories in Genesis were written down as early as 900 B.C.E. That's half a millennium earlier. The entire Hebrew Bible had been completed before Athens reached its peak.

And make no mistake: Hebrew Scripture is overflowing with love. The stories are at times romantic, painful, marital, extramarital, and sexual. To leave out the Hebrew Bible from the larger history of love is to commit a shameful error, yet that's exactly what's been done for centuries. So what should the Hebrew Bible be given credit for?

To answer that question, my final visit in Jerusalem was to a woman who had devoted her life to studying relationships in Hebrew Scripture. Judy Klitsner was born in Wilkes-Barre, Pennsylvania, where her grandfather sold clothing to coal miners. In Jewish day school, she was denied access to holy texts because of her gender. "When the boys would study Talmud, the girls were sent to learn sewing," she said over lunch. "You'll need those skills in a few years when you get married and have kids," she was told.

Instead Judy moved to Israel, apprenticed under a prominent female Bible scholar, and became a beloved teacher. (She also married and had five children.) Did she ever have a moment when she considered abandoning Scripture? "Many," she said. "But my answer has consistently been, 'They don't get to keep it.'"

I asked her how big a role she thought love played in the Bible.

"The greatest contribution of Hebrew Scripture to world thought is the line, 'Love the Lord your God with all your heart and with all your soul and with all your might,'" she said. "Jesus called it the most important commandment in the Hebrew Bible. God doesn't want us to fear him, respect him, or blindly follow him. He wants us to love him.

"But I think we misunderstand what love means in this context," she continued. "To me the more critical line is what Jesus calls the second most important commandment in the Torah, 'Love your neighbor as yourself.' What's amazing about that statement is that it presupposes love of self. That sounds easy. We know exactly what motivates us. But it's actually one of the hardest things for most of us to do."

Judy began rearranging the items on the table to demonstrate her point. She put a saltshaker in front of me. "Think of love as a series of concentric circles," she said. "It begins with love of self." Next she put a pepper shaker next to the salt. "From there you move outward to love of neighbor." She placed a fork next to that. "Then to love of stranger." Finally she placed a water glass at the outermost edge. "And that leads to love of God. If you ask me to summarize the Torah on one foot, that would be my answer."

This emphasis on love in the Hebrew Bible, hundreds of years before classical Greece or Rome, is easily the earliest, most comprehensive discussion of the subject in the history of the West. British philosopher Simon May, in his book **Love: A History**, is one of the few scholars to recognize it. "If love in the Western world has a founding text, that text is Hebrew," he writes. Still, even this discussion involves a mostly nonsexual, generalized loving kindness toward others, what the Greeks would later call **agape**.

But the Bible illustrates romantic love, too. "The Song of Songs," in the second half of the Hebrew Bible, contains a riveting, explicit portrait of two lovers pining for each other. It begins, "Let him kiss me with the kisses of his mouth! For your love is better than wine." From there it goes on to discuss heaving breasts, flowery orgasms, even fellatio. In an image that many see as a play on the Adam and Eve story, a woman rhapsodizes her lover this way: "As an apple tree among the trees of the wood, so is my beloved among young men. With great delight I sat in his shadow, as his fruit was sweet to my taste." The passage ends: "He brought me to the banqueting house, and his intention toward me was love."

Even as early as the book of Genesis, Jacob is described as loving Rachel from the moment he sees her. Forced to work for seven years to earn her hand, "it seemed to him but a few days because of his love for her." When his labor is completed, he confronts her father hungrily. "Give me my wife, for my time is fulfilled, that I may consort with her." Even after Jacob is forced to marry her older sister first, his feelings endure, "because he loved Rachel more than Leah." When it appears, romantic love in the Bible is red blooded and hard suffering.

But if the Hebrew Bible introduces this idea into the world, where precisely in the Bible is this idea introduced? Most critics credit the patriarchs and matriarchs, but this is grossly unfair to the Bible's first couple. A main reason for this oversight, I believe, is that we rarely read the story of Adam and Eve even open to the idea that it might contain love. When we do a surprising thing happens.

The first time human beings are described in the Bible, it's that passage in Genesis 1:26 in which God creates the twin-gendered or ungendered human "in our image, after our likeness." In the next verse, God divides this single human entity into male and female. Here's the way the distinguished translator Robert Alter renders this poetic passage:

And God created the human [**ha-adam**]
in his image,
in the image of God he created him
male and female he created them.

Whatever else is going on in this passage, the sequencing is clear. First God creates humankind; then humankind is separated into male and female. Before there was male and female there was a mixture of male and female.

Today, when sexual identity is widely discussed as being more fluid than ever; when individuals are described as being on a "gender continuum"; when young people are rejecting binary distinctions like male and female, gay and straight; when transgender transitions fill our television screens, our workplaces, and our family reunions, finding this idea in the opening chapter of the Bible is both startling and enlightening. More to the point, the Bible may be trying to tell us something about the nature of human relationships, something we haven't been able to hear because we haven't stopped to listen.

The first thing worth observing is that as unusual as it might seem to contemporary readers that the Bible somehow suggests humans had a mixed-gendered past, it would not have been unusual to readers in the past. In fact, the idea that human beings possessed both sexes at some point in prehistory was widespread among philosophers, scientists, rabbis, and preachers from antiquity all the way into the modern world.

The early Jewish commentator Philo and the Gnostic Gospel of Philip both said that the original human being was androgynous. The Talmud concurred. Rashi, the single most influential Jewish interpreter, said God created **adam** "with two faces, then separated them." Since Rashi's commentary, written in the Middle Ages, was considered indistinguishable from the Torah for many Jews, he guaranteed that the idea would be embraced for centuries.

And it wasn't just religious leaders. The greatest thinkers of the classical world believed we had hermaphroditic origins. The most sweeping discussion of love in ancient philosophy was Plato's **Symposium**, which chronicles a dinner party in which five men offer tributes to the god of love. The third speaker, Aristophanes, argues that in prehistory humans were round, with two faces, two sets of limbs, and two sets of genitals. These roly-polies came in three sexes—male, female, and androgynous. The gods found these creatures threatening, so Zeus chopped them in half "like people cut an egg in two." Not just their bodies were cut, but their souls, too. Ever since, humans have forlornly wandered the earth, searching for their other half. "Love is just the name we give to the desire for and pursuit of wholeness," Aristophanes says.

What's significant about this legacy of unified sexual origins is that it's responsible for one of the more enduring ideas about human relationships: that each of us has a missing half out there that can make us whole again. We all carry around within us an existential yearning to reunite with our lost selves. The urge for love precedes the search for love. "The need has invented the solution," in Alain de Botton's elegant phrasing. A goal of being human is to guide ourselves to our complement and restore our original nature.

Sure enough, once this idea was introduced into the world it's never really gone away. The Sufi poet Rūmī wrote, "Lovers don't finally meet somewhere / They're in each other all along." Freud described the "oceanic feeling" of lovers who meet and feel like they've always known each other. Virginia Woolf spoke of "two sexes in the mind corresponding to the two sexes in the body" that must rejoin to achieve happiness.

The way we speak about love today still echoes this notion. We "find our soul mate," "fit well together," "feel whole" with someone we love. "You complete me," Jerry Maguire says to Dorothy.

To me, Genesis 1 deserves credit for introducing this now universal concept. It begins the discussion of human relationships with the idea that the first man and woman weren't just thrust together because they were the only choices available; they were made for each other. And once they were divided in half, they became the first to engage in what became an overriding quest of their descendants: They went looking for their match. They went searching for love.

I asked Judy whether she thought Adam and Eve were in love.

"Yes," she said without hesitation. Then she tilted her head and leaned forward. "But it's complicated. The word 'love' is not actually used in the story, but it's on display in many ways. I'd say there's a description of love more than a presentation of it."

"Where do you see it described?"

"In Genesis 1, there's this wonderful sense of

equality. Every single thing that's true about the man is also true about the woman. God says to both, 'Be fruitful and multiply.' 'Go out there and master the earth.' 'Rule over all the animals.' There's something touching about that.

"Then in the second story, in chapter two, it gets more complicated," she continued. "First you have this thing that sounds like genuine love. The man leaves his father and mother and clings to his wife. He declares her 'bone of my bones and flesh of my flesh.' She becomes his 'helper.' You get a sense of how they feel about each other. And they don't just say, 'Yes, honey.' Part of love is about challenging the other person. It's about helping them to improve."

She squirmed a little.

"But here's where being a woman Bible student comes into play," she said. "There's this beautiful stuff about clinging and becoming one, but notice how it's phrased. It's very one directional. She is his helper. He is clinging to her. She is one flesh to him. Everything revolves around him. It sounds a lot like control. Then in chapter three, with the snake, the fruit, and being kicked out of the garden, everything falls apart. We have the beginnings of power, competition, and rivalry."

I gestured toward the salt, pepper, fork, and glass in front of me. "I get that," I said. "But if what you say about the Bible on one foot is true—that we are called by God to love ourselves, then the other, then God—then mustn't that also be true for Adam and Eve? They must love each other. They have no choice. Even if it's a struggle."

She took a bite of cucumber.

"Honestly, I'm not as negative as I sound," she said. "I think it's enormously significant that the first story of man and woman begins with love. Then there's a crisis, and with that crisis comes an upturn in romantic tension. I see that as an opening. The same when they leave the garden, that's when the real work of their relationship begins.

"But even there, I have a feeling of optimism," she continued. "Adam and Eve are everyone. Their message should apply to all of us. And let's face it, relationships are tough. So fine, it's tough for Adam and Eve, too. That allows us to find ourselves in them."

We parted warmly. As I walked down the street, I reflected on the swings Judy described. Having embarked on this journey to find lessons for today in the story of Adam and Eve, I found much more in the opening chapter of Genesis alone than I ever would have expected.

One: Before Adam and Eve was the story of two people, it was the story of one God.

The most important moment in the lives of Adam and Eve occurred before they were even created. It was the innovation of a solo God. Without companions of his own, this individual God creates human beings and allows them to become individuals themselves. "In discovering God, singular and alone," wrote the former chief rabbi of Britain Lord Jonathan Sacks, human beings "eventually learned to respect the dignity and sanctity of the human person, singular and alone."

Two: Before Adam and Eve were two human beings, they were one.

The Bible's oldest couple begin life as a single creature. Their fundamental equality is so central to their identity that they enter the world unseparated from each other. They are the original conjoined twins. The symbolism of this cannot be overstated: Long before there was a tradition of hierarchy surrounding Adam and Eve, there was an assertion of parity.

Three: Adam and Eve introduce the main tension in what I call a two story: learning to live as one.

"In love," Octavio Paz wrote, "everything is two and everything strives to be one." That's the unspoken outcome of what happens at the end of Genesis 1 when God separates male from female. They will want to reunite. Among the most persistent expressions of love, concluded Simon May, is its "craving to 'return.'" Adam and Eve are the first to experience this craving, which is one reason they're first to experience love. Because on day one they were one, they yearn to live out their days as one. They both need the other to be fully themselves.

That all these ideas are found in the opening lines of the Bible reminds us why this story still demands attention. At the starting line of humanity, there is unity. We are not discovering a new way for the sexes to relate today; we are recovering it.

But while equality may be the theme of these initial verses, that parity does not last—either in the narrative or in how the narrative has been remembered. To understand that part of the story, I had to travel 1,500 miles to the east—and nearly that many years into the future—to unpack what happened to Adam and Eve when they came face-to-face with the heart of Christianity.

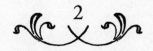

MEET CUTE

Who Was Present at the Creation?

THE SUN WAS JUST DIPPING over St. Peter's Basilica one summer evening when Cesare Massimo walked up to the enormous bronze doors of the Vatican Museums and knocked hard. Commissioned for the Jubilee of 2000, the fortlike doors were forged by a local sculptor to honor the story of creation. Pope John Paul II said at their dedication, "The subject of creation . . . harmonizes well with that of art and seems to invite the visitor to marvel at the mystery of the Creator Spirit."

More practically, the doors allow the museum to more efficiently funnel in twenty-five thousand people a day, primarily to marvel at the works of two scandal-ridden artists whose statues adorn the old entrance: Raphael, who appears with a palette and paintbrushes, and Michelangelo, who is shown with a chisel and mallet.

"I hope they remember we're coming," Cesare whispered.

When I first decided to go back to Rome to explore how Michelangelo had shaped the history of Adam and Eve, I blithely set a goal that I wanted to be in the Sistine Chapel alone. The better to appreciate the artwork as the artist had intended, I thought; the better to see them in peace and quiet.

I had no idea how hard it would be. Outside of joining a conclave, there are three principal ways to enter the chapel. One, buy a ticket, wait in line, and get ten minutes along with two thousand other people, during which you're not allowed to sit down, take pictures, or talk. Two, spend hundreds of dollars to join one of a handful of after-hours tours that are bought out by huge travel companies. Or three, spend thousands of dollars to rent out the joint for yourself. One Roman I know helped a client do just that for his sixtieth birthday. The man paid sixty thousand dollars, flew in sixty guests from around the world, put them up in local hotels, only to have the Vatican call the morning of the party and announce that Porsche had swept in and paid more.

Cesare was something else entirely. A twentieth-generation Roman with a ponytail, moustache, and what might be described as graduate-student good looks, he had deep and somewhat mysterious ties to the Church. A great-great-great relative had been the first librarian of the Vatican. An alumnus of Cambridge, Cesare returned to the city of his youth, where he now wrote novels, made art, and was working on a virtual reality app about the chapel.

After several tense minutes, the door cracked open, Cesare whispered to the guard, and we were pulled inside. We walked past a security desk and took an elevator to the fourth floor, then headed down a marble corridor about the size of an airport jet bridge.

"OK, here we go," Cesare said, and suddenly we were inside the chapel. I was a little disoriented at first. With no people inside, the full impact of the mosaic marble floor, exquisite walls, and storied ceiling was more overwhelming than I had expected. The entire structure seemed to revolve, with the walls pushing in, then pushing out, like a three-dimensional kaleidoscope or virtual reality fantasyland.

But there's nothing virtual about this place. The great jewel box of Western art is among the most famous rooms ever created—and the most influential. It has defined the faces, the bodies, even the hands of Adam, Eve, and God for the last six hundred years. "God provided the words," Michelangelo is said to have uttered. "I provided the images."

And though it's often forgotten today, those images were shocking at the time they were created. The reason: They represented a radical rethinking of the creation story. As the son of an art teacher, I always thought the heart of the Sistine Chapel was the arresting image of Adam and God extending their index fingers to each other. I was wrong. For Michelangelo, the crux of the story was the unheralded third player in the narrative. The Florentine's seminal insight is that the divine is not the heart of life on earth, nor is his first human creation, Adam. The centerpiece of life is the figure he chose to put in the exact center of the Sistine Chapel ceiling.

Eve.

THE FIRST CREATION STORY ends in chapter 2, verse 3, with the formation of the seventh day, a time of holiness, reflection, and rest. Then, without warning, in verse 4, the tone, content, and subject matter change sharply. The second creation story begins with scenes of botany, meteorology, and God playing in the dirt. God forms man "from the dust of the earth," then blows "the breath of life" into his nostrils.

While the first creation story is more high level, the second gets into what Robert Alter calls the "technological nitty-gritty" of human origins. We've gone from God as poet-creator to God as hands-on surgeon—cutting, molding, shaping, breathing. Also, we've gone from a situation of pure equality, with men and women being formed simultaneously, to a more specific sequencing of male and female. With these differences begins a centuries-long debate about what this ordering means and which sex, if either, might be God's favorite.

Man is clearly created first, and the story contains a play on words to suggest how intimately this human creation is connected to God's terrestrial creations: the man, **adam**, is created from the earth, **adamah**. Using soil to create human beings echoes the creation stories of Mesopotamia, though Uri Gabbay told me that in those accounts humans were created out of clay, because the Tigris and Euphrates basin is wetter, while the Bible suggests dust, in keeping with the moisture level in Israel.

But should God's use of soil be considered a compliment?

Over the years, commentators have interpreted this choice in competing ways. Some viewed it positively, saying Adam was exalted because his body was a microcosm of the earth. The rabbis of the Talmud, for instance, said God collected soil from all over the world, so wherever Adam died he'd feel at home. Others viewed it more negatively, suggesting Adam was lowly because his body was made from "filth and dirt." John Calvin said God chose dirt so humans would not be too prideful about their bodies.

Regardless, once God forms this human, he immediately creates a new patch of earth for him to live in. God plants "a garden in Eden, in the east," and places man within it. The garden contains "every tree that was pleasing to the sight and good for food," though two specific trees are named: the "tree of life" and the "tree of the knowledge of good and evil."

The formation of the garden ends with God offering man free rein to till, tend, and eat anything in it he wishes. But God warns the man not to eat from the tree of the knowledge of good and evil, "for as soon as you eat of it, you shall die." Man is barely alive and already he's being threatened with death.

Then comes one of the more pivotal statements in the entire story: God says, "It is not good for the human to be alone." As in chapter 1, the word often translated as "man" here is actually **ha-adam**, which suggests not just males but females, too. A better way to understand the meaning would be, "It is not good for humans to be alone."

What's striking is the use of the expression "not good." Until now, God has declared things in his new world to be either "good" or "very good." Aloneness is the first thing he declares to be "not good." What does the word "alone"—in Hebrew, **levaddo**—mean in this context? The Hebrew root **levad** is used 158 times in the Hebrew Bible, mostly referring to inanimate objects and mostly suggesting singularity or uniqueness. When the term is used to describe individuals, as when Jethro tells Moses it's not good for him to be sole magistrate, the word suggests without help. To be alone is to be helpless.

This idea that humans need what Yeats later

called the "sensual music" of horizontal relationships has echoed through Western thought. The great thirteenth-century commentator Ramban observed that God is suggesting humans should not live a static, unchanging life but should instead live face-to-face with an other. Hobbes wrote that human relatedness emerges out of the primary isolation of humans who require "all kind of engagement to each other." Adam is the original human who requires engagement with others.

God's response to this feeling of loneliness is to commit to creating an other for Adam. He vows to make "a fitting helper"—in Hebrew, **ezer kenegdo**—for him. The phrase **ezer kenegdo** is notoriously difficult to translate. The King James Bible renders it "helpmeet"; others "sustainer," "partner," or "an aid fit for him." The first part, **ezer**, is used sixteen times in the Bible to describe God's service to others, which suggests the type of help intended for Adam is not meant to be subservient. **Kenegdo** is much rarer, rendering the meaning of the entire phrase unclear.

What is clear, though, is that while we expect the creation of woman to follow immediately, that doesn't happen. Instead we get a curious moment in which God serves as a divine match-maker, parading every animal, beast, and bird before Adam to see if any hold appeal. The first speed dating. And as in the hook-up app Tinder—swipe left to reject, swipe right to meet—Adam swipes left on each of the animals.

The way the text describes Adam's feelings is key. "For Adam no fitting helper was found." As powerful as it is when God has the insight that it's not good for humans to be alone, it's even more powerful when Adam has the insight him-self. The animals around him have mating part-ners, but they don't have what he's looking for. They don't have companionship, intimacy, or a commitment to be each other's helper.

They don't have love.

Adam is looking for love. "Every human ac-tion," wrote philosopher Henri Bergson, "has its starting point in a dissatisfaction, and thereby in a feeling of absence." Knowing one's incom-pleteness is a necessary precondition to the search for completeness. Or as Wallace Stevens wrote, "Not to have is the beginning of desire."

And Adam is not alone in his aloneness. Some of the greatest love stories in history begin with a protagonist who feels isolated, misplaced, or adrift. The Cornish knight Tristan is cut off from home before he falls for the Irish princess Isolde. Romeo is out of favor before meeting Juliet. Swann is mired in solitude before he swoons for Odette.

To be human, it seems, is to seek comfort in love. "We are born helpless," C. S. Lewis said. "As soon as we are fully conscious, we discover loneliness. We need others physically, emotionally, intellectually; we need them if we are to know anything, even ourselves."

Given that God understands Adam's need for companionship, why not go ahead and give him what he needs? Why the diversion with the animals? The answer, I believe, is to deliver a message: God cannot help us if we don't first admit that we need help ourselves. In the familiar language of the self-help movement, "Hi. My name is Adam, and I'm lonely."

It's not just literature that understands the human need for connection; it's become a central pillar of biology, too. Empathy and attachment have been shown to be deeply rooted in our DNA. Babies in the womb have the capacity to hear and sense their loved ones outside. Newborns learn to speak by mimicking the facial expressions and vocal tones of those around them. All of us have mirror neurons that fire both when we act and when we observe others acting, meaning when someone smiles at us, we smile back, and when they express compassion, we feel more compassionate.

Social science, too, has begun to zero in on loneliness as a social problem. I had lunch some years ago with John Cacioppo, a distinguished professor at the University of Chicago and one of the leading neuroscientists in the world. Cacioppo almost single-handedly brought loneliness to the forefront of psychology. "When people are asked what pleasures contribute to happiness," he told me, "the overwhelming majority rate love, intimacy, and social affiliation above wealth, fame, or even physical health."

Loneliness, by contrast, is the biggest detriment. Those with higher rates of loneliness have higher rates of depression, anxiety, hostility, pessimism, and neuroticism. They also have increased rates of dying from heart disease, cancer, respiratory diseases, gastrointestinal diseases, and every other cause of death studied. Social isolation is on par with high blood pressure, obesity, lack of exercise, and smoking as a risk factor for illness and early death.

Why? Cacioppo's research has shown that being lonely is like being in a hostile environment. It triggers cellular changes in the body that make the immune system less able to protect vital organs.

I bring all this up because religion and modern science are often said to be incompatible. The ideas of one are thought by many to contradict the ideas of the other. But here's an exquisite example where that's not true. A central assertion about human nature in Genesis and a central finding about human nature from neuroscience agree: Human beings are not meant to be alone.

If you're the kind of person who thinks the Bible has been rendered moot by modern science, here's a beautiful illustration of why that's not always true, either. If you're the kind of person who thinks the Bible contains all the wisdom you need about living a meaningful life and that contemporary science has nothing to add, this example weakens that case as well. That both worlds agree on the centrality of relationships makes the insight all the more powerful and our need to heed it all the more urgent.

So how does God respond to this urge?

By taking part of the already depleted man and using it to create the companion he craves. God "casts a deep sleep upon the man," and while he sleeps, he takes one of his "ribs"—in

Hebrew, **tsela'**—and closes up the spot. "And the Lord God fashioned the rib that he had taken from the man into a woman."

Though **tsela'** has been commonly translated for centuries as "rib," a consensus has emerged in recent years that this usage is probably misleading. The word **tsela'** is used thirty-eight times in the Hebrew Bible. None refers specifically to the body part, while twenty-three refer to "side" and fifteen to "side room."

Anne Lapidus Lerner, the former vice chancellor of the Jewish Theological Seminary, writes, "Given the fact that **tsela'** is seen meaning 'rib' only in the context of the creation of woman, it is unlikely that it is a correct reading." The more likely reading, she concludes, is that woman is taken from man's side, suggesting they stand less in hierarchy to each other and more as partners, side by side.

Even more relevant to their relationship is Adam's reaction to her appearance. He's elated. He awakens from his sleep to find his dream fulfilled. The result is the first time a human speaks in the Bible, what Simone de Beauvoir calls a cry of "ecstatic union": "This one at last!" God speaks when there is one human; the human speaks only when there is another human.

Our one story has now become a two story. Befitting this emphasis on two, Adam's phrase "this one" appears twice in his joyful greeting.

> This one at last
> Is bone of my bones
> And flesh of my flesh.
> This one shall be called Woman

The heart of our lonely hunter is lonely no more. Having been diminished by losing a part of his body, he feels enhanced by gaining an extension of his body. Even the great medieval commentator Rashi announced that Adam had found love. "His heart's longings were not satisfied until he met Eve."

And we should see it as love. The occasion of Adam and Eve's first greeting is a moment of great consequence. A "meet cute" they call it in Hollywood, a scene in which a future romantic couple meets for the first time in a way that's unexpected, amusing, or mildly contentious. Giving up a body part to a total stranger would seem to qualify.

Yet Adam does not complain about losing part of his side. Instead he falls head over heels. Those same social scientists who gave us wisdom about loneliness have also found that men fall in love faster than women. Men are more visual, more impulsive, more motivated by sex. That certainly holds true in the Garden of Eden. Adam has barely laid eyes on the woman—and he doesn't even know her name—before he lustily declares her "bone of my bones and flesh of my flesh." That's what my mother might have called being forward. Unlike Jerry Maguire, he doesn't even bother with "Hello."

Yet it's a moment for the ages. The imaginative biblical commentator Avivah Zornberg compares Adam meeting Eve to Cortéz encountering the New World, a moment of "wild surmise," in Keats's phrase, in which the man discovers a part of himself grown immeasurably more valuable in its new otherness. This notion of love as finding a part of yourself is yet another idea that Adam and Eve introduce into the canon of ideas.

That famed lonely heart Jane Eyre, for instance, uses strikingly similar language when she and Rochester declare their love. First Rochester, sitting under a tree in his "Eden-like" garden, reveals he has a "queer feeling" toward her. "It is as if I had a string somewhere under my left ribs, tightly and inextricably knotted to a similar string situated in a corresponding quarter of your little frame," he says.

Later, Jane affirms that she is the one who feels supremely blessed for being "the apple of his eye." "No woman was very nearer to her mate than I am; ever more absolutely bone of his bone and flesh of his flesh." Of course one woman was as near to her mate as Jane. It's Jane's progenitor, the first woman to be loved, and, as Michelangelo memorably showed, the first to entwine her flesh and bones with those of her lover.

ADAM AND EVE were never intended to appear in the Sistine Chapel. Originally called the Great Chapel, the private prayer chamber of the Apostolic Palace was constructed between 1473 and 1481 under the supervision of Pope Sixtus IV, after whom the room is named. The fortresslike building mirrors the dimensions of Solomon's temple—134 feet long, 44 feet wide. When the chapel was dedicated to Mary on the Feast of the Assumption in August 1483, the side walls were frescoed with elaborate depictions from the lives of Moses and Christ, while the flattened vaulted ceiling was painted in blue and studded with gilt stars.

The idea of putting the first couple in the chapel wasn't even considered when Sixtus IV's successor, Julius II, commissioned Michelangelo to paint the ceiling in 1508. Michelangelo's original charge was to paint the twelve apostles on the triangular pendentives that support the vault. But according to his version of events, Michelangelo demanded the freedom to paint what he wanted. He chose to paint the entire 12,000-square-foot ceiling, focusing on nine panels down the ceiling's spine that he filled with three images each from the first three stories in Genesis—the creation of the world, the creation of humans, and the drunkenness of Noah.

Michelangelo was in many ways an odd choice for this commission. A Florentine not a Roman, he had virtually no experience as a painter. His reputation was as a sculptor, and an intuitive one at that. "I saw the angel in the marble," he said of one work, "and I carved until I set him free."

Even when he turned to painting, his chief interest remained the human body. The thirty-three-year-old was one of the most enthusiastic practitioners of a new, illegal fad in the Renaissance: dissecting corpses. Michelangelo even set up his own secret dissecting room in a church, where he made anatomical sketches of corpses provided by a friendly friar. Michelangelo's goal was to depict realistic bodies by moving outward from the bones, to the muscles, then to the flesh. His artwork is said to have included at least eight hundred different anatomical parts.

"What matters to me about this room is that it's a temple to genius," Cesare, my Vatican insider and guide, said once my head rush had subsided. "You've got the innovation of three-dimensional imagery at its very inception. The first visitors privileged to see this room were said to be struck dumb."

"What were they dumbfounded by?"

"How he uses artistic license. It's very modern, and he's very conscious of it. He references a very orthodox source, the Bible, but depicts it in a very cutting-edge way."

One thing that surprised me about being in the chapel without crowds was how well sound carried. Each step, each word, each note reverberated in a deep, physical way. It's as if the walls were made of reeds from a Renaissance wind instrument.

"There are three ways the Church achieves that affect," Cesare said. The Church does it with music; it does it with liturgy; and it does it with art. "When we stand in here today, we're experiencing it without the music or liturgy," he said, "so the chapel is speaking with only a third of its voice."

But what a voice it is. The most arresting image in the entire room, certainly to Michelangelo's contemporaries, was the sixth panel in the central aisle, the **Creation of Adam**.

"It's ironic to me that on the ceiling you have the introduction of the archetype for the super-hero into imagery," Cesare said. "You have an old, bearded man flying through the air with a billowing cape. No one had done that before. No one had shown God baring his knees, wear-ing no shoes, catapulting through the sky. God made humans in his image; Michelangelo made God in ours."

More than being original, Michelangelo's willingness to rethink God's physicality was also risky, especially considering who was paying for his work and where it was located. Early Jews and Christians believed that the book of Exo-dus, in saying that no person should see God's face, forbade depicting God in visual form. By the Middle Ages, some artists began showing God's hand or sometimes his face, but painting his full body was still unthinkable. When Renaissance artists did venture to show God's face, they depicted it with a long beard to make his usually stern appearance seem more patriarchal and forbidding. Michelangelo went in a radically different direction. His God was active, balletic, lithe. An old head on a young body.

"Often it's said that God isn't an old man in a beard," Cesare said. "But what if Michelangelo never came up with that image of God in a beard, flying through the air? There's no guarantee anyone else would have thought of it. Or that Superman would look the way he does."

As for Adam, he, too, is shown with internal contradictions. He has a lifeless face but a taught, tensile body, about to spring to life. All he awaits is the breath of God. The text suggests Adam comes alive when God "blows into his nostrils," a CPR-like image that would surely have presented challenges in a room like this. Michelangelo's answer was to capture this moment with two index fingers reaching for each other, one from a limp-wristed man, the other from a virile God.

"To me it's a beautiful detail," Cesare said, "the way the fingers touch. And it references what's been sung in the conclave since before

Michelangelo, **Veni Creator Spiritus**, about how man is created from the index finger of God."

Cesare believes the outstretched fingers hold an even larger message: Michelangelo has taken a story that is largely about communicating with words—"And God said,"—and made it about communicating without words.

"I believe the Sistine Chapel is rightly celebrated as the word made image," Cesare said.

In the first of the three panels in this series, he went on, God creates Adam and has a wordless connection with him. In the second, God creates Eve and has a similar connection with her. By the third, God has retreated and Adam and Eve have that connection with each other, before they're kicked out of Eden.

"Surely the paradise they lose is the ability to speak without words," Cesare continued. "The Hebrew alphabet, which I adore, reformats the brain in order to comprehend a single God. But it also burdens us with language. Language redefines the world, and complicates it."

"What does it mean to communicate without words?" I asked.

"It's the message of this entire room," he said. "It's love. Love means being able to look at someone and communicate imaginatively, nonverbally. What Michelangelo is saying—what the Church is saying, in effect—is that originally that ability is a gift from God, because God is love. Only when we love God can we re-create that love with another person."

THERE'S AN OLD JOKE about Adam and Eve that goes like this:

One day in the Garden of Eden, Eve called to God, "Lord, I have a problem."

"What's your problem, Eve?"

"I know that you created me and put me in this lovely garden with all the animals. But I'm just not happy anymore."

"Why not, Eve? What's gone wrong?"

"Well, Lord, I guess that I'm getting lonely. These animals don't talk. And to tell you the truth, fresh apples just don't do it for me anymore."

"Eve, I have a solution. I'll create a man for you."

"What's a man, Lord?"

"Well, he's a bit like you, but flawed. He's tough and not easy to get along with. But he will be bigger and faster than you so he can help out when needed. But he'll be a bit dimmer than you, and you'll have to help him figure out what to do."

Eve thought for a few moments, scratched her head, and asked, "What's the catch, Lord?"

"Well, there will be one condition attached."

Eve smiled wisely and asked, "And what's that, Lord?"

"You'll have to let him think that I made him first."

One curious feature of the Sistine Chapel is that it doesn't just tell the story of Adam and Eve, it's actually part of the story itself. The images Michelangelo painted in those panels didn't just capture centuries of biblical discussion that preceded them; they also shaped centuries of discussion that followed them.

That was never more true than with what may have been the Florentine's biggest challenge to orthodoxy: his depiction of Eve. For the first time in such a prominent place, Eve was not merely Adam's inferior or even his equal; she was something more remarkable—his conduit to Jesus, his bridge to God. Before the Sistine Chapel it was possible in learned circles from Jerusalem to Rome to discount or even dismiss Eve; after what the pope's handpicked artist frescoed on that ceiling, few could do so without challenge. Simply put: Michelangelo was Eve's biggest booster, and he did so in the malest place on earth.

How exactly this happened was on my mind when I went to a different entrance to the Vatican the following morning at 7 a.m. Located just off St. Peter's Square, the St. Anne's Gate is one of the international borders between the Vatican and Italy. As such, it was protected by a member of the Swiss Guard, a stockinged and pantalooned patrolman, draped in billowing red, blue, and butterscotch and looking very much like a dollop of tricolor toothpaste.

I was there to meet Daniel Gallagher, a mild-mannered American monsignor from the Midwest. Handsome, with an easy smile and neatly brushed sandy hair, Dan looked born to play the small-town mayor in a Broadway musical. In real life, he's a chief Latinist for the papacy. It's his job to transmit the pope's official utterances into Latin, including sermons, homilies, even tweets. The pontiff's Latin Twitter feed has half a million followers. In his spare time, Dan also translated **Diary of a Wimpy Kid** into the language of the popes.

Dan had invited along Liz Lev, an African-American art historian with russet hair pulled into a bun and a ready supply of books and papers tucked into a backpack. Liz is a native of Boston and two-decade resident of Rome who was working on a book about Michelangelo and women. A onetime lapsed Catholic, she had worked closely with Pope Benedict XVI on a project about faith and art that led her to renew her own practice.

We began walking up the Royal Stairs, the official welcome path for state visits to the Vatican, for what I thought was going to be breakfast. About halfway up the broad steps, Dan paused and pointed down a corridor. "These are called the stairs of the dead, because they're the shortest route from the papal apartments to the basilica and thus the path deceased popes take to their final resting place. When John Paul II died, people caught a glimpse of this because the cameras were following his corpse."

I mentioned something about the conclave, and he said he had something to show me. We walked through a large wooden door, watched over by yet another Swiss guard, and just like that I was standing again inside the empty Sistine Chapel. Having spent months trying to gain access, suddenly I was here for the second time in twelve hours.

What Dan wanted to point out was a burnt spot in the corner where officials place a temporary stove to burn ballots during the closed-door sessions that elect a pope. After the color of the smoke was indecipherable during the 2005 conclave that tapped Benedict, black-and-white dye was added for the gathering that tapped Francis.

"While it's great that tourists can visit the chapel," Dan said, "the room doesn't really come alive until there are liturgies in here. There is hardly a passage in Scripture that is not reflected on the walls or ceiling. And when someone is reading a passage, everyone, including the pope, scans the chapel to find the corresponding scenes. We're all contorting to look at the figures, and the figures seem to contort right back at us."

I asked Liz what stood out to her in the chapel.

"To me the most important thing about this room is that if you take Michelangelo's work as a whole—not just the nine Genesis scenes but also the dozens of sibyls, prophets, and ancestors that fill out the space—he makes the point of having a woman alongside every man. And in a room where women are not permitted to be in until 1700!"

The women on the periphery of the ceiling

are painted especially lovingly, Liz said. Their hair, their costumes, the way their children interact with them all indicate that Michelangelo was actually observing women closely in everyday life.

"This is a man who was out looking," Liz said. "And the idea that he portrays women so realistically in here is truly exceptional. It shows that women are more hardwired into the Church than people might think."

The link between how Adam and Eve were discussed in religious circles and the way women were treated by early Judaism and Christianity is profound, but not in ways that are always clear cut. Let's start with Jews. A number of commentators argued that the way God handcrafts Eve from Adam's body, then escorts her to his side, is a mark of exaltation. One midrash has God adorning Eve with twenty-four pieces of jewelry as a sign of her loftiness.

But by far the more common interpretation was that being created from Adam's body is inferior to being created from earth. One midrash has God putting Adam to sleep before creating Eve because "the beginning of a man's downfall is sleep: being asleep, he does not engage in study." Another says bone is clearly inferior to dirt. "Why is it that woman must perfume herself but a man does not?" asks one rabbi. Because man is made from earth and earth doesn't stink, while the inverse is true for bone. "Consider! If you leave a bone three days without salt, it immediately begins to stink."

The hierarchical view of man and woman can be summed up in this colorful passage from Genesis Rabbah:

> I will not create her from his head, lest she be swell-headed; nor from the eye, lest she be a coquette; nor from the ear, lest she be an eavesdropper; nor from the mouth, lest she be a gossip; nor from the heart, lest she be prone to jealousy; nor from the hand, lest she be light-fingered; nor from the foot, lest she be a gadabout; but from the modest part of man, for even when he stands naked, that part is covered.

The Christian view of Adam and Eve is more complex. Adam and Eve don't play a huge role in the New Testament, though Jesus is called "the son of Adam." Jesus refers to the first couple only once, when asked about divorce, and he appears not to favor one sex over the other. "Haven't you read that at the beginning the creator 'made male and female' and said, 'For this reason a man will leave his father and mother and be united to his wife, and the two will become one flesh.'"

Paul, however, makes his view clear: Man is superior. "I do not permit a woman to teach or to assume authority over a man," he writes in 1 Timothy. "She must be quiet. For Adam was formed first, then Eve."

As Christianity evolved, the connection between the first couple of Genesis and the first family of the New Testament only deepened. Adam and Eve's failings serve as contrasts for the primary players in the Christ story. Adam is a worldly figure, Paul argues; Jesus is an otherworldly one. Adam is mortal; Jesus is divine. "The first man is of the earth, earthy," Paul says. "The second man is the Lord from heaven."

Michelangelo draws on this connection between Adam and Jesus, but he's far more interested in another connection—between Eve and Mary. That association grew up in the years after the New Testament. The second-century bishop Irenaeus was the first to write that just as Eve, a virgin who disobeyed God, brings death

Panels from the ceiling of the Sistine Chapel
depicting the downfall of Adam and Eve, the
Creation of Eve, and the **Creation of Adam.**
Michelangelo painted the **Creation of Eve**
in the center of the chapel.

into the world, it would take Mary, a virgin who obeyed God, to bring salvation.

Once introduced, the idea that Mary was the "second Eve" spread quickly. It was fueled by the fact that the Latin name **Eva** spelled backward is **Ave**, the familiar greeting the angel Gabriel gave Mary and that echoes in the wildly popular **Ave Maria**. As Mary's stature grew in the Church, Eve's stature grew alongside it, until this mystical kinship found its greatest expression in the Sistine Chapel.

After we settled into the room, Liz walked Dan and me step-by-step through how Michelangelo used his portrayal of Adam and Eve to systematically elevate women in the Church.

"Let's start with the **Creation of Adam**," Liz said. "Adam is very much a passive figure about to receive this energy from God." Michelangelo is always a "moment before" guy, she said. He likes showing things just before they happen.

"But once God activates Adam, he's going to need a partner," Liz continued. "So look at God's other arm, it goes around Eve, suggesting she's part of his plan. There's something lovely about how this is painted. Eve's hand comes up and touches God's arm. There's a confidence and an intimacy. The more I look at it, the more connection I see between them."

I mentioned that one of my daughters had first suggested to me that the woman under God's left arm might be Eve.

"I'm amazed your daughter saw that," she said. "She should be doing art history."

"That would make my mother very happy," I said.

"But I think your daughter is right," Liz went on. "This room is all about Mary." The man most responsible for this room, Sixtus IV, is the one who gave us the Feast of the Immaculate Conception, she explained, which takes Mary and puts her on a plane with Jesus. The biggest piece of art in the room, the **Last Judgment**, places Mary immediately to the right of Jesus.

"The entire room is designed to send a signal that Mary is central to salvation," Liz said. "Making Eve the central figure of the ceiling is a way of building up Mary."

That led to the second panel in the series, the **Creation of Eve**. In this genre-bending image, a slumbering Adam lies prone under a dead tree trunk, while an upright God, in a white robe and golden beard, stands gesturing with his right hand. Between these two male figures is Eve, her right foot tucked behind Adam's left side and her face and clasped hands pointing in the direction of God. The way the panel is designed, Eve's face and torso fill the center. I asked Liz the significance of the fact that Eve, not Adam and not God, is the navel of the entire room.

"I believe Michelangelo is emphasizing that Mary is a Co-Redemptrix alongside her son," she said. "In the Church, the Son of God is obviously the most important figure, but Mary is a close second. Putting Eve here is a way of emphasizing that the most important mortal who ever lived was not a man, but a woman. Think how radical that was in a place like this."

And what a radical image of Eve it is. Far from the graceful, ethereal women of Botticelli, Michelangelo's Eve is strong, with muscular legs, a potato-y midsection, and bulging biceps. She's just as tall as Adam and God, and, counter to the commentaries, she's hardly some afterthought, plucked from a second-rate part of Adam's body and destined to live out her life in his shadow. Michelangelo not only respected this woman. He may have feared her a little, too.

"I personally wish she were a little bit more sensual," Liz said. "I understand, at the end of the day, she has to be a chunky figure. We are not linked to God by something fragile. And like many Renaissance painters, Michelangelo would have used a man to model Eve in this image. You only used female models when they were your wife, your girlfriend, or your prostitute, and Michelangelo had none of these."

But what she lacks in conventional beauty, Liz said, she more than makes up in stature. In every way, she is Adam's equal.

This equality of stature is most evident in the third and final panel of the series. In the first panel, the **Creation of Adam**, Adam and Eve are on opposite sides of the composition, separated by God. In the second panel they are joined at Adam's side, with God alongside them. By the third panel they are fully entwined—intimately, erotically, sexually—with God nowhere in sight. In a bold statement of their equivalence, both Adam **and** Eve in this image reach for the forbidden fruit.

Even more shocking, Eve's face in this image is positioned directly alongside Adam's exposed, slightly engorged member. Were she to turn her head away from the serpent and back toward Adam she would create a scene unfit for papal consumption. This fellatory image was considered so scandalous the Vatican forbade it from being reproduced for centuries.

"What I find fascinating," Liz said, "is that

Adam and Eve's bodies are complementary in this panel. They just fit together. He's much more forceful in the way he reaches for the fruit, and she's more yearning. Plus, they're beautiful. Those are the bodies of gods."

"Are they in love?"

She smiled. "It's always love," she said, "because God is love. The question is defining what kind of love it is. It's not 'I have a cuddly feeling' kind of love. It's 'They're made of God's love so they're made for each other' kind of love. In that way their love relationship is a model for ours."

The first tourists were starting to file into the chapel by now. Dan had to go off to work. In less than twenty-four hours, I had rethought a lifetime of conventional ideas I had about the Sistine Chapel. No longer did I view it as a temple of maleness, a place where God and Adam effortlessly assert their patriarchal control over the world. No longer did I view Adam as the central figure in the room and Eve the forgotten one.

Instead I saw the chapel as a bulwark against those ideas, a corrective to centuries of belittling Eve. I saw it as a restoration of the idea that Adam and Eve share credit—and blame—for what happened in Eden.

And in delivering that revolutionary message,

Michelangelo reminds us of the revolutionary message in the early verses of Genesis. For all the differences between the first and second creation stories, there is one overriding similarity: Both portray man and woman as containing a piece of the other within them. It's the same shared physicality that comes across in Michelangelo's panels, and that anyone who's ever been in love has experienced in one way or another. "Every fall into love involves the triumph of hope over self-knowledge," wrote Alain de Botton. "We fall in love hoping that we will not find in another what we know is in ourselves." But as Adam and Eve show, that's not really possible, because part of what we find in the other is the piece of ourselves that we feel is missing.

As we prepared to leave, I asked Liz the question that had begun my journey here years earlier, when one of my daughters looked at Michelangelo's **Creation of Adam** and said, "Where am I in that picture?" Is it possible, in the twenty-first century, that these images have anything to teach us about our own lives?

"It's the same question I've been asking myself since I first came here as a young art history student," she said. "I looked up at the ceiling and thought, 'It's dark. It's unwelcoming. I don't want to be here.' But about fifteen years ago, when I started working on Michelangelo's depiction of women, I began to ask a different question. 'How can this room, painted five hundred years ago for old white guys in dresses, a room I wouldn't even have been allowed in for hundreds of years, be a place where I feel so completely at home?'

"And that's when I began to realize," she continued, "that everywhere in this room where there's a hero, there's a heroine, too. There's a partnership between man and woman that's a reflection of the partnership between humans and God. That's what I would tell your daughters. You can take the path in life that allows you to navigate on your own. It may lead to tremendous fortune and success, but I'm not sure it leads to serenity, joy, or a real sense of fulfillment.

"Or you can take the other path. The one that leads you to form relationships. And when you come into a room like this and look at the ceiling, you realize that our earliest ancestors were in relationships. They were the first to do this thing we're all still trying to figure out."

"So what can we learn from them?"

She thought for a few seconds.

"First, that we're made for love. That's what that initial image shows: We were made out of love, and we were made for love.

"Second, that real love is gentle. The gentleness with which God awakens Adam is a powerful expression of how we are supposed to love. Not the forceful, 'Come here, do what I say,' but the gentle giving of ourselves. God gives of himself to awaken Adam, then Adam gives of himself to awaken Eve.

"Finally, that real love is about completion. That's what happens when Adam and Eve leave Eden: They learn that they are incomplete without each other. Love is not a brief flash of pleasure. Nor is it a long, dutiful trudge. Love is an opportunity to find a situation with another person that will lead you to greater holiness. Ultimately, you're trying to build on the inside what Michelangelo depicts on the outside: two people, equal in size and stature, that with the grace of God are growing into something that's more like God, something that's very good."

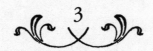

THE DEVIL
MADE ME DO IT

What We Do for Love

Around four o'clock in the afternoon is a great time to visit a cemetery in London. The light has usually mellowed. The rain-stained crypts seem to soften under the lengthening shadows. And children on their way home giggle, shout or play hide-and-seek among the gravestones. These sometimes forbidding monuments become approachable, even gregarious, and, if you're lucky, their ghosts are free to talk.

Late one summer afternoon, I stepped through the entrance of Bunhill Fields Burial Grounds on the eastern edge of old London. I was accompanied by Lance Pierson, a genial, balding, sixtysomething Oxford-educated actor with a passion for Shakespeare and Renaissance poetry.

He wanted to show me what might be considered the birthplace of marital bliss.

"Even most Londoners don't know about this place," he said.

At a little under ten acres, Bunhill Fields is hardly the largest of London's cemeteries. Opened in 1665, after the city's churchyards overflowed during the plague, it wasn't an especially desirable place to be interred. It is the final resting spot of some of the country's most notorious religious rebels—John Bunyan, Daniel Defoe, William Blake, and the "Mother of Methodism" Susanna Wesley.

But soon after it opened, Bunhill Fields became the front yard and unwitting inspiration for another notorious rebel, a golden-tongued diplomat who rose to the highest levels of English government, only to be disgraced, thrown into prison, and exiled to live out his days across the street from a graveyard.

John Milton was right at home at death's door. By the time he moved here at age fifty, he had buried his mother, his father, two wives, a son, a daughter, countless friends to hanging, and more than a few to disemboweling. He was also ill, suffering from gout, and completely blind. One of his contemporaries wrote that he used to sit in a gray, coarse cloth coat at the door of his house, enjoying the fresh air and receiving visits.

"It's very evocative to me that he could be just there and we could go and talk to him," Lance said.

"And what would you ask him?"

"How do you find the will to go on living?"

The answer is that he retreated into the company of the earliest heroes of his faith and reimagined their story as no one else had. In the process, Milton gave life to an idea so commonplace today it's hard to remember that it was once a crime. The idea was that people should love the person they wed, and if they don't, they should be allowed, even encouraged, to divorce them. The inspiration behind this unlikely crusade was his own failed marriage, along with his lifelong desire for emotional intimacy and his belief that romantic companionship was the ultimate answer to loneliness.

John Milton, scholars believe, invented the idea of what we today call companionate marriage. And to bring this notion to life, he used the story of history's most famous couple. At the time, few people considered the inhabitants of Eden paragons of a good marriage. Milton single-handedly changed that, and he did so against extraordinary challenges: He composed his epic while entirely blind.

Paradise Lost is many things: the greatest poem ever written in English; the bane of high schoolers everywhere; the cri de coeur of an angry, bitter, thrice-married man. But above all it is the step-by-step argument for the idea that Adam and Eve are the first and best example of a loving relationship.

In the march of Western civilization, one of the great hinges in the evolution of love from abstract philosophical ideal to messy, elevating reality was the invention of a heartsick poet and pamphleteer who lived across the road from a cemetery. In marking this achievement, John Milton deserves credit for doing more than anyone in history to advance the belief that Adam and Eve is a love story.

IN 1597, eleven years before John Milton was born, William Shakespeare published **Romeo and Juliet**, or, as it was known at the time, **The Most Excellent and Lamentable Tragedie of Romeo and Juliet.** That play helped popularize the idea that a love story must be built around pain. As philosopher Robert Solomon puts it, love is not just a momentary passion but an emotional development, an arc, a narrative. And the crux of that narrative is a difficulty that must be surmounted.

"The heart of the love story, what makes it romantic, is the 'problem,'" Solomon writes. "Love is a challenge, an enormous and often pathologically stubborn effort to overcome misunderstanding, tragedies and apparent betrayals."

While this formula is sometimes attributed to Shakespeare or the classic Greek plays he was inspired by, no place more brilliantly brings it to life than the opening verses of Genesis. In the story of Adam and Eve, the chief conflict is whether the protagonists will eat from the tree of the knowledge of good and evil, and the chief tempter is the serpent.

The narrative of the tree begins in chapter 3 and the first thing to note about it is that almost everything we think we know about it—that the snake is the Devil, that Eve is the victim, that her succumbing initiates the descent of evil into the world—is not in the original text. Even the word "fall" does not appear. These interpretations are layered onto the story by the almost exclusively male commentariat.

The biblical narrative begins with Adam and Eve in a state of wedded bliss, as captured in the last line of chapter 2: "The two of them were naked, the man and his wife, yet they felt no shame." Chapter 3 opens with an ominous, even peculiar shift, the introduction of a heretofore unmentioned character, a talking snake. "Now the serpent was the shrewdest of all the wild beasts that the Lord God had made," the text says. "He said to the woman, 'Did God really say: You shall not eat of any tree of the garden?'"

Serpents have a long association with deception in the ancient Near East. Mesopotamians considered them symbols of guile; Egyptians used them to represent black magic. The Bible alone links serpents to divination, the Devil, and dragon monsters. But serpents were also associated with health and wellness, as in the serpent-entwined Rod of Asclepius, still in use by the American Medical Association. Like so many elements of the story, the true symbolism of the snake is twisted in mystery.

The serpent immediately zeroes in on the tree and tries to undermine God's command. What exactly is this tree? Eden actually has two named flora. The first is the tree of life, a common symbol that appears throughout the Bible as a sign of divine presence. The second is the tree of the knowledge of good and evil, an awkward name that suggests it bestows godlike powers on anyone who consumes its fruit. The tree becomes the subject of a taut back-and-forth between the serpent and Eve. She responds, "We may eat of the fruit of the other trees," but of this particular tree God has said, "You shall not eat it or touch it, lest you die."

The serpent counters, "You are not going to die, but God knows that as soon as you eat of it your eyes will be opened and you will be like divine beings."

Now comes the test. Eve must decide whether to follow the will of God, even though she never hears it directly, or follow what she sees with her own eyes. With remarkably little wavering, she sides with her own eyes. "When the woman saw that the tree was good for eating and a delight to the eyes, and the tree was desirable as a source of wisdom, she took the fruit and ate."

What exactly has she eaten? All we are told is that the woman eats the fruit, or **peri**, of the tree. Over the years, countless interpretations have been offered for what type of fruit it is, including pomegranate, carob, pear, quince, apricot, and date. The most popular choice, "apple," seems unlikely on the surface since apples are not native to the ancient Near East. This association began with the Vulgate, the popular fifteenth-century Latin edition of the Bible, which used the Latin word for evil, **malus**, in the name "tree of the knowledge of good and evil." The Latin word for "apple" is the similar-sounding **malum**, and the association stuck.

An apple also plays up the sexual overtones that came to be associated with the story. "The Song of Songs," with its heavy allusions to Eden, compares apples to female breasts. Ancient Greeks and Romans spoke euphemistically of sexual relations as "stealing apples." In another linguistic oddity that many believe has erotic origins, the larynx, or voice box, which is noticeably more prominent in men than in women, came to be called the "Adam's apple" after the idea that the forbidden fruit got stuck in Adam's throat as he swallowed.

There is clear sexual innuendo in yet another possible fruit that's alluded to in the Jewish commentaries and picked up by Michelangelo in the Sistine Chapel. In the third panel of his Adam and Eve sequence, at exactly the moment Eve's head is stationed alongside Adam's scrotum, Eve reaches for two figs shaped unavoidably like a

pair of testicles. We know that figs, unlike apples, are actually in Eden, because when Adam
and Eve discover they are naked immediately
after they eat the fruit, they cover themselves
with fig leaves. Some observers have also pointed
out that in the Italian of Michelangelo, the word
for "fig," **fico**, sounds remarkably like **fica**, a
Renaissance Italian vulgarism for female genita-
lia and the root for the verb **ficcare**, which means
to drive and thrust.

Regardless of what fruit it is, what happens
when Eve tastes it? We are poised to expect
thunderclaps, lightning bolts, instant annihila-
tion. Plenty of times in the Bible when God is
defied, he responds with immediate, bloodcurdling death. Surely this first transgression will
be met with definitive retaliation.

Instead, here's what happens: nothing. Eve
doesn't die. She's not even wounded, injured,
hobbled, or roughed up in any way. God, at least
in the internal logic of the story, appears to be
wrong.

Even more surprising, the serpent turns out
to be right! The story reports what happens next
in a remarkably understated way: "She also gave
some to her husband, who was with her, and he
ate." Adam and Eve have both eaten of the fruit

of the tree of the knowledge of good and evil, and both have lived to tell about it. They end their minidrama exactly where they began: bound together as one.

IF ONLY.

The story of how this narrative has been interpreted over the centuries is elaborate, at times deeply misogynistic, and profoundly consequential to the history of male-female relations in the West. Jews put meaning enough into these events, but Christians made them the centerpiece of their entire worldview, a precondition for the rise of Jesus Christ. The popular American spiritual "Them Bones Will Rise Again" captures the connection:

> That's all there is, there ain't no more.
> Eve got the apple and Adam got the core.
> That's the story of the Fall from Grace.
> Until Jesus saved the human race.

Looking back, it seems fair to say the two-hundred-word set piece about the forbidden fruit became the pivotal story in the first two thousand years of Judeo-Christian life. Before

examining how we might read this story today—
or how Milton read it in his time—it's important to understand the consensus interpretation
that built up in the first millennium of organized religion.

For many early commentators, the responsibility for eating the fruit was clear: It was the
girl's fault. The earliest source to link Eve's eating the fruit with the larger decline of humanity
was a Jewish text from the second century B.C.E.,
the Wisdom of Jesus Ben Sirach. "From a woman
sin had its beginning, and because of her we all
die."

Christian interpreters picked up on this theme
and homed in on why the serpent chose Eve.
One commented, "Not daring to accost the man
because of his strength, he accosted as being
weaker the woman." No less an authority than
Martin Luther wrote, "Because Satan sees that
Adam is the more excellent, he does not dare to
assail him; for he fears that his attempt may turn
out to be useless."

Yet just because Eve took the brunt of the
criticism didn't mean Adam got off easily. If
anything, many commentators were even more
withering toward him. At least Eve had an excuse; she was duped by the serpent. Adam had

no one to blame but himself. "Better had it been that the earth had not produced Adam," wrote one rabbi. Again it was Jews who started this line of attack. The first century C.E. text 2 Esdras says, "O Adam, what have you done? For though it was you who sinned, the fall was not yours alone, but ours also who are your descendants." But it was Christians who carried the idea through the centuries. "Sin entered the world through one man and through sin death," wrote Paul.

By the Middle Ages, the belief that Adam and Eve were failures whose weakness introduced iniquity, disease, and demise into the world was nearly universal. Before the Fall, wrote one sixteenth-century commentator, the stomach digested food better, the liver produced purer blood, and the heart was more resilient. After the Fall, "the body and all its limbs are feeble, dull, lazy, reluctant and frail." Given this consensus, it was all the more remarkable that in the seventeenth century one man could tilt into the headwind of such ecumenical scorn and reintroduce Adam and Eve as a couple not just capable of sin and devastation but of deep, abiding love.

.   .   .

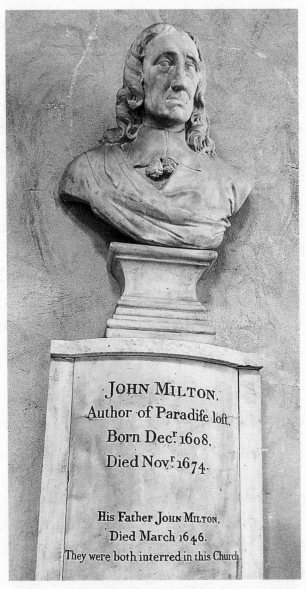

JOHN MILTON,
Author of Paradise lost,
Born Dec.r 1608,
Died Nov.r 1674.

His Father JOHN MILTON,
Died March 1646.
They were both interred in this Church.

A bust of Milton near his burial site in St. Giles' without Cripplegate, a church in London.

MOST OF THE PLACES John Milton lived were destroyed in the Great Fire of London of 1666, which wiped out 13,200 houses, 87 churches, and the homes of 70,000 of the city's 80,000 residents. Only six people died, but the character of the entire city was altered. In 2008, on the four-hundredth anniversary of Milton's birth, Lance Pierson decided to celebrate his favorite author by creating two live shows and a walking tour of his life.

The first place he took me was a small alley not far from St. Paul's Cathedral in what is today the city's financial district. Tucked away on the wall was a large marble plaque.

JOHN MILTON
was BORN in BREAD-STREET, on Friday, the 9th day of December, 1608

"London was a walled, medieval city at the time," Lance said. "And this was the market. All the streets were named after trades—bread, fish, meat, milk. But the neighborhood had a lot of money, and for Milton's father it was an ideal place to have his office as a scrivener, a mix of lawyer and moneylender."

For the elder John Milton, who had been disinherited by his Roman Catholic father after he became a Protestant, his profession and ideal location earned him significant wealth. His son took ample advantage, with private tutors and the best education money could buy, first at St. Paul's and then Cambridge, where he ranked fourth in his class. Following university, Milton continued studying on his own and completed his version of a Grand Tour, visiting France and Italy. While it's tempting to imagine him inside the Sistine Chapel, he left no record.

"This whole decade was his way of completing his education," Lance said. "Meeting everybody who was everybody and reading everything he could find."

Milton dreamed of becoming a poet-priest, and from his earliest writings, he showed fervent interest in love. Sex was the theme of one of his first elegies: "What is lovelier than she as she voluptuously bares her fertile breast and breathes the perfume of Arabian harvests." In his twenties he took pride in preserving his virginity for religious obligation, a decision that appears to have stoked his fantasies. "Losing no time he swung on the girl's eyelashes, then on her mouth, then jumped between her lips," he wrote in one poem. "I burned inwardly with love."

The elder Milton hoped his son would become an Anglican priest, but the younger Milton followed his father's lead and rebelled against the religion of his youth. Inspired by the corruption he witnessed in Rome, Milton turned against similar corruption he saw in the Church of England. Milton became a Puritan, arguing that power in the hands of bishops should be rejected, Scripture alone should determine matters of religion, and everyone should be his own prophet. The next place Lance took me, Milton's burial place at St. Giles' without Cripplegate church, captured this asceticism. The only marker is a modest stone.

"To me this chasteness is very appropriate," Lance said. "Milton believed that if churches needed to exist, they should be plain, with nothing to obscure an individual's direct relationship with God."

Once he tiptoed into the culture wars of the day, Milton could not be stopped. He became a fierce antiroyalist during the Civil Wars that pitted Republicans against the Crown and wrote detailed pamphlets advocating freedom of speech and separation of church and state, both decades before these ideals were widely adopted. When Parliament briefly seized government,

Milton was named secretary of foreign tongues, meaning he translated official correspondence into Latin.

But his most enduring contribution was in the arena of marriage. In 1642, thirty-four-year-old Milton paid a call on a justice of the peace near Oxford named Richard Powell. He returned a month later with a bride, Powell's eldest daughter, seventeen-year-old Mary. The lifelong romantic was ecstatic. Yet barely a month into their marriage, with the dowry not even paid, Mary returned to her family and refused to have any relations with her heart-stricken husband.

Instead of feeling sorry for himself, however, Milton channeled his pain into a diatribe for the ages. He published five lengthy tracts—over sixty thousand words—arguing that divorce, then permissible only in cases of infidelity or abandonment, should be legal and socially acceptable. The primary aim of marriage, he insisted, was fellowship of the mind and spirit, not the oft-cited reasons of procreation and relief of lust. Even loveless sex, he said, was nothing but slavery, a mere grinding "in the mill of an undelighted and servil copulation."

A devout Christian, Milton based his argu-

ment almost entirely on the Bible. The fundamental basis of marriage, he insisted, is what
God declared in the Garden of Eden, "It is not
good that man be alone." A successful bond is
built on the "apt and cheerful conversation," he
said, not the imperative of having children,
which comes later in the story. "The prime end
and form of marriage is not the bed," Milton
wrote, "but conjugal love and mutual assistance
in life."

Clearly drawing from his own misbegotten
marriage, Milton noted that nothing is worse
than a wife unfit for companionship because of
"dullness" and "deadnes of spirit," a personality
that's "mute and spiritless," an "unaffectionate
and sullen masse whose very company represents
the visible and exactest figure of loneliness."

The pain in these documents, and their sheer
volume, shows how much the man who had
long dreamed of love felt crushed. The phrases
he used to describe a true soul mate are extraor-
dinarily evocative: the person should be a "fit
conversing soul," "an intimate and speaking
help," "a ready and reviving associate." It's worth
remembering this is the 1640s, not the 1960s.
By using his voice to rail against meaningless
sex and loveless marriage Milton laid the ground-

work for a rethinking of how society considered intimacy. And his views became the foundation for his revolutionary retelling of Adam and Eve.

Despite being such a vocal advocate of dissolving marriage, Milton himself never got divorced. Mary Powell returned to her estranged husband three years later, and the two went on to have four children, before she died following childbirth. Milton's second marriage, to Katherine Woodcock, was happier. But she too died, two years later, after giving birth to a daughter, who also died.

Milton, by this point disgraced and out of a job following the Restoration of the monarchy, married for a third time after moving across from Bunhill Fields. His new wife was thirty-one years younger, a caretaker mainly, and, as Lance pointed out, perhaps not a very good one. "The slightly worrying thing is that when he died it took place over the space of forty-eight hours," Lance said. "She knew he was alive on Tuesday and discovered he was dead on Thursday. It doesn't suggest she was taking very close care of him!"

We were standing now at the final stop of our tour, in the home Milton occupied immediately after he was released from jail. Appropriate for a blind man who feared for his life, the narrow street was located on the extreme edge of town. Its name: Jewin Street, because it was the one place Jews were allowed to live in London. For a deeply symbolic man like Milton, the meaning could not have been lost. Exiled from the Promised Land, he found himself in the wilderness, with no place to turn to except his faith. Sure enough, it was here that he returned to his earliest dream—to become a poet-priest, to fulfill his classical learning, to realize his longstanding desire of finding everlasting love. It was here that he began writing **Paradise Lost**.

I asked Lance why he believed Milton latched onto this story.

"Because Adam and Eve were the progenitors, the originals of the human race," he said. "He saw himself writing an epic poem that would out-epic all the previous ones."

But even more than that, he went on, there was something about this story that Milton related to personally. "Milton endures a huge amount of disappointment, frustration, and tragedy in his life," Lance said. "And by the time he moved here, he had just lost his second wife. He was abidingly lonely. I feel for him. But he found comfort in our first parents. The fact that everything started out well between Adam and Eve, then everything went wrong, then after they got kicked out of Paradise, they had to start all over again.

"There's a beautiful lesson in that," Lance continued. "Milton wrote about Adam and Eve because he believed their story could help people like him. Because he believed God wanted us to find partners with whom we could have a lifelong conversation, a 'sweet and gladsome society,' as he called it. And if that type of intimacy was good enough for Adam and Eve, why not for us?"

BEFORE DISCUSSING the achievement of **Paradise Lost**, we should acknowledge that not everyone has loved it. Candide called the poem "obscure, bizarre, and disgusting." Samuel Johnson said, "**Paradise Lost** is one of the books which the reader admires and lays down, and forgets to take up again. None ever wished it longer than it is." And the legendary twentieth-century critic Northrop Frye wrote of Milton's protagonists, "Adam and Eve are suburbanites in the nude, and like other suburbanites they are preoccupied with gardening, with their own sexual relations, and with the details of their rudimentary housekeeping."

Still, **Paradise Lost** represents a high-water mark for writing about the Bible in English. The Bible experienced a boom in seventeenth-century England, fed by the publication in 1611 of the King James Bible. The first translation in almost two thousand years that drew heavily from the Hebrew, the widely printed volume kicked off a frenzy of lay engagement. People hung hand-painted biblical quotations directly on their walls; they ate dinner on tablecloths and plates decorated with biblical scenes; they posted instructions for maintaining biblical households in their kitchens. Children often learned to read from the Bible, and it was a source of entertainment for the population at large. As Defoe put it, "Preaching of sermons is speaking to a few of mankind; printing of books is talking to the whole world."

With all this attention on biblical stories, it was hardly surprising that Milton, burned by politics, turned to the Bible's first couple for his final reach for grandeur.

First published in 1667, **Paradise Lost** ultimately contained twelve books and ten thousand lines of verse. It includes two narrative arcs.

The first focuses on Satan and other rebel angels waging war against Heaven, losing, and being banished to hell. The second is a groundbreaking domestic epic that examines the intimate relationship between Adam and Eve. "Our parents" are presented for the first time in world literature as having a complete, well-rounded, nuanced marriage. "Hail wedded love," as Milton puts it.

Barbara Lewalski, a professor of English at Harvard and one of the world's leading Milton scholars, summed up his achievement this way: Milton "explores through Adam and Eve the fundamental challenge of any love relationship: the uneasy, inevitable, and ultimately creative tension between autonomy and interdependence."

Before coming to London, I went to see Professor Lewalski at her home in Providence, Rhode Island. In her mideighties, widowed, with short, sandy hair and irrepressible spunk, she welcomed me with a cup of tea and a blunt take on why Milton matters.

"Some people thought you shouldn't write epics about the Bible," she said. "Imaginative literature requires invention, and you can't go around inventing about the Bible. But that

didn't bother Milton. He spent his whole life interested in love, and he wanted to imagine how
our first parents experienced it. Plus, he got to
write about how they experienced sex."

I was little taken aback. "He did?"

"Oh, certainly. Go back and look at Book
Four. They go into their hideaway and have sex.
And it's good sex! A wonderful celebration of
the joys of conjugal love. It's also the essence of
Milton's philosophy: God doesn't want us to be
miserable. He wants us to be happy."

When we first meet Adam and Eve in **Paradise Lost**, they are blissfully enmeshed in paradise: "Reaping immortal fruits of joy and love,
uninterrupted joy, unrivaled love." But soon Eve
begins to crave more. She wanders off by herself
and encounters a beautiful image in a lake, for
which she feels "sympathy and love." In a moment that embodies Judy Klitsner's idea that the
first kind of love is self-love, the image turns out
to be Eve's own reflection. She considers staying
but instead elects to return to Adam.

"Milton is great on choice," Barbara said.
"You don't go around forcing people. They have
to make their own decisions. Here she chooses
to be with her partner, and Adam chooses to
forgive her. It's a real moment by a real couple,
albeit an imperfect one."

But tensions continue. In a scene unprecedented in other accounts of their lives, Adam and Eve have a bitter, back-and-forth fight about equality. Eve says there's so much work to be done tending the garden, that they should divide the labor equally. Don't be absurd, Adam says, nothing can be lovelier than a woman who supports her husband. Outraged, Eve threatens to go off on her own, but Adam warns she'll encounter someone who "envying our happiness" will "disturb conjugal love."

"Frail is our happiness if this be so," she retorts dryly.

Adam, not wanting to threaten her independence, backs down. The stage is set for Milton's audacious move: reimaging the Fall as something not altogether horrible.

I asked Barbara where Milton got his radical view that love could be a negotiation between partners.

"There is great interest in romance during this period," she said. "There are romantic plays, romantic verse. But those are primarily courtship stories. The girl and boy love each other, and they have obstacles to overcome before marrying. It usually ends with them living happily ever after, but what happens after that? The writers never show it. I think there's something pretty unusual about what Milton does, which is discuss what love is really like."

Milton, in this case, is part of a larger evolution. The earlier focus on love as being controlled by divine intervention had been waning for some time. Now love was beginning to be seen as grounded in human behavior. This movement was consistent with the larger shift in the Renaissance toward humanism, in which the focus of life turned away from church and more toward human beings. God is still the ultimate figurehead, but the new concept of "true love" contains within it sexual satisfaction and earthly pleasures. The art of courtly love, which arose in France during the late Middle Ages, is often mentioned as the source of this idea, but it was more limited, a game of seduction played between a married man and his mistress. "Love can have no place between husband and wife," wrote the twelfth-century French author of **About Love.** The most ennobling love, by contrast, was secret, inspiring, unobtainable. Courtly love did contain one innovation: Women, for the first time, had some modicum of power over men. Men could express their desires, but women got to choose whether to take them up on it.

The biggest impact of courtly love was that it

helped spawn a burgeoning self-help literature. Books like **Advice on Love** and **Advice to the Ladies** offered techniques about flirtation, seduction, and concealing your true feelings. The game of romance, as we know it today, began to emerge.

Inevitably, this new spotlight on relationships fell on the first relationship in the Bible. Protestant writers in Milton's era were particularly eager to elevate Adam and Eve as exemplars of romantic affection: "Two sweet friends, bred under one constellation, tempered by an influence from heaven," wrote one author. Scores of plays about the first couple were written during these years. With all this attention, Milton's fascination with the origins of romantic love was no aberration. Where he went further was in applying this interest to what many thought was Adam and Eve's greatest sin.

From the outset of Christianity, the central theological view of Eve and Adam's decision to eat the forbidden fruit was that it introduced sin into the world. The Fall, as it came to be called, was the precondition for the return of Jesus.

But while this doctrine was being passed down, a rival interpretation was bubbling up, that eating the fruit, while a sin, was a necessary

one, because it allowed humans to have the un-
godly lives that Jesus would redeem. The Church
Father Irenaeus was the first to suggest this in
the third century. In time this alternate doctrine
came to be called "felix culpa," the "fortunate
fall." In the words of one seventeenth-century
writer: "Oh happy Fall, and happy unhappiness,
which was the occasion of so great happiness."

While popular, this new way of looking at
Eden also left an awkward gap. If Adam and
Eve didn't eat the fruit because it was wrong,
what motivated them? Milton's answer was radical.

He gave their actions a positive motivation.
In Eve's case, he made her decision about pursuing wisdom. After separating from Adam, she
meets the serpent, who has been occupied by
Satan and transformed into an advocate for
self-improvement through learning. "Do not believe those rigid threats of death!" the serpent
says. "Ye shall not die!" The fruit, he says, "gives
you life" and "knowledge."

Eve hesitates, but soon succumbs to this
promise of wisdom. God "forbids us to be wise?"
she asks. No way! She plucks the prize and
greedily eats. As happens in Genesis, she doesn't
die.

But then Milton invents a breathtaking moment. In debating whether to share the fruit with Adam, Eve casts her choice as a decision between sharing all she's gained or keeping it all for herself. Should Adam "partake full happiness with me?" or should she "keep the odds of knowledge in my power?" She even suggests that keeping wisdom in her hands would be a win for the "female sex." It would "render me more equal," even "superior," she posits. Eve considers all this and yet can't make the power play, "So dear I love him."

Eve hurries to Adam's side and announces that everything he's heard about the fruit is a lie. Join me in eating, she says, and we'll share "equal joy, as equal love." Adam freezes, overcome with "blank, white horror chill." Yet he knows he has no choice. "How can I live without thee," he says. "How forgo thy sweet converse and love so dearly joined."

The use of the phrase "sweet converse" is telling; it's the same idea Milton laid out in his divorce tracts twenty-five years earlier. "No! No!" Adam cries. I won't be lonely again. I won't give another rib. We must remain together, "bliss or woe." Adam chooses "not death" but "life."

Adam chooses Eve.

I asked Barbara whether **Paradise Lost** represents the return of love to the center of the Adam and Eve story.

"I think so," she said. "It makes it a love story. It is a love story. Adam wants a mate, and he gets what he wants."

"But what kind of love story is it?" I asked.

"It's a messy one," she said. "Yes, they're interdependent, but they're autonomous, too. And that's not particular to Eden. That's what it means to be married. What's remarkable about Milton's achievement is that he portrays a complicated, mature, complex love, with all these choices to be made all the time. Some people say there can be no such thing as love in a continuing marriage, but Milton didn't believe that, and that's what makes this poem so terribly powerful."

THE DAY AFTER my Milton walking tour I took the train an hour northwest of London to the village of Chalfont St. Giles. It was here, in the summer of 1665, that Milton moved to escape the plague that was devastating the capital. One fifth of the city's population died. By mid-July, five hundred people a week were going to

Milton's timber-framed cottage in the village
of Chalfont St. Giles.

the grave, many in the massive burial pits in Bunhill Fields. Defoe said it became so bad that the delirious would simply run and fling themselves in.

Milton, along with his third wife and grown daughters from his first marriage, took up residence at the edge of town in a modest brick-and-shingle cottage. Today the home is a small museum, the second oldest literary shrine in Britain after Shakespeare's home in Stratford-upon-Avon. It was also struggling financially for lack of visitors.

"In this monarch-crazy country, Milton is still getting a bit of a bum rap for his political views," explained Keith Sugden, a member of the museum's board. "But if the republican regime had survived, Milton wouldn't have written the book for which he's known."

Keith showed me around, ending in the drawing room with its large stone hearth. Several first editions of **Paradise Lost** were on display, along with a lock of Milton's hair, and a list of words Milton invented. A Cambridge don trawled the **Oxford English Dictionary** looking for neologisms and concluded that Shakespeare had coined 239 words, John Donne 342, and Ben Jonson 558. Milton's tally was

630. Those include: gloom, impassive, dismissive, irksome, self-esteem, didactic, pandemonium, padlock, unhealthy, terrific, fragrance, outer space, self-delusion, jubilant, unconvincing, exhilaration, and—no surprise given his interest in romance—debauchery, besotted, sensuous, and love-lorn.

"Milton always had a rich inner life," Keith said. "He would wake up around four thirty and sit before the fire, where he'd compose, rewrite, and edit entirely in his head. Then the family got up, everyone had breakfast, and Milton would summon whatever amanuensis was at hand, usually one of his daughters, to write down what he had composed."

Keith excused himself, and I stepped into the garden, which was bursting with crab apples, peonies, lilies, and hydrangeas. In the back was someone's idea of literary drollery, a marble statue of a naked Eve with a child's inflatable purple pool floatie curled around her feet. The floatie was in the shape of a snake.

Since the start of my search into what Adam and Eve might tell us about relationships, I was struck by certain parallels between the biblical account and modern insights into human behavior. I'd already learned how much Adam and

Eve embody one pillar of contemporary psychology, that being a fully realized person requires a high degree of connectedness. Loneliness
is a key part of unhappiness; togetherness is a
key ingredient to happiness.

But there's another pillar of psychology that
the incident with the fruit embodies, that being emotionally healthy requires a high degree
of self-directedness. The founder of this line of
thinking is Edward Deci of the University of
Rochester in New York, and I spoke with him
about Adam and Eve at his summer home in
Maine.

Ed began studying motivation in the early
1960s and found above all that people don't like
being controlled by others, whether it's through
rules, money, or any other means of coercion.
Instead they like to feel independent and motivated from within. "We believe that human beings, doesn't matter culture, doesn't matter
gender, doesn't matter age, need to feel autonomy in order to be psychologically healthy," he
said. "That's an absolute proposition of self-
determination theory and we have hundreds
and hundreds of studies showing it to be true."

It's also true in relationships, he said. The
more each person promotes the autonomy of the

other, the better both parties feel. This can be done by listening carefully to your partner, understanding their perspective, and giving them choices rather than imposing your will. Milton, by showing Adam letting Eve go off on her own and Eve letting Adam decide whether to eat the fruit, illustrates the power of autonomy.

I asked Ed to apply his theory to the biblical story, beginning with the question, "Why does Eve eat?"

The first thing he observed is that Eve is subject to a lot of control—both coercive, in the form of the mandate not to eat from the tree, and seductive, in the form of the snake. So why does she defy convention and succumb to seduction? "It could be rebellion," he said, "which wouldn't be the healthiest reason, or it could be a more affirmative motivation that she wanted more meaning in her life." The story seems to hint at that, he said, when it says the fruit was "desirable as a source of wisdom." "For Eve, eating the fruit appears to be an autonomous choice," he said.

This fits the pattern in the story in which Eve is the more assertive actor. Eve provokes the marital crisis by going off into the garden by herself; Eve engages the serpent in debate; Eve plucks the fruit and eats it; Eve offers the fruit to Adam and gives him the choice whether to eat it. Barbara Lewalski uses a wonderful expression to describe **Paradise Lost**. She calls it an "Eviad." The founding text of Western civilization is not a male-first story; it's the female who takes the lead.

What makes Milton's version even more contemporary is that what Eve is looking for in this narrative is not power, fame, love, or money. It's knowledge. In Shakespeare's comedies, the conflict is often resolved when the man and woman reverse roles. Specifically, when the woman becomes the teacher. "Love," says Lord Berowne in **Love's Labour's Lost**, is "first learned in a lady's eyes." They are "the books, the arts, the academies."

Eve is the first teacher, the first to trust her eyes, the first who wants to know. In so doing, she becomes the first to commit the ultimate modern act of not accepting the meaning of others but insisting on making meaning yourself. She writes her own story.

To be sure, this act can be viewed negatively, as a way of saying "I know better than you." But it's also a way of saying "If I don't know for myself, I cannot know at all." And knowledge, in this instance, is empowering. As Dorothy Parker quipped, "The cure for boredom is curiosity. There is no cure for curiosity."

So that's Eve, but what about Adam? Why does he eat? Ed pointed out that there are three possible motives that guide people's decisions: They're coerced, they rebel, or they're motivated from within. "What I look for in healthy individuals is a deep commitment to acting out their personal interests," he said. "In this case, Adam seems to do that. He makes the autonomous decision to be with Eve."

As with her, his move could be viewed negatively: He's jealous. Psychologists have identified what they call the "endowment effect," meaning we fear losing something we have more than gaining something we don't. Adam does not want to lose his bride.

But to see him as merely reactive is to miss the point: He's active, too. He has free will. He could cast his lot with God and lose Eve, or cast his lot with Eve and lose God. He opts for the latter, and in so doing he chooses love over obedience. Who among us cannot relate to that?

"Love is born of an involuntary attraction that our free will transforms into a voluntary union," wrote Octavio Paz. "Voluntary union is love's necessary condition, the act that turns bondage into freedom."

Put more simply: He loves her. And not until that moment is he forced to identify his own feelings. Having been handed his love on a silver platter when God simply presents Eve to him, Adam for the first time now must get off the fence. And he does. "O I willingly stake all for you," Whitman wrote.

Now, at last, man and woman can be together as equals. Having both taken autonomous steps, they are finally autonomous from God. Only when each faces down death alone can they face life together. "Learning to be oneself," wrote Thomas Merton, "means learning to die in order to live."

The Bible is obsessed with vertical authority. God is on high, humans are below, animals are even lower than that. Figures are always climbing up mountains, rising to new heights, reaching to a higher plane. With all these heights come lots of falling. Israel falls, Moses falls, and, of course, Adam and Eve fall.

But as Milton understood, there's another way of looking at this story. In breaking away from the vertical, Adam and Eve commit to a horizontal partnership with each other. They propel their life story—and, in effect, the human story—forward. "Even God was secretly pleased," wrote Katha Pollitt in her poem "The Expulsion." "Let History begin!"

Only by eating the fruit could Adam and Eve be fruitful. Only after falling from grace can Adam and Eve fully fall in love with each other.

It's this sense of alignment in the face of what lies beyond Eden that Milton chooses to focus on at the end of his epic. Adam and Eve, having been banished by God, are left only with each other. Let us "lighten each other's burdens," they vow. Once we are out of Paradise, they say, we'll be in a "far happier place," enjoying "far happier days." And in perhaps the most beautiful image in the entire history of Adam and Eve, they walk out of the garden, side by side, both together and separate unto themselves.

The world was all before them, where to choose
Their place of rest, and Providence their guide.
They hand in hand with wand'ring steps and slow
Through Eden took their solitary way.

This haunting portrait of Adam and Eve captures one of the untold secrets of relationships that Milton had to learn for himself. Love binds you intimately to your lover, yet it can never entirely allay the loneliness. Even as you achieve interdependence, you still must preserve your independence. Even as you walk "hand in hand," you must still make your "solitary way."

CHORE WARS

Who Needs Love?

ON JULY 4, 1929, Friedrich Ritter, a blond, blue-eyed German doctor and lay philosopher, and his mistress, Dore Strauch, a former schoolteacher and devotee of Nietzsche, boarded a freighter in Amsterdam and sailed for the Pacific, where they intended to settle on an uninhabited island on the Galápagos and re-create the lives of Adam and Eve, right down to the naked farming. Ritter and Strauch, both married to other people at the time, had met in Berlin when he treated her for multiple sclerosis using the unconventional approach of applying mind over body.

They fell in love. "We had a feeling that we were intended for each other," Strauch later wrote, "as though we were a joint tool in the hand of a spirit using us to unknown ends." She would visit him daily at his office, and the two would sneak away to the roof for assignations. It was here, overlooking the crowded city, that they hatched their dream. "We lay up there in the sun letting our fancy wander where it would, pretending that the clouds that drifted by were our remote island of refuge and the blue sky the ocean in which our earthly Eden was set."

Ritter and Strauch arranged for what must have been an unimaginably awkward joint meeting with their spouses. Strauch's husband was a stern high school principal who wanted little more than a hausfrau; Ritter's wife was an opera singer who had given up her career for her husband. Under Ritter and Strauch's scheme, the two couples would simply switch partners and everyone would be happy. It worked! There was some fear about what the neighbors would think, but somehow the spouses agreed and the lovebirds were free to seek their new life as philosopher-gardeners, or as Ritter called them, "Homo solitarius."

In a final precautionary flourish, Ritter extracted all of his and Strauch's teeth and replaced them with rustproof steel dentures to prevent dental decay. Then they were off. The couple made their way to Ecuador, then to the island of Floreana, once called Charles Island after Darwin's storied visit in 1835. There, surrounded by tortoises and marine iguanas, they set up camp in an abandoned volcano overflowing with papayas, oranges, bananas, pineapples, guavas, lemons, and coconuts.

"We had chosen a place where no one was," Strauch recalled, "for we had learned that it is the contact with unlike natures that destroys the inner harmony of lives. We were to try and found an Eden not of ignorance but of knowledge."

What they didn't know is that the world they had left behind would soon make its way to their door, "to ruin what we made," in Strauch's words. When word of Ritter and Strauch's experiment in biblical asceticism leaked out, the two became instant celebrities. "Adam and Eve in the Galápagos" hailed **Atlantic Monthly** in a three-part, twenty-thousand-word exclusive. This fame inevitably attracted copycats, and soon others began popping up in paradise. One of those was a pistol-wearing, whip-yielding Austrian who insisted on being referred to by the fictional title "baroness" and who arrived with her three lovers and a plan to build a grand hotel on the island, called "Paradise Regained."

"I felt as Eve must have felt on learning that the serpent was the Evil One," Strauch wrote in her memoir, which she pointedly entitled **Satan Came to Eden**. Sure enough, within two years, two people were dead and two more were missing in what is widely regarded as a double homicide.

Along the way, the self-styled Adam and Eve of the Galápagos became yet another illustration of the three-thousand-year-old quest to perpetuate the idea of Eden. And they proved yet again that Adam and Eve, in their long history, have not just been figures of the Bible. They have been—and to many still are—exemplars of the deepest questions of human yearning: What does it mean to live in paradise? What does it mean to coexist with another? What does it mean to be in love?

THE INCIDENT WITH the fruit represents a critical turning point in the story of Adam and Eve. Up to now we've been in the "things are going along nicely" stage; now we enter the phase in which "things go horribly wrong." Afterward we have, in rapid order, Adam and Eve realizing they're naked, the confrontation with God, the exile from Eden, the birth of Cain and Abel, the introduction of murder and death.

Viewed through the rubric of the classic Hollywood three-act structure, we're now at what's called the "midpoint." In the first act, the "setup," the plot is put in motion. In this case that involves the formation of Adam and Eve, and their coming together as "one flesh." The first act ends when the protagonist experiences a complication that introduces a goal he or she wants to achieve. Eve, in this case, is the protagonist, and her dilemma is that despite being with Adam, she craves independence and goes off on a quest of self-discovery.

The second act in the Hollywood formula covers about half the story and is called the "confrontation." It focuses on the main character's struggle to achieve his or her goal. In this instance, the protagonist, Eve, meets an antagonist, the serpent, and she must decide whether to eat the fruit. About halfway through this act, the "midpoint," the formula calls for a critical plot turn in which the main character experiences what appears to be a devastating reversal of fortune. Here, the midpoint is eating the forbidden fruit, which results in Adam and Eve being booted from the garden. The final act is the climactic showdown in which the protagonist achieves (or does not achieve) the goal. In this case, will Adam and Eve live happily ever after?

Given that we're at this critical juncture, it seems a good time to pause and ask some questions that have bedeviled commentators for centuries but that we haven't had time to consider. First, where exactly does this story take place?

For most of the history of Adam and Eve, nearly everyone who heard the story believed the Garden of Eden was real. The earliest descriptions were often ethereal and glimmering, reminiscent of the bejeweled fantasy worlds my daughters conjured when they were young. The book of Ezekiel describes Eden this way: "Every precious stone was your covering, carnelian, chrysolite, and moonstone, beryl, onyx, and jasper, sapphire, turquoise, and emerald." The word "paradise" to describe this ideal place was introduced when some Israelites emigrated to Persia in the sixth century B.C.E. The Persian word **pari-daeza**, which means a "walled garden," became the Hebrew word **pardes**, which eventually made its way into English.

As early as the fourth century, Augustine was among the first to suggest that maybe Eden was not a "corporeal" place but an "allegorical" one. His contemporaries were horrified, and he had no choice but to reverse course. A typical example of how Christians viewed paradise in this era comes from the fifth-century text known as Pseudo-Basil. The Garden of Eden was an "ideal spot," "admirable and splendid." Summer brought no wilting flowers, autumn brought no drought, winter brought no ice. The trees always had fruit, the meadows were always filled with flowers, and "the roses had no thorns."

Yet as more of the world came to be mapped in the coming centuries and no one found a walled garden, the issue of where Eden was exactly took on added urgency. Early medieval cartographers placed Jerusalem in the center of their maps and Eden on the perimeter. As that became untenable, speculation placed Eden in Mesopotamia or Armenia. The most popular location was somewhere along the equator. Christopher Columbus, for one, believed this. When he sailed on his third voyage, in 1498, he fully expected to spot paradise. "I believe that, if I pass below the Equator, on reaching these higher regions I shall find a much cooler climate," he wrote. "For I believe that the earthly Paradise lies here, which no one can enter except by God's leave." Soon, however, even this idea became impossible to sustain, and by the time Darwin sailed on the HMS **Beagle** in 1831,

Eden was no longer a place on a map but a place that lived on in imagination.

The next question commentators debated was how old Adam and Eve were during their tenure in the garden. The Bible gives no age. Jewish interpreters like Genesis Rabbah imagined them created as fully developed human beings of twenty. Some Christian observers insisted they were thirty, since that was the "perfect age" of Jesus during his ministry. Later authors insisted the perfect age was fifty, while others put it at eighty.

While this debate may seem ancillary or even amusing today, it hints at the larger struggle people had over the centuries trying to fathom the depth of emotional connection Adam and Eve shared. Are they mere youngsters just figuring out who they are, or seasoned adults capable of well-reasoned decisions? Especially in light of a century of Western thought that says that your relationship with your parents helps define your relationship with your lover, the absence of any parental figures raises the tantalizing possibility that the lack of romantic role models partly explains why Adam and Eve rarely express their feelings directly to each other.

Another question that troubled readers was

how long Adam and Eve were actually in the garden. The Talmud created a timeline: "The day consisted of twelve hours. In the first hour, Adam's dust was gathered; in the second, he was made into a crude shape; in the third, his limbs were formed; in the fourth, a soul was infused into him." This exhaustive pace continued until hour twelve, when he and Eve were expelled. Christian interpreters tended to speed up this timetable, with Adam and Eve in the garden for a mere six hours. A Cambridge don, writing at the time of Milton, imagined creation at nine o'clock in the morning, the Fall at midday, and the judgment of God at three in the afternoon. One reason for such haste is that in the story, Adam and Eve don't eat anything before the forbidden fruit, so interpreters had to explain why they didn't starve.

All these interpretive puzzles paled next to the most important conundrum of all: What exactly was the relationship between Adam and Eve? Were they married, betrothed, besotted, living in sin, living in chastity? The Bible never says. It certainly never says outright that they're married, even though commentators eagerly read matrimony into a succession of phrases in chapter 2. After God declares it's not good for man to be alone, he vows, "I will make a fitting helper for him." After fashioning woman from man, the text says God "brought her to the man." The rabbis especially loved that phrase, suggesting God braided her hair, fluffed her dress, and ushered her to her husband, thereby revealing that "God acted as best man to Adam."

In perhaps the most telling phrase of all, the Bible states, "Hence a man leaves his father and mother and clings to his wife, so that they become one flesh." This line is especially curious, because Adam has no father and mother to leave. That linguistic oddity suggests that Genesis is trying to introduce and explain the origins of the later institution of matrimony.

Still, even saying Adam and Eve were married in Eden doesn't say very much about their relationship, because marriage in the ancient world was hardly a place of love. The Hebrew Bible does have a few loving relationships between spouses. Rachel and Leah side with their husband over their father; Michal protects David. Proverbs says, "He who finds a wife has found happiness." But the laws that Hebrew Scripture promulgates about marriage were heartless at best and grossly unequal at worst. These include male dominance over property and sexual relations, the obligation that brides (and not grooms) be virgins, divorce laws that favor husbands over wives.

The Greeks and Romans were no better— and in most ways were worse. Marriage in classical Greece was an institution built for economic, social, and political reasons, as well as for procreation. No one expected the couple to be in love. Athenian men were expected to have three women—a wife for home, a concubine for sex, and a courtesan for pleasure—along with a young boy on whom they were expected to shower love. The wife was the least important and was usually chosen by the two families when she was as young as six. Any man who opted out of this system was deemed "an idiot," the origin of that word.

In Rome, love between husband and wife was considered so déclassé that when Pompey actually fell in love with his fourth wife, Julius Caesar's daughter, his contemporaries mocked him. "Let his fondness for his young wife seduce him into effeminate habits," wrote Plutarch.

The early Church adopted an even harsher view toward marriage, casting it as unwelcome competition to a life devoted to Jesus. Outside of Mary and Joseph, the New Testament contains few examples of loving couples. Jesus himself suggests celibacy might be preferable to matrimony, "for the sake of the Kingdom of Heaven." The fourth-century bishop Gregory of Nyssa called marriage "the first thing to be left behind" in a journey toward Christ.

Even when Protestants played up marriage as a way to separate themselves from Rome, they hardly portrayed it as a source of mutual fulfillment. The woman was second class. All one needs for a "happy and tranquil marriage," Luther wrote, is a subservient wife, which shouldn't be hard because women had been "created for no other purpose than to serve men and be their helpers."

The reason all of this matters to our understanding of Adam and Eve today is that it helps explain why few people viewed their relationship as something worth emulating. Strip away all this accumulated bias, though, and look closely at the original story, what you find is a couple whose age, maturity, and locale are left purposefully vague, perhaps to increase their universality, who are struggling to figure out what it means to live alongside each other. This state of insecurity may make Adam and Eve less idyllic, but it makes them far more real, which in turn makes them far more relevant for anyone struggling to figure out the same issues many centuries later.

LIKE, FOR INSTANCE, Friedrich Ritter and Dore Strauch.

The Spanish were the first Europeans to reach the Galápagos, in 1535, and the islands appeared on the first modern atlas in 1570. From the very beginning, they fit many of the requirements for the collective vision of paradise. An isolated archipelago of thirteen large islands and dozens of smaller ones, the "Enchanted Isles," as they were called, are a watery wilderness spanning the equator. They have otherworldly geological formations, active volcanoes, red and black beaches, unusual vegetation, and an alphabet of endemic species—tropical penguins, spitting iguanas, and the largest tortoises on earth, called "Galápagos," which eventually gave the islands their name.

But when buccaneers, pirates, and whalers starting coming here in the seventeenth century, the landscape didn't strike them as paradise at all. It struck them as a special kind of hell. "Take five-and-twenty heaps of cinders dumped here and there," wrote Herman Melville, "imagine some of them magnified into mountains and the vacant lot the sea; and you will have a fit idea." Two of history's more memorable novels of humanity's showdown with nature—Defoe's **Robinson Crusoe** and Melville's **Moby-Dick**— were inspired in part by the Galápagos. Even Darwin compared the volcanic islands to dark industrial foundries, and said, "Nothing could be less inviting than the first appearance." Worse, he said, the few residents who live there complain a lot.

One unintended side effect of Darwin's visit is that while his ideas are often said to have been a blow to the biblical idea of paradise, his journey proved to be a boon for the idea that the Galápagos itself was paradise. For many, the Galápagos became "the new Eden," a place to reimagine what it means to be alive. There may have been some poetic justice to that. Of all the books Darwin took on board the **Beagle**, he preferred one. "Milton's **Paradise Lost** had been my chief favourite," he wrote in his autobiography. "And in my excursions during the voyage of the **Beagle**, when I could take only a single small volume, I always chose Milton." He spent five weeks on the islands; it's tempting to picture him scampering over the lava and strolling among the tortoises reading Milton's vision of Adam and Eve in love.

The idea of returning to paradise was the forty-three-year-old Friedrich Ritter's primary motivation. He was turned off by the complexity and emptiness of modern living, he wrote, in which everyone "was chasing madly after the ephemeral and valueless things of life." His goal was an idyllic life for two—"a special Adam, a special Eve, and special Paradise"—though he conceded that something this perfect could likely never be realized.

Sure enough, he and Strauch did face problems. Eden was not so Edenic after all. Their first challenge was the surroundings. "The tender shoots of our second planting had hardly peeped through the ground when the insect hoarders descended upon them like one of the plagues of ancient Egypt," he wrote. The bug brigade included huge black cockroaches, brilliantly colored beetles, long fuzzy caterpillars, and rival armies of ants. "Anyone familiar with the tropics will understand how we were transported from the joys of heaven to the uttermost depths of hell by such ruthless destroyers." Worse were the four-legged tormenters—dogs, hogs, asses, and a huge black boar, which Ritter branded Satan.

As for how this couple fared in their compound, which they called Friedo, a combination of their first names, Ritter seems to have been completely uninterested in a relationship. Publicly he said of the woman whose life—and teeth—he pried from their natural habitat, "Fortunately, I had in Dore a companion who fully shared my point of view." But that was as tender as he got. They hadn't been on the island more than a few weeks before she felt betrayed, lonely, and unloved. "Frederick did not move in the sphere of mundane feeling," she wrote. She loved flowers, for instance, but he dismissed them as "foolish decoration." When she planted some anyway and begged him to water them when she fell ill, he went outside and ripped them up.

"He did not even see that I needed to be loved and treated kindly," she wrote. "So I lived beside him in a solitude too bitter to be described. I had forgotten that he had ever talked of love to me, and when I tried to recall the Berlin prelude to our life it seemed that I was only dreaming it."

When others started arriving, Strauch initially was elated. First was another German couple, Heinz and Margret Wittmer, and their twelve-year-old son, who needed treatment for delicate health. Strauch couldn't stand the uneducated Margret, and as for Margret, the die was cast when she showed up for their first meeting in a dress only to find her new neighbors completely naked. The two became bitter rivals.

But the real Satanic mills didn't start grinding until the arrival of Eloise Wehrborn de Wagner-Bosquet, who first called herself the "baroness," but jettisoned that title for the "queen of Floreana," and later moved on to "empress." Her arrival proved to be a nightmare for Ritter and Strauch: their mail was stolen, their crops destroyed, and their animals killed. The baroness's three-male harem didn't last long either. First her Ecuadorean laborer fled the island after she shot him in the stomach; then one of her German lovers, Lorenz, took up residence with the Wittmers after he lost out to his rival, Philippson. Soon after, the baroness told Margret she and Philippson were heading to Tahiti to start their hotel, and Lorenz announced he was going to say good-bye.

The baroness and Philippson were never seen again, and everyone who's ever investigated the story assumes they were murdered, probably by

Lorenz on March 27, 1934. A month later Lorenz himself fled but his ship wrecked and he was found dead of dehydration on a nearby island.

All of this would be something of a macabre sideshow in the history of Edenic fantasies, if not for what happened next. Four months later, Strauch went running to her bitter enemies, the Wittmers, to announce that Ritter's tongue was swollen and she thought he was dying. She was right. Margret says he became ill from eating spoiled chickens, which would be odd for a devout vegetarian, and speculated that Strauch had poisoned him. Strauch, meanwhile, agreed it was poison, but said it was from another source. She had eaten the chicken, too, and felt no ill effects.

Strauch also emphasized that after their early difficulties the two had reconciled. "We had found perfect harmony and peace together," she said. "All differences had been smoothed out and we had reached that infinite understanding which no words can tell." She went on to offer a description of their relationship that anyone would envy.

> Frederick had become considerate and tender. All storms had ceased. And

amid the debris of its outward peacefulness the inner life of Friedo's found-
ers had achieved perfection. A stillness
and happiness that we had never
known before united us in the last
month in more than human oneness.

Milton, for one, would have longed to feel
this about one of his wives. And whether this
description is self-justification, self-glorification,
or even self-exoneration is beside the point.
Their experiment was always an exercise in literary wish fulfillment, an application of Ritter's
beloved philosophy of mind over body.

Instead, what's poignant about Strauch and
Ritter's story is having set out to re-create the
Garden of Eden—not for religious reasons,
mind you, but for philosophical ones—they had
inadvertently stumbled into a central lesson of
the original Garden of Eden: It's hard to live in
paradise. The nature of human relationships
makes it inherently hellish to live in close prox-
imity with another human being for long periods of time. That the geographic location once
considered the likeliest spot for the actual Eden
could produce such a startlingly similar result as
the original Eden suggests the biblical account

may have hit on a larger truth: Eden is not so much an actual place; it's a place we must create for ourselves, especially when it seems most challenging to do so. Strauch, in her own heart-rending epitaph, captures this feeling best: "Although our Eden was no peaceful one, it was an Eden just the same."

THE GALÁPAGOS TODAY is no less extraordinary than when explorers first arrived four hundred years ago. Twenty-five thousand people now live on the islands, but they're tucked away in a few towns. Ninety-seven percent of the land is a national park. Not long after my trip to London I visited the Galápagos with my family, and I quickly found I couldn't escape the first couple. Everything you read about the place describes the mystical landscape as being "like the Garden of Eden."

Once you set foot on the islands—a heavily controlled process that involves sanitizing your shoes so as not to relocate biomatter—you come face-to-face with the uncommon animals and their unusual mating patterns. Fleshy sea lions like Titian nudes congregate in harems. One bull tends up to twenty-five cows, darting from front to back fending off rivals until he becomes so worn out he's replaced by another male. Female flightless cormorants share nesting, incubation, and feeding with males, until the female bolts to find another mate, leaving the father to do further parenting. A male saddleback tortoise rams its chosen mate, then mounts her and emits the only sound he ever makes, a succession of bellows, grunts, and groans. After a week in the Galápagos it's impossible not to appreciate how Darwin changed the conversation about how males and females relate to each other.

In many ways, Charles Darwin was the last person one would have expected to disturb the tranquillity of Victorian religion. His father was a prominent doctor; his mother an heir to the Wedgwood china fortune. He was an undistinguished student at Cambridge and rejected his father's wish that he become a doctor, agreeing to become a small-town pastor instead. Far from having it out for religion, Darwin was a few weeks away from becoming a country vicar when he joined the **Beagle** in 1832. His brief stay on the Galápagos was a sidebar on the five-year voyage, and it wasn't until he returned home that he pieced together his theory of natural selection.

There were many consequences to the publication of **On the Origin of Species** in 1859, but blaming it for single-handedly torpedoing belief in the Bible is grossly overblown. The book appeared in the midst of a much larger challenge to biblical literalism, including the difficulty the new field of archaeology was having in proving events of the Bible and the success the new field of higher criticism was having in showing that the Five Books of Moses were likely not written by Moses. Darwin was only one part of a larger conversation that had been going on for 1,500 years: Is the Bible real?

Specifically regarding Adam and Eve, Darwin changed their reputation immeasurably. The normal way this is discussed is to say that Darwin undermined the first couple by showing once and for all that their story is more allegorical than historical. There's some truth to this, but not as much as you might think. First, the Bible is full of parables, so even many biblical readers are comfortable viewing Adam and Eve as having allegoric qualities. Second, the clear majority of believers today—that includes Jews, Catholics, and Protestants—accept evolution and believe it's not incompatible with biblical teaching. In the much-hyped cage match between Darwin and Adam and Eve, both sides are still standing.

More intriguing to me is a topic I rarely hear discussed: In what ways did Darwin actually enhance the story of Adam and Eve? Put differently, what can we learn about Adam and Eve by looking at their story through Darwin's eyes? Specifically I'm thinking of one critical question: Why do humans experience love in the first place?

To help answer that question I went to see the only person I know who's both a world-renowned anthropologist and a passionate student of religion. Melvin Konner was born into an Orthodox Jewish family in Brooklyn and grew up believing that Adam and Eve were real. During his freshman year in college, he had a crisis of faith and turned to anthropology.

Mel went on to do pioneering fieldwork in Africa and to write a series of academic books, as well as several popular books on the theory and practice of religion. Nearing seventy, with a thin, gray beard and an avuncular manner, he now teaches at Emory, which is where I visited him. I started by asking why it's important that the Bible has a man and a woman at the beginning of the human story.

"If you go back to the origins of life, all individuals could reproduce themselves," he said. "We were all basically female. So the real question is why do we have males? And the answer appears to be that if you clone yourself, you're much more vulnerable to disease. You need male and female in order to have a stronger species." Once you have two sexes, he went on, you need some way to bring them together to produce offspring.

"That's where sex comes in, and in the case of humans, love."

One of Darwin's greatest insights is that human beings, like all species, are driven to reproduce. "Reproduction is the sole goal for which human beings are designed," wrote science journalist Matt Ridley. The Bible, in its own way, shares that imperative. The first commandment God gives to Adam and Eve is "Be fruitful and multiply." The human initiative cannot succeed, God seems to be saying, unless the two of them have children. In a book about creation, Adam and Eve must create.

But sexuality is not the only urge that drives us. Our closest relatives, chimpanzees, live in promiscuous groups in which females seek multiple sex partners and males solicit intercourse by waving their penises in the air. Put a bunch of chimps on a plane for a few hours and it would quickly turn into an orgy. Humans, by contrast, put curbs on our sexual desires. We have dating apps, sock hops, condoms, wedding dresses. Why do we need all of that if our only objective is to pass along our genes?

The answer is that we don't live by sex alone; we also live by culture. The human brain is seven times larger than that of similarly sized animals, and our bigger brains are capable of keeping track of myriad connections and maintaining complex communal ties. Among the urges of our social brains is to avoid the pain of loneliness by nurturing close interpersonal relationships, including partnerships that last the rest of our lives. We need these partnerships in part because it takes so long to raise our children to maturity.

In essence, our lives are a tension between our genetic impulse to have children and our cultural need to form long-term social connections—i.e., the family—in order to successfully raise those children. This tension is vividly captured in the lives of Adam and Eve. It's the trade-off between living vertically—caring only about passing on your genes—and living horizontally—caring also about the person you're passing on those genes with.

That horizontal instinct is love, the greatest creation of human beings and the cultural innovation that most ensures that our society continues to exist. Rabbi Jonathan Sacks calls love "the most beautiful idea in the history of civilization." Without it, we would all be copulating all the time; with it, we stick around and form families, the basic building block of human society.

I asked Mel what purpose romantic love serves.

"That's a question I think about a lot," he said. Animals shy away from pair-bonding, he explained. Only 9 percent of species are monogamous. That includes a third of primates and 90 percent of birds. Humans, then, are outliers in our commitment to commitment. Even accounting for infidelity, polygamy, and the occasional harem, lifetime relationships are still the norm among humans. "I'd say we're more or less monogamous," Mel said, "but more more than less."

"But why?"

"Human life is built around a simple formula," Mel said. "Easy males and picky females."

Males compete for female attention, while females choose which ones they like. Females get more power to select because they must invest considerably more time in carrying and rearing a child. Studies show that women look at a broader range of social, economic, and personality issues than men, who tend to focus primarily on youth and attractiveness. "You can see the difference in what we fantasize about," he said. "Pornography is a male fantasy world of short-term sexual satisfaction while romantic comedy is a female fantasy world of long-term mating."

What women get out of this equation is obvious. They get someone to help when they're pregnant, nursing, and raising a child. The real question, Mel said, is what do men get out of it? The answer brings us back to the main purpose of our conversation. The men get children they can be confident are their own. They get a relationship that, at least in theory, brings them stability and satisfaction. In a word, they get love. In return, they have to give up the ability to have sex with whomever they want.

The sociologist Philip Slater, in his book **The Pursuit of Loneliness**, captures this remarkable bargain. "The idea of placing restrictions on sexuality was a stunning cultural invention, more important than the acquisition of fire." In this invention humans found a source of energy that was seemingly limitless. That source he identified as deprivation, longing, loneliness. The one remarkable force that could counteract that otherwise bottomless source: courtship, romance, love.

So why do we have love? It's the cultural currency that men and women trade with each other in order to bind them together. It's the glue that makes civilizations stick, though glue isn't exactly the right image, because what love generates is not a permanent bond. It's more of a porous, flexible adhesive, with a give-and-take, Sturm und Drang, in which each party helps create the other and in the process cocreates something new.

Early in his career, Mel and his wife lived in the Kalahari Desert in southern Africa and did fieldwork among hunter-gatherers. Mel told me he still thinks of the conversations he and his wife witnessed around the campfire and how they were round-the-clock, in-your-face, frank exchanges over feelings and relationships. "They were one long marathon encounter group," he said.

In many ways, that's still the vision of love he

carries in his mind. "You get into marriage," he said. "You're naive, you start having children, a thousand and one things happen, then twenty years later, you look across the table at someone you collaborated with through all these trials, if you're lucky there's still a sexual spark, then you know what love is. Love is what keeps you together through the trials of being together."

"And what can the rest of us learn from that?"

"The same thing we can learn from Adam and Eve," he said. "Think of romantic love as the first part of their story. It's the state of grace when you think you're in Eden and you think you're always going to be there. But then life slaps you around a few times, you get the knowledge of good and evil, and then you either say, as some people do, 'I've got to get out of here.' Or you say, 'I can't do this by myself. I need you.'

"That's what happens in the second half of their story," he went on. "She gets unhappy and goes looking for a little excitement; they give in to temptation and lose their home; they go off into the wilderness and have children; their family doesn't work out as well as they'd like. These are things everyone can relate to. And it's in that part of the story that their relationship is tested. And sure enough, they get through it. At every turn, they say, 'I don't want to go back to being alone.' It's when you say that—and you say it repeatedly—that you know you've found love."

IN THE SPRING OF 1838, two years after returning from the Galápagos, twenty-nine-year-old Charles Darwin was getting enormous pressure from his family to get married. But Darwin wasn't sure if he wanted to. On April 7, he took out of a piece of paper and made two columns: "Marry" and "Not Marry." At the top he wrote, "This is the Question."

In the left-hand column he listed all the advantages of marriage: "charms of music & female chit-chat," "Home, & someone to take care of house," "Children—(if it Please God)," "constant companion (& friend in old age)," "better than a dog anyhow."

In the right he wrote a much longer list of negatives: "fatness & idleness—Anxiety & responsibility—less money for books &c," "feel duty to work for money," "London life, nothing but Society, no country, no tours," "Eheu!! I should never know French,—or see the continent—or go to America, or go up in a Balloon, or take a solitary trip to Wales."

At the bottom of the sheet, he wrote out his conclusion: "Marry Q.E.D."

Six months later Darwin proposed to the youngest of his eight cousins, Emma Wedgwood, a woman with whom he had little relationship and had spent virtually no time alone. They remained happily, even ecstatically married for the next forty-three years and produced ten children. Love, the great scientist might have observed, takes many forms.

There's a narrative we've had about love that it's the reason people get into marriage but that marriage itself slowly eats the love away until there's nothing left. Certainly that's what the jokes say. "Keep your eyes wide open before marriage and half-shut afterwards," Ben Franklin quipped. Oscar Wilde said, "One should always be in love. That is the reason one should never marry."

But there's another narrative of love. This narrative may not be true for all people but it's surely true for more people. And that is: Love is not that temporary, giddy passion that often gets labeled love. Love is what emerges from the slow, dispassionate accumulation of good deeds, kind gestures, the occasional forgiveness, and the ongoing service to the other person. Robert Solomon makes this point beautifully. Love, he says, is something that is cultivated and grown rather than simply found or experienced. "We have lost the idea that love takes time, that love is a process and not just an experience, that love is a lifelong development and not something found and enjoyed, ready-made."

To me that sense of cultivation elegantly captures the relationship of Adam and Eve. They had to learn to love. They didn't have some delightful, storybook courtship. If anything, they had the ultimate arranged marriage. **"So how'd you two meet?" "God set us up."** Seconds later they were paired for life.

It was only after their relationship began that they realized they had to figure out how to be in a relationship to begin with. And it was challenging, as such things are. Maybe he was just looking for a helpmeet or didn't respect her as an individual. Maybe she wanted to go out more or flirt with the tennis instructor. Maybe one of them had the seven-year itch, or in their case, the seven-hour itch. Whatever it was, they were guinea pigs on the treadmill of love.

But when these otherwise normal missteps

proved catastrophic and they were kicked out of the garden, that's when the real work of their relationship began. Suddenly they had to survive by "the sweat of their brow." They had to labor to eat. They had to struggle to build a home. The Egyptian hieroglyph for love depicts a hoe, a mouth, and a man with his hand in his mouth, which suggests a planting, a growing, a nourishing. A similar connection between landscape and love surrounds Adam and Eve.

To be fully in love they had to build their own garden.

One of the central themes of the Hebrew Bible is the value of passing things down. God passes down his commandments, the patriarchs pass down their birthright, the house of Israel passes down its name. When this idea of passing down is coupled with the parallel idea of climbing up—to Sinai, to Zion, to Heaven—it becomes possible to see the story of the Israelites as a giant y-axis. It's an unending vertical line that stretches from God through the Bible to all of us.

But there's a counternarrative that carries equal weight and that often gets lost. That's the horizontal narrative, the idea that we must step away from our loved ones, go into exile, create new relationships. This is the x-axis of the Bible, and it appears in the very first relationship. God forms Eve out of Adam's side; God then brings Eve to his side. Adam leaves his parents and clings to Eve; Eve clings back. In every beat of this story, the movement is not up and down, it is side to side.

If the y-axis of the Bible is the love of parent (or God) for child, the x-axis is romantic love, the love of two individuals for each other.

And while it might be nice to think that every gesture along that axis is made out of affection, it need not be. Sometimes the act is made out of desperation, frustration, or obligation. But the impact can still be immense. Even if every act we make toward our lovers is not done out of love, the cumulative effect can still be love.

"Action and feeling go together," William James said. By changing our actions, we can change our feelings. Positive psychology has picked up on this idea and shown that acting a certain way can inspire certain feelings. Smiling can make you feel happier; expressing gratitude can make you feel more grateful; acting in a loving way can help you feel more loving.

In **Fiddler on the Roof**, there is a moment in the second act in which Tevye, the beleaguered milkman struggling to hold his family together in a Russian shtetl in 1905, is forced to accept that the second of his five daughters has chosen to marry for love instead of using a matchmaker. "It's a new world. Love," he says. The experience calls into question his own marriage to his sharp-tongued wife, Golde. Tevye comes to Golde in a quiet moment while she's doing chores and sings, "Do you love me?"

"Do I what?" she barks.

"Do you love me?"

For twenty-five years, she begins, I washed your clothes, cooked your meals, cleaned your house. And now you want to talk about love?

The first time I met you was on our wedding day, he responds. I was nervous and scared. But my parents told me we would learn to love each other. Were they right?

She continues to dissemble and grumble for a few tense minutes. I lived with you, fought with you, suffered with you, shared a bed with you. And then she gives an answer that might have been given by Charles and Emma Darwin, by Dore Strauch and Friedrich Ritter, and by half the long-term couples I know.

And, yes, it might have been given by Adam and Eve.

"If that's not love, what is?" Golde says.

"Then you love me!" Tevye cries.

"I suppose I do."

"And I suppose I love you, too."

THAT LOOK IN THEIR EYES

How Sex Became Evil, Then Unbecame It

I WAITED AS LONG AS I could before sticking my hand in Mae West's corset. While Ms. West was obviously not wearing the undergarment at the time, I would be lying if I didn't admit that it wasn't something of a thrill. The item was also, I should confess, a little smaller than I expected.

It was early afternoon on a late summer day in downtown Los Angeles and I was standing inside the frigid storage facility of the largest clothing collection on the West Coast. The fifteen thousand objects at the Fashion Institute of Design & Merchandising Museum include apparel from Fred Astaire and Marlene Dietrich, an inaugural gown worn by Nancy Reagan, and Oscar-winning costumes going back twenty-five years. The collection also contains more than a dozen pieces of lingerie worn by the Brooklyn bombshell, who became the public face of sexual-boundary pushing in the early twentieth century and in the process earned herself the highest wages of any woman in America and the indelible nickname, "the Statue of Libido."

"This bustline may not seem very big," explained Carolyn Jamerson, the collection's manager and an expert in Victorian gowns. "But the way the wood is laid at an angle and these hip plackets are stitched, when the whole thing is pulled tight it gives the body an hourglass shape." America had just been through the flapper era in the 1920s, Carolyn went on, which was all about flat-chested, boyish figures. "Mae West is credited with bringing back the full-figured shape. I, for one, am very grateful she did."

I had come here not to gawk at century-old underwear but to understand one of the more colorful incidents in the history of Adam and Eve and the one that shines the clearest spotlight on the explosive sexual ramifications of what happened in the Garden of Eden. On Sunday, December 12, 1937, Mae West appeared on the **Chase and Sanborn Hour** at 8 p.m. on NBC. Broadcast live from the network's studio at 5515 Melrose Avenue in Hollywood, the radio show was the most popular in the country that year. West was at the pinnacle of her career, coming off a string of hit films including **She Done Him Wrong** and **I'm No Angel**. "More people had seen me than saw Napoleon, Lincoln and Cleopatra," she said. "I was better known than Einstein, Shaw or Picasso." **Variety**, noting her penchant for provoking free-speech controversies, said, "She's as hot an issue as Hitler."

A music and variety hit since 1929, the **Chase and Sanborn** show was on its third host, the breakout star Edgar Bergen, along with his ventriloquist dummy, Charlie McCarthy. The night's bill included music by Nelson Eddy and Dorothy Lamour, jokes about holiday gift buying, and a risqué skit in which West vamped that Charlie McCarthy had come up to her apartment to show off his stamp collection. "Nothing happened!" the dummy assured a horrified Bergen, before turning to the audience and whispering, "He's so naive." The exchange slyly played off West's most famous line, "Why don't you come up some time and see me?" (She later changed it to what it's remembered as today, "Come up and see me sometime.")

But the other skit the troupe performed that

night would become one of the most infamous incidents in the long-running standoff between Hollywood and religion. The two-act play was set in the Garden of Eden and featured Don Ameche as Adam, West as Eve, and McCarthy as the snake. As soon as it aired, the skit ignited a scandal so intense it engulfed NBC, enraged the federal government, and generated a backlash severe enough that it resulted in Hollywood's biggest female star being banned from radio. It also served as an awkward introduction of Adam and Eve into the media age and showed that despite the rapid changes that love, sex, and relationships were undergoing in the modern world, the first couple still stood at center stage.

CONSIDERING HOW MUCH shock and horror have been generated about the sex lives of Adam and Eve over the centuries, it comes as something of a jolt to read the original account and find no direct mention of sexual relations at all. There's no first kiss, no first cuddle, no first time. No sheets are ruffled, no fluids are exchanged, no base is crossed. There's no dissolving to fireworks at midnight, no cutting to the couple lying blissfully in each other's arms the next morning. The clichés of romance have not yet been invented, and Genesis doesn't invent them.

Instead, all that appears in the text is a measure of innuendo that would make Mae West proud. In essence, there are two key moments in which sexuality is implied but not stated outright. These moments bookend the eating of the forbidden fruit. The first occurs at the end of chapter 2, when God escorts the newly formed Eve to Adam. He greets her using the erectile imagery "bone of my bones" and the carnal language "flesh of my flesh," then immediately embraces her and the two become "one flesh." What precisely happens here is not spelled out. The encounter could be as romantic as a rose-filled honeymoon suite or as awkward as the backseat of a Chevy. The only clue is that the text announces they are comfortable with the outcome. "The two of them were naked, the man and his wife, and they felt no shame."

The second moment occurs immediately following the incident when Eve hands Adam the fruit and he eats it. The text describes a rapid series of events. First, "the eyes of both of them were opened." Next, "The two of them perceived they were naked." And third, "They sewed together fig leaves and made themselves loincloths." No explanation is given for these occurrences, but considering that the action of tasting from the tree generates a series of bodily reactions— eyes opened, nakedness noticed, genitals covered—it seems safe to assume the fruit has some sort of sexual connotation. Also, given that the moment immediately preceding the incident with the tree is described as one of satisfaction and lack of shame, the clear implication is that eating the fruit has produced dissatisfaction and shame.

So what is going on here?

The first thing to observe is that whatever is happening between Adam and Eve in these encounters brings them closer together, not further apart. The expression "the two of them," in Hebrew, **sheneihem**, appears only twice in the entire Adam and Eve narrative. The first is right after they become one flesh when "the two of them" are naked and feel no shame; the second is right after they eat the fruit when "the two of them" are naked and feel shame.

This highlighting of their "twoness" sends a clear message. Adam and Eve are described in their earliest intimate encounters as being not "one" but "two." Sexual relations, by their very nature, are not something you do alone.

The second thing to observe is that in these sequences about sex, the Bible introduces yet another truth about relationships. Once again, it's a truth that's been confirmed by every love story ever told and every study of love ever done. Love is in the eyes.

Eyes are mentioned three times in the story. First, when the snake says after Eve eats the fruit, her "eyes will be opened." Second, when Eve catches sight of fruit she finds it "a delight to the eyes." Finally, when Eve and Adam have eaten the fruit, "the eyes of both were opened."

Eyes have become inseparable to how we understand love. Many of the iconic expressions involve seeing. We speak of "love at first sight," "gazing into each other's eyes," "peering into someone's soul." We don't say love is all knowing; we say "love is blind."

Science has confirmed this connection. When we experience feelings of love, our pupils dilate, our tear ducts activate, our eyes glisten. Long stares are not just a sign of affection, they actually generate affection. Psychologist Zick Rubin compared couples' self-reported feelings of love with how long they made eye contact with each other when they spoke. The more love a couple feels, the longer they look at each other.

What Adam and Eve initiate, the most famous love stories of all time continue. Nine times Romeo invokes Juliet's "twinkling," "wondering," "heavenly" eyes in their famous balcony scene. The "finest thing" about Emma Bovary, Flaubert tells us, "was her eyes." "What did you love me for?" asks the heroine of Thomas Hardy's **A Pair of Blue Eyes**. "I don't know," says her suitor. "O, yes, you do," she replies. Finally he confesses, "Perhaps for your eyes."

And when Marius and Cosette meet (in a garden, no less) in **Les Misérables**, it's their eyes that connect first. In a "proceeding known to Eve from the day the world began," Victor Hugo wrote, "a single look had done it." Hugo could have been thinking of Adam and Eve when he explained, "We scarcely dare say in these days that two persons fell in love because their eyes met. Yet this is how one falls in love and in no other way."

There's another meaning of Adam and Eve's eyes that may be even more illustrative of their feelings. By opening their eyes and recognizing they're without clothes, Adam and Eve illustrate the power of noticing. Love turns even the most unobservant person into a virtuoso of observation. Suddenly you become "an anthropologist of the beloved," in Alain de Botton's wonderful phrase. You decode every gesture, dissect every word, break down every touch, and read meaning into every interaction, no matter how minute.

On top of that, you overthink and second-guess your own behavior. Love forces you to look at yourself through the other's eyes. Not who am I, but who am I to that person? The moment you feel most secure because you've just connected with your other is also the moment you feel most insecure because you're freshly exposed. Genesis captures this sense of vulnerability when it says of Adam and Eve that when their eyes are opened they "know" they are naked.

The final thing to observe about these sequences is that everything the story has been suggesting about sexuality is deeply insightful. Sex fuses people to each other. Shelves of works of social science confirm that when humans engage in the ultimate form of social connection—sexual intercourse—orgasm floods the body with a cocktail of substances, including endorphins, prolactin, and the "cuddle drug" oxytocin, that together induce calm and attachment. These reactions help lower blood pressure, relieve stress, and maintain the bond between partners.

The feelings that arise in these moments are

often called—or at least mistaken for—love. The English word "love" actually comes from the Sanskrit word **lubh**, meaning "to desire." The connection between love and sex runs as deep as the rivers of Eden.

While often wonderful, this link can also be dangerous. Centuries of parental warnings to children were not untrue: Sleeping with the wrong person can trigger feelings of closeness that are just as strong as sleeping with the right person. "This unconscious bonding is one of the underappreciated reasons why having sex with someone you're not sure about can be a bad idea," writes John Cacioppo in **Loneliness**. "The chemical infusion can create a fixation on a single individual that otherwise might not make much sense."

But when it works, the attachment sex generates is the strongest adhesive there is and one of the building blocks of human society. Sex thrills us, writes de Botton, "because it marks an overcoming of loneliness." He goes on, "The pleasure we take is not rooted purely in stimulated nerve endings and the satisfaction of a biological drive. It also stems from the joy we feel at emerging, however briefly, from our isolation in a cold and anonymous world."

The sexual awakening of Adam and Eve ends their anonymity, and, in effect, reintroduces them to each other. The text captures this moment of rebirth by having the couple, immediately after eating the fruit, discover in each other one of the signatures of being newborn: their nakedness. Now that they're together, Adam and Eve realize they've been in the altogether up till now. How they feel about this realization harkens back to what they felt before eating the fruit. Then they feel "no shame"; now they feel shame.

That it's shame and not guilt they feel in this instant is important. Guilt comes from inside; it's a feeling of responsibility or remorse for some offense or wrongdoing. Shame comes from the outside; it's a feeling of humiliation or embarrassment at not living up to the values of others. That Adam and Eve are now shameful suggests that knowledge of good and bad has introduced social conventions—in essence, civilization— into their lives. It's a critical sign that the two are becoming human, finally apart from God.

Add all these details together, look beyond the centuries of commentaries, read the text with your own baby blues and a truth becomes clear: Adam and Eve, upon becoming one flesh, upon gaining wisdom, upon seeing each other anew, do not drift apart. They come together. They both open their eyes; they both feel vulnerable; they both cover themselves. Sexuality, at least in its initial form, is not a source of division between Adam and Eve. It is a source of union.

So WHEN DID all this change? And why?

One only has to consider another iconic Hollywood depiction of sexuality to appreciate the horror that has trailed Adam and Eve. In the opening of **Carrie**, directed by Brian De Palma, the lead character, played by Sissy Spacek, is showering in the girls' locker room. Blood starts coursing down her legs. She screams, but the other girls taunt and harass her, tossing tampons. Back at home, instead of finding sympathy, Carrie is further attacked by her devout mother, who views all sex, even between husband and wife, as the work of the Devil.

"And God made Eve from the rib of Adam." she screams. "And Eve was weak and loosed the raven on the world. And the raven was called Sin . . . and the first Sin was Intercourse."

The story of how we went from Adam and

Eve frolicking blissful and naked in the Garden of Eden to blood, rage, and ravens is one of the most tortured, consequential, and just plain sad stories in the history of religion.

The Bible itself can't really be blamed. In the ancient Near East, sex was considered a gift from the gods. The gods had sex with each other and with humans, and when humans had sex with each other they were mimicking the gods. The God of the Bible, by contrast, no longer has sex and grants this right exclusively to humans.

Sex appears, in one way or another, on nearly every page of the Bible, and for the most part it's positive, a way to produce children and occasionally pleasure. The Good Book uses every euphemism in the book to describe carnality—from "laying" to "getting with" to "coming into." The Hebrew Bible finds especially creative ways to encourage men to please their wives. "Find joy in the wife of our youth," says Proverbs. "Be infatuated with love."

Early Jews deepened this embrace of sexuality. In Jewish law, sex is a mitzvah that begins immediately after a wedding. A couple disappears for a time of **yichud**, or "togetherness," an expression that's derived from the word **echad**, first used when Adam clings to Eve. The rabbis specified sexual frequency by profession: "For men of independence, every day; for laborers, twice a week; for ass-drivers, once a week; for camel-drivers, once in thirty days; for sailors, once in six months." Eventually sex became a mandate for everyone on Shabbat.

Some early Christians echoed their Jewish ancestors and embraced sexuality. The second-century Church Father Clement of Alexandria said intercourse was not sinful but part of God's "good" creation. But any pro-sex attitude in Christianity was quickly overwhelmed by deep strands of prudery. Early Christians, eager to set themselves apart from the licentiousness of Greeks and Romans, aggressively made sex the antithesis of holiness. Paul said, "It is good for a man not to have sexual relations with a woman." Gregory of Nyssa suggested God had intended Adam and Eve to remain virgins. Had they done so, he argued, God would have arranged for humans to multiply in nonsexual ways, just as angels do.

But no person was more influential in the history of sexuality than the fourth-century bishop Augustine of Hippo. Born in North Africa in 354 to a Christian mother and a pagan father, Augustine had what he called a raging, hedonistic sex life. "Love and lust together seethed within me," he wrote. "In my tender youth they swept me away over the precipice of my body's appetites and plunged me in the whirlpool of sin."

After rejecting Christianity and living with a lover with whom he had a child, Augustine moved to Rome and, at thirty-one, had a dramatic conversion and returned to the faith of his childhood. In some of the most detailed and voluminous writings about the creation story, Augustine built an entire theology of sin around the sexual conduct of Adam and Eve.

Augustine argued that Adam had been born with free will and autonomy, which he squandered when he ate the forbidden fruit and had sexual relations with Eve. But this travesty wasn't theirs alone. Everyone who came after them inherited this "original sin." As a prime example of how humans could no longer control their desires, Augustine cited the fact that he became aroused despite his conscious attempts not to. His member was disobedient on account of the disobedience of Adam and Eve. "Because of this," he wrote, "these members are rightly called **pudenda** [parts of shame] because they excite themselves just as they like."

Though some of his contemporaries resisted this unforgiving attitude, Augustine eventually prevailed. His views of the inherent immorality of sex became the predominant view of Christianity for the next millennium and a half. Even those who didn't subscribe to traditional Christianity were affected. Everything from Puritan modesty to Victorian virtue to the rigorous censorship codes that bedeviled Hollywood are directly traceable to how a fourth-century bishop and guilt-stricken father interpreted the first man and woman.

How this legacy came to be overturned is a critical story in the history of Adam and Eve. One small though memorable player in that story was the Brooklyn-born daughter of a Bavarian corset model and her prizefighter husband.

YOU CAN LEARN A LOT about a person by looking at their underwear. The first thing I learned about Mae West is how short she was, even for Hollywood. The museum had about a dozen pairs of her shoes. All were double decker, meaning she had altitudinous heels, underneath which was an additional prosthetic that lifted her frame even higher. The part of her shoes containing her feet were hidden underneath her clothing, while the fake shoes were what stuck out. The total height: nine inches.

"Honestly, I think it's great how she's trying to create an image," said Carolyn, the manager of the collection. "But she's going to kill herself!" West's signature walk, in which she slid her feet away from her body as if figure skating, was the result of not being able to lift her feet, Carolyn explained.

The next thing I learned is that her hourglass figure wasn't all that natural either. "She was hippy," Carolyn explained, "so putting on the corset was a way of moving the fat around. The garment doesn't get rid of the weight; it just pushes it someplace else."

Finally, she knew exactly what she was doing. All the clothing I looked at was flesh-colored—peach, salmon, cream—so you couldn't tell where the clothing ended and her body began. "She knew all the tricks," Carolyn said. "You think you're seeing something, but you're actually not. That's one thing movie stars today don't get. They show everything!"

Born in 1893, Mae West learned her tricks from her mother, whose morals were more European and who advocated a social climber's approach to getting ahead: Do whatever it takes. Though Mae briefly married a fellow vaudevillian in her teens, she came to equate wifehood with servitude and thought monogamy was for the birds. "Haven't you ever met a man who makes you happy?" Cary Grant asks her in **She Done Him Wrong.** "Sure," she answers. "Many times."

Most of all, she didn't accept that the body was inherently evil. "Sex is not more vulgar than eating," she said. "Why is it necessary to weep or gnash teeth over the processes of nature?"

The fact that West became such an enormous star in the twenties suggests that public views on sexuality were changing. In the early twentieth century, magazines began publishing articles on birth control and divorce; songs were full of suggestive lyrics; and movie houses were filled with sexually provocative story lines. As one newspaper observed, "For the first time in the history of the world it is possible to see what a kiss looks like."

But this loosening of standards also came with pushback. These years saw the first organized backlash against the licentiousness of popular culture. In 1926, West scored her first starring role on Broadway in **Sex**, a play she wrote, produced, and directed. Police raided the theater and arrested her on morals charges, and she was sentenced to ten days in jail. In typical fashion, West managed to dine with the warden and got out two days early for good behavior.

By the time West moved to California in the early thirties, the censorship movement had gained momentum. The original Motion Picture Production Code of 1930 categorized sex in general, and any passion outside of wedlock, as "impure love" and insisted they be shown as wrong and not be implicitly tolerated with jokes. But the code lacked teeth and wasn't enforced.

By 1934, the Catholic Church, then at its peak influence in American life, was leading a movement to attack Hollywood. The Church got a whopping eleven million people—nearly 10 percent of the population—to sign a pledge objecting to "vile and unwholesome" movies, branding them "a menace to youth, to home life, to country, and to religion." That year, a Catholic layman was put in charge of upholding censorship rules in Hollywood, and the Hays Code, as it was called, became much more onerous. No less a liberal than Eleanor Roosevelt applauded the move. "I am extremely happy the film industry has appointed a censor within its own ranks," she said.

It was this climate that West faced when she stepped to the microphone in December 1937 to play Eve. NBC had hyped the occasion by releasing a publicity photo of a lingerie-clad West in bed with a tuxedo-clad McCarthy. The announcer introduced "the event itself." Let us turn back time, he said. Step into the Garden of Eden and meet "the most fascinatin' woman of them all, Eve." Under a spreading fig tree, "Mr. Adam" sprawls lazily in the sun, while Eve, "bored all the way to the bottom of her marriage certificate," is looking for a little action.

"Listen, tall, tanned, and tired," she tells her man. "Ever since Creation, I've done nothin' but playin' double solitaire. It's disgustin'!"

Adam defends the place like a shill from the Chamber of Commerce: The weather's perfect! The food is plentiful! What more could she want? What follows is a classic Mae West moment, in which the words she utters are safe enough to pass the censor (which they had) but her delivery makes her intentions abundantly clear.

"But I want somethin' to happen!" she coos. "A little excitement, a little adventure! A girl's gotta have a little fun once in a while."

Eve disappears into the garden by herself. But in a twist cooked up by the writers to play off West's reputation, instead of being seduced by the snake, she does the seducing. "Hello, long, dark and slinky," she says. Eve points to the apple tree and enjoins the snake to pick her a "big one." "I feel like doin' a Big Apple!" she purrs.

Adam will never go for it, the snake protests, but Eve says she knows how to persuade him. "I'll turn the apple into applesauce!" When Adam does dive into her nectar, thunder crashes, and the two of them are thrown out of Eden. Adam is horrified, but Eve is thrilled. "I just made a little history," she says. "I'm the first woman to have her own way." The skit ends with Eve giving Adam what she calls a big, wet "original kiss."

What happened next seems predictable in retrospect, but at the time was unheard of. The episode produced the biggest outcry in radio history. NBC was besieged with letters. "I deeply resent these rats invading my home to destroy spiritual life," wrote one irate Illinois mother. "My daughter now scoffs at religion. The damage done is beyond repair." A professor of religion at Catholic University introduced a statement into the Congressional Record calling West "the personification of sex in its lowest connotation," and accusing her of injecting "her own sexual philosophy into the Biblical incident of the fall of man."

With Congress fulminating, the government had to react. The head of the FCC sent a blistering letter to NBC deeming the skit "offensive to the great mass of right-thinking, clean-minded American citizens" and insisted the network take action. It did, dubbing the star "an unfit radio personality" and banning her from its airwaves.

There are two ways of looking at this story. The first is that it demonstrates how Adam and Eve were still untouchable in the early twentieth century, that religion still held a grip on American life, and that sex was still considered a dangerous threat to civilized society. There is some truth to this view.

But on closer inspection, an alternative explanation arises. The letter-writing campaign turns out to have been highly organized by a few vocal organizations. NBC, fearing greater regulation, made its priority clear: protect its own star, the dummy. McCarthy issued a rare statement, playing dumb. "Ho hum, this is one time I'll let Mr. Bergen do all the talking."

The powers that be, in other words, conspired to throw West under the bus. Her career was the only one to suffer. Her reputation and stature never recovered. In hindsight, the **Chase and Sanborn** Adam and Eve incident was less an example of sexuality shocking the public and more an example of the oldest lesson of all: When all else fails, let the woman take the fall.

I asked Carolyn what she thought. After explaining that she was a minority in Hollywood, a church-going Christian, Carolyn said she believed West was a victim of her own success. "I wonder if she was happy with her image. A lot of times the person within is struggling."

Carolyn was in her late twenties, dressed conservatively in a modest blue skirt and yellow scalloped sweater. Was she offended by West's persona?

"Absolutely not," she said. "She was a nonbeliever. If she professed to be a believer, I might be, like, 'Well, ma'am, we might want to talk about this area of sin.' But since she was a lady of the world, she's going to do what the world does."

"And what's that?"

"Make everything about sex."

I asked her if she thought much about Adam and Eve.

"Of course," she said. "They're part of the Bible."

"And what lessons do you draw from them? Is there a message in the Bible about relationships or is it simply, 'No sex before marriage'?"

"Oh, I strongly support that," she said. "But I understand I'm an outlier." She turned serious. "Look, I'm happy to be single. I think there's providence in it. But I'd love to be in a relationship. We are meant to be the helper."

I did a double take. "You don't find that demeaning?"

"Oh, no. I'm not under the man; I'm by his side. But he's still the leader. I have been honest with my boss from the get-go that if a guy comes along, this job will go down to part time, and when children come along, nothing."

"What if the guy says he wants you to be happy and you need the money?"

"I think a lot of what the world says we need to survive on are unnecessary. But if he says that, he's the leader, and I would work to the best of my ability, while also leaving time to take care of the house."

I mentioned the irony that we were having this conversation while standing over an open box of Mae West's lingerie. "Why is this topic of religion and sexuality so charged?" I asked.

"Because there's a divide between people of the world and people of faith," she said. "Some of the garments in here I really can't bear to look at. They're explicit and antibiblical. But I'm fine with that. I'm not trying to save people. My friends know that."

"Then what are you trying to do?" I asked.

"Uphold the Bible," she said. "When I look at Adam and Eve, I see myself in them. I'm tempted, just as Eve was tempted. But I don't want to make the same mistakes she did. It ultimately comes down to honoring God and not honoring the world. If I do that, I'll be content, because that's where my real happiness lies."

JOHN MARK COMER STEPS to the stage of the Reality LA Church just off Hollywood Boulevard in the heart of trendy West Los Angeles. Barely thirty, he's wearing an outfit that suggests he fits right into the neighborhood—tight black designer jeans, untucked navy shirt, fashionable shoes—and is boy-band handsome with tussled brown hair lined with blond streaks. "It's not dyed, I promise!" he says with a sheepish, almost apologetic tone. He looks a bit like Kevin Bacon in **Footloose**.

Actually he's a preacher, a fundamentalist one

at that, and the second-generation leader of a thriving Christian community in downtown Portland, Oregon, called Bridgetown: A Jesus Church that, among other things, has the hippest religious Web site I've ever seen. He's come here tonight to give a seminar on the topic that most concerns his followers: the Christian way to understand sex.

John Mark asks the hundreds of millennials in the audience to open their Bibles to Genesis 1. "If you have a book, use that. Otherwise, just open your app." He starts reading the story about Adam and Eve and quickly does three things I don't expect. First, he teases the crowd about how un-Eden-like their city is. "You call that concrete ditch a river? You gotta come visit us in Portland," he says. Next, he makes a joke about evolution. Adam's pickup line to Eve— "She will be called woman"—is lame, he says. "Keep evolving, guys." Finally he tells a story about how he lost his virginity.

John Mark points to his wife, Tammy, a sunny, curly-haired brunette in the front row, and says that for them it was love at first sight. "I know it sounds cheesy, but it's true!" he says, and you believe him. He was eighteen. They met at a party. Within days he knew she was "the one." "My friend said, 'Dude, you haven't even been on a date!'"

But the electricity was all he ever dreamed, he said, and soon they were engaged. "Her parents wanted us to wait until after I turned twenty-one, so we were married the following Saturday night," he said. "That will tell you all you need to know about my personality."

John Mark and Tammy were both virgins when they were married, he went on. "That meant our first night as a married couple was **so much fun**. Awkward, but fun." On their honeymoon, they went to see **Romeo and Juliet**. "About halfway through the play, during the überdepressing part, my wife turned to me and whispered, 'Wanna get out of here and go make love?' The answer to that question is always yes!" Their son Jude was born the following year.

Soon, however, their marriage soured. John Mark is introverted, he explained, along with being driven, high strung, and melancholy. "Generally not that fun to be around," he said, though you don't believe that. Tammy is extroverted, the life of the party. "One day we were driving, listening to the radio, and an ad for eHarmony came on," he said. "At the end, the

founder said, 'Opposites attract, then they attack.' I reached over and turned off the radio.
Awkwaaard."

John Mark realized he had no idea what marriage is for, he said, "And I'm not alone. In the
last few years, we've had a volcanic, passionate
debate in this country about **who** marriage is
for. But what's shocking is that through it all
we've had very little discussion about **what** marriage is for—other than the tax write-off and
health insurance, which is awesome, but not
enough. I've come here today to talk to you
about why we need companionship, why we
have love, and why healthy, joyful sex is crucial
for both."

The harsh antisex theology that Christianity
adopted in the wake of Augustine was powerful
but not universal. Strands of pro-sexuality lived
on in the margins of Church society all through
the Middle Ages. One example was a sect of lib-
ertines who were said to have held naked assem-
blies and were known, after the original naked
man, as "Adamites."

Over time, this openness pushed closer to the
mainstream. Eighteenth-century philosopher
Jean-Jacques Rousseau rejected the idea of original sin and said bodily urges are inherently

good. Nineteenth-century Romantics helped legitimize sexual desire as a path to individual fulfillment. And of course in the twentieth century, Freud helped make sexuality a central obsession of modern life. The "nucleus" of love consists in "sexual love with sexual union as its aim," Freud wrote. Love, which was once a way of serving God, now became a way to serve yourself. Sex, which for a long time was evil in the eyes of Christianity, now became a way for people to express who they are.

For a long time organized Christianity pushed back against this sexualizing of public life—and many leaders still do. It's not difficult to find prominent voices sermonizing against promiscuity, prostitution, porn, premarital sex. Church officials have used any number of biblical passages to argue against equality of the sexes, and to say homosexuality is evil. But many leaders specifically trace their beliefs back to the Garden of Eden, especially to the understanding that women are supposed to be men's helpers, that sex is sanctified only between a man and a woman and then only within marriage, and that the body after the Fall is inherently dirty.

More recently, though, a vocal minority of Christian leaders has said, "Stop! What we've been doing for centuries is not working." John Mark Comer is one of those voices. This movement he's a part of is not particularly well organized, he told me, but it's real. What members have in common is they're determined to change the way the church speaks about sex. They're committed to doing it without sacrificing their beliefs. And they're focused on doing it in a way consistent with the Bible.

After his seminar, I spoke with John Mark about what inspired his sex-positive crusade. "We have countless young people in our church," he said. "It's not the demographic you'd expect, especially for a church on the more conservative side." Two thirds of his members are single, between eighteen and twenty-eight. "And they're just trying to navigate what it's like to live in a sex-crazed culture and make decisions about relationships, dating, and love. It became the number one issue I was dealing with."

And he found little help in the church, he said, which had mostly avoided the conversation. "When my father started our church in the 1970s, he was not dealing with these issues," John Mark said. "But my generation grew up in the sociological and psychological aftermath of divorce. From my point of view as a pastor it's been catastrophic. We have scores and scores of educated, intelligent, successful young people who don't know the basics of how to be in relationships because they grew up with educated, intelligent, successful parents who were disasters at relationships.

"The church," he went on, "instead of filling the void, was silent, either because 'We don't talk about that kind of stuff' or because our language was hung over from the Middle Ages." As a result, young people got their messages from the culture at large, he said, which is all about doing what feels right.

"What I'm trying to do is tell an alternative story," he said. "For too long the church's message on sex was 'don't'—'Don't masturbate,' 'Don't make out,' 'Don't sleep around,' 'Don't watch porn.' I want to lead with the 'do.' I want to show that in Scripture, sexuality is created by God as a beautiful, affirming, positive experience. It's more than just play for grown-ups. It's two bodies, two souls, fusing as one."

Exhibit A, in his effort, are Adam and Eve.

"If you look at Genesis 1 and 2," John Mark said, "and if you can get past the talking snake and all that, I see the most profound, insightful, illuminating story that makes sense of who we are. Whether it's historical or not, I don't care. To me it's a parable, the same way Jesus was a master of parables.

"And the basic message," he said, "is that God's creative intention is that we live in relationships and be in love." Companionship is part of the reason for that, he said. God doesn't want us to be alone. Building communities is part of that.

"But the thing that makes God's entire enterprise work is sex," he said. "That interpolation at the end of Genesis 2 makes it clear. 'Adam and his wife were both naked, and they felt no shame.' There's no tremor, no tension, no conflict. They were friends, yes; they were partners. But they were also lovers. God created sex because it's the secret that holds relationships together."

That idea is the essence of John Mark's appeal: God's mandate to humanity—to have children, to create nations, to build societies—depends on relationships, which in turn depend on love, which in turn depend on sex. Stop making sex the enemy when it is so clearly the intention of a relational God, he said. It's this God who created humans in his image to be relational themselves. John Mark even goes so far as to blame Augustine for burdening the Church with a theology that pleasure is evil. "With humility and respect," he told me, "I do trace many of the Church's biggest mistakes to Augustine."

There are limits to how far a fundamentalist preacher can go. John Mark's positive message about sexuality applies only to couples who are already married. He counsels young people, as he did that night, to resist having sex before marriage, to stay far away from tempting situations that could compromise that position (including kissing), and to resist the inclination to play God and make up their own rules. He's against divorce. He's against pornography. He steadfastly believes the church needs to be more welcoming to anyone who's involved in those activities, but his embrace of sexuality does have limits.

Still, since my purpose was not to explore what different religious groups say about sexuality but to discern what role Adam and Eve might play in contemporary life, John Mark's Eden-centric vision was a revelation. Adam and Eve, for centuries the public face of a campaign by traditional Christians to make sexuality the enemy of a holy life, could now be used by traditional Christians as the public face of a holy life. John Mark may not speak for all conservative Christians, but the fact that he speaks for any is a signal that even conservatives are prepared to adapt to the changing moral views of their followers.

Even more intriguing is the possibility that sexuality, which for decades has caused a divide between progressives and traditionalists, believers and nonbelievers, might once again be a source of shared connection. Adam and Eve, instead of being lightning rods in the debate over the human body, might once again be common ancestors.

Mae West, in other words, may have won.

And why not?

The story of Adam and Eve, as it appears in Genesis, celebrates sexuality. At the end of Genesis 1, after God creates male and female and orders them to "be fruitful and multiply," he declares what he has done "very good." At the end of Genesis 2, after God leads man to join with woman and the two become "one flesh," the story declares them to be naked and happy. Before the Fall, Adam and Eve share body, joy, and purpose.

"God is a God of pleasure," John Mark told

me. "Sex is about creation, and it's about recreation. It turns out that 'be fruitful' is a really fun command to obey." And he insists what he's doing is not discovering a new interpretation; he's only recovering what was there all along.

So how does this go over with this flock?

"There are three basic responses," he said. "For people who grew up in conservative churches who have this hangover Catholic guilt or Fundamentalist shame, it's freeing. It's hearing that sex is good, it's part of who you are, it can be a beautiful thing.

"For those who grew up outside the church, whose soul is in bad shape because they've been sleeping around or are addicted to porn, whose heart is wrenched and whose morality is wrecked, for them it's all about walking them through a radical healing and toward a higher bar of human flourishing.

"And for the third category, folks who are kind of believers but not really in the boat yet, my message is something you don't often hear on the conservative end of the church: It's not that what we're saying is right versus wrong; it's that it's better versus not as good. If you try to live this way, you'll get in touch with something that's timeless, enriching, and true."

"And when you stand up in one of the hippest parts of the country," I said, "in an epicenter of youth and technology, and preach that something as old-fashioned as Adam and Eve can teach them something about their lives, do they roll their eyes or does it resonate?"

"Oh, it massively resonates," he said. "I get a barrage of e-mails, texts, and posts from people who say this message shaped their relational journey. I can only conclude there's a hunger in our me-addicted world to believe that some things are so eternal they've been unchanged since the Garden of Eden."

"And sex is one of those things?"

"One hundred and ten percent."

THE OTHER WOMAN

The Dark Side of Love

IN THE SPRING OF 1927, Ernest Hemingway, who had just published his first successful novel, married Pauline Pfeiffer, an independently wealthy writer from the Midwest. The two spent an extended honeymoon in le Grau du Roi, a small fishing port in France, where they dined, drank, swam, and fished, while in the afternoons he wrote. Hemingway had met Pauline two years earlier in Paris at a party he attended with his first wife, Hadley Richardson. The three became close, and Pauline often accompanied the couple on vacation. That is, until Hadley, the mother of Hemingway's two-year-old son, learned her travel companions were having an affair and insisted on getting a divorce.

Twenty years later, and by this point divorced from Pauline after having cheated on her, Hemingway began writing a novel inspired by those earlier events. The plot centers on an American writer who has just published his first successful novel and is spending his honeymoon with his wealthy wife in le Grau du Roi until an affair unravels their marriage.

Hemingway worked on his novel off and on for a decade, eventually writing an unwieldy 1,200 pages, or 200,000 words. But he was never fully satisfied with it, and the book was left unfinished at the time he committed suicide in 1961. Twenty-five years later, the novel was resurrected by his estate, cut down by two thirds, and published posthumously to international sensation and mixed reviews. A film was made of it.

The name of the novel: **The Garden of Eden**.

The parallels with the original Garden of Eden are both unexpected, and, given the author, kinky. Le Grau du Roi is a paradise cut off from the rest of the world. David and Catherine, the characters who are figures for Hemingway and his wife, are deliriously fused together at the outset. The two even share an androgynous connection after Catherine decides to cut her hair like David's.

But soon the newlyweds undergo a psycho-sexual shift that makes their connection with Adam and Eve even more intriguing. First, Catherine transforms into a devilish, masculine figure; next, this male persona makes sexual advances on David; finally, Catherine begins sleeping with Marita, a young woman they meet.

So what's going on here? David, the classic Hemingway doppelgänger, is clearly modeled on Adam, but Catherine is just as clearly not modeled on Eve. Instead, she's modeled on a different figure. She's patterned on the long-rumored third wheel in the union of Adam and Eve, the symbol of sexual deviance who tries to wreck the first couple's Eden, the demonic succubus who has shadowed the first man and woman for nearly as long as their story has been told.

Catherine is Lilith. And you can't fully comprehend what happens in the Garden of Eden, the relationship between Adam and Eve, or the true meaning of love, unless you contend with her.

You didn't think Adam and Eve could survive all these years without a sex scandal, did you?

For as long as there have been stories of romantic harmony there have been stories of sexual aberration. The same goes for this earliest of love stories. In some ways it's oddly comforting that underneath Adam and Eve's otherwise decorous relationship lies a seamy underside of infidelity, fantasy, and intrigue.

For Jews the idea was that Adam had a first wife named Lilith, whose sexual dominance proved so threatening to his masculinity that she fled to the wilderness and became a baby-snatching stalker. For some Christians the idea was that the Devil assumed the head of a woman and the tail of a snake in order to ensnare Eve in a homoerotic entanglement. For most everyone, it seems, the idea was that nothing could be as idyllic as it appeared for Adam and Eve in Eden.

There must be another side of the story.

The concept of the dangerous, otherworldly woman actually predates the Bible. The ancient world was full of tales of female fiends or maniacal goddesses that threaten the sanctioned world. In Mesopotamia, glowing maternal goddesses were shadowed by horrific, menacing goddesses modeled on the "bad mother" who ignores or harms her unwanted children. In

Sumer such creatures were called "dark maids." In Syria, "flyers in a dark chamber."

A Babylonian writer describes one of these creatures as having the head of a lion, the body of an ass, and the howl of a jackal. "Raging, furious, fearsome, terrifying, violent, rapacious, rampaging, evil, malicious, she overthrows and destroys all that she approaches," the text says. "Wherever she appears, she brings evil and destruction. Men, beasts, trees, rivers, roads, buildings, she brings harm to them all. A flesh-eating, bloodsucking monster is she."

Mesopotamians were not alone. The Greeks had Lamia (the name means "jaws"), a spurned lover of Zeus whose ghost hunts down babies and devours them. The Romans had a cadre of bloodsucking, child-stealing female demons called **Striges**, or "night owls." "Greedy birds are they," Ovid said. "They fly around at night. / They seek out children, when their wet-nurse is away. / They carry them off. / They maul their bodies with their claws."

The name Lilith became attached to this figure as early as 2000 B.C.E. in the Epic of Gilgamesh, which labels her a "maiden who screeches constantly" and "one who steals the light." It's under this name that she makes an appearance in the Bible, though far removed from the Garden of Eden. The book of Isaiah, in describing an inhospitable wilderness, says jackals and owls shall live there, wild wolves of the desert shall meet with hyenas there, "and Lilith shall also rest there." The fact that no further introduction is given suggests no further introduction was needed. Everyone already knew who Lilith was.

Having made the jump into the Judeo-Christian tradition, Lilith spread quickly. In the late Roman period, Lilith's name begins to appear on magical bowls that were used to protect pregnant women from the demon's ability to steal their babies. In the Talmud, Lilith is deemed a sexual predator who steals men's sperm and gives birth to devilish children. "A man should not sleep alone in a house, because whosoever sleeps alone in a house will be attacked by Lilith."

Finally, around the ninth century, Lilith enters the story of Adam and Eve. A half-Aramaic, half-Hebrew text called the Alphabet of Ben Sira gives Lilith her enduring role: the first wife of Adam. The text exploits the fact that the first and second creation stories appear to be different and concocts an explanation: Adam was married before Eve.

The story begins with a straight echo of Genesis. God creates Adam, then observes his sadness. "It is not good for man to be alone." God promptly fashions a woman out of the earth and calls her Lilith. Immediately the two begin to quarrel—not about knowledge, fruit, or anything else that appears in the Bible. They argue about sex, specifically who gets to be on top.

"I will not lie below you," Lilith says.

"I will not lie below you," Adam replies. "I will only be on top. For you are meant to be in the inferior position, while I am meant to be superior."

Lilith retorts, "We are both equal, because we are both created from the earth."

Adam refuses to back down.

With neither party listening to each other (now there's a relatable couple!), Lilith speaks the magical name of God and flies away to the Red Sea. God dispatches three angels to bring her back, but she rebuffs them. "Leave me! I was created for no other purpose than to harm children." Every day, a hundred children will die at her hand, she vows. The only thing that will prevent her is when she sees God's name on an amulet. The story concludes, "That is why we write her name on an amulet for small children. And when Lilith sees it, she remembers her promise and the child is saved."

Like any malignancy, once Lilith infected Adam and Eve, she never really departed. In the Jewish world, fears of the demon sorceress multiplied exponentially. This growth is traceable because of an explosion in the number of amulets women hung around their homes, a tradition that still continues. Anti-Lilith amulets are for sale on Etsy.

The idea of a devilish woman who threatened the first couple popped up in Christianity around this time, too. Instead of focusing on Adam's relationship with this figure, though, Christians focused on Eve's relationship with her.

Not long after the Alphabet of Ben Sira, a new image entered Christian art: the female-headed serpent. Genesis makes no mention that the serpent had female qualities, and a depiction of the serpent as female is absent from the first millennium of Christian art. Suddenly, though, around the tenth century, the serpent takes on features of a woman—and a fetching blond one at that.

One medieval writer explained that the Devil chose to approach Eve as a woman because "like prefers like." The serpent appears with female characteristics in the Notre Dame Cathedral in

Paris, the Brancacci Chapel in Florence, and, most famously, in the Sistine Chapel. In the third panel of Michelangelo's creation sequence, the serpent has not only the head of a woman, but also the shoulders, arms, breasts, buttocks, and knees of one. Indeed, the serpent's translucent skin, broad torso, and pointed nose bear stunning similarity to Eve.

So what's the origin of this idea? Scholars have identified a host of possible sources, from vipers to sirens, but one source they've singled out seems particularly intriguing: Lilith. This would make sense because of the timing: the female-headed serpent was unknown before the Alphabet of Ben Sira. Also, we know Christian artists drew heavily from Jewish commentaries. Merging the archetype of the spurned woman with that of the satanic temptress seems inevitable.

However the leap to Christianity began, the presence of Lilith in Christian writings only grew. In Goethe's **Faust**, Mephistopheles describes Lilith as Adam's first wife, "Beware of her. / Her beauty's one boast is her dangerous hair." When Lilith winds her hair "tight around young men," the Devil goes on, "she doesn't soon let go of them again." Everyone from Flaubert to Hugo to Keats to Coleridge used versions of the dark temptress in their writing. By the twentieth century, Lilith had become so tightly wound with other outsider women—fairies, mermaids, witches—she could never be untangled again.

What explains the persistence of this idea?

"The duality of light and dark, official and nonofficial, what one should be and what one wants to be, is the core of civilization," said Esther Perel, the famed psychotherapist and the author of **Mating in Captivity**, a study of eroticism. I went to see her in her office in Manhattan to discuss why this history of sexual nonconformity hangs over the first couple.

"If everybody just fantasized about lying with their partner on a bed of roses all the time, we wouldn't be having a hard time," she continued. "But the fact is people lust, they want, they aspire to all kinds of things that are not part of their identity or their belief system. That's why these stories endure. They provide an outlet for nontraditional thoughts."

"You say this is part of civilization," I said. "But I thought it was the job of civilization to keep these ideas away?"

"Yes, but we have the superego and the id," she said. "There's the code of conduct, social control, the idea of civilization. But then there's your instinct, your animalistic urges, your unruly impulses. That's the whole point of Freud's **Civilization and Its Discontents.** You have to have a system that contains both, otherwise we'd all be going to underground bacchanals all the time."

I mentioned that what I found interesting about this undercurrent of darkness in the Garden of Eden is how equally it was distributed. Adam has his dalliance and his opportunity for ongoing fantasy in Lilith, while Eve has her dalliance and her opportunity for ongoing fantasy in the serpent. Both man and woman have both light and dark inside them.

"And yet neither succumbs," I said. "They end the story with each other."

"Because that's the way it is in real life," she said. Esther is writing a book about infidelity, and she said her research confirms this pattern. More than half the relationships that involve cheating survive.

These couples fall into three groups, she said. The first she calls "supplicants," those who swallow the poison, live with the resentment and mistrust, and leave the violation at the heart of their relationship. The second she calls "survivors," those who view the experience as a temporary state of insanity and return to their prior way of life. The third she calls "explorers," those who view the affair as a catalyst that allows them to be more open and honest with each other.

"Which one is Adam and Eve?" I asked.

"I think Adam and Eve are number three," she said. "Because they dig each other. They're not just together because it's the right thing to do. They're together because they love each other. And I think they understand why both of them did what they did, and they were willing to learn from it."

"So what can we learn from them?"

"What's relevant about these stories is not the specifics," she said. "It's the concept. And the concept in this case is that we all have a dynamic tension within us between order and chaos, good and bad. Accepting that does not mean we need to kill off marriage. It means we need to have enough common sense to embrace contradictions and come back together and make up."

IT'S PRECISELY THIS CONTRADICTION that Hemingway explores in **The Garden of Eden.**

From his earliest childhood, Hemingway experienced gender elasticity. His mother, who was obsessed with twins, dressed young Ernest in identical clothes as his older sister, Marcelline, born eighteen months before him. Sometimes they appeared as boys, other times as girls. Ernest's hair was shoulder length and curled to make their appearance match. Photographs in the family scrapbook labeled him, "summer girl."

"At some point, though, in his edenic infancy," wrote one biographer of these practices, Hemingway "awakened to an understanding of the situation in which his mother had placed him. . . . He thought of himself as a victim of treachery long before he knew what to call it." All through his life, Hemingway referred to his mother as "that bitch."

As an adult, Hemingway could not escape questions about his sexuality. Though we tend to think of him as a paragon of twentieth-century masculinity, the Marlboro Man with a pen, his friends wondered about his sexual orientation. Gertrude Stein called him "yellow" in **The Autobiography of Alice B. Toklas**, a tag Hemingway is said to have interpreted to mean "unmanly" or "queer," and the writer Max Eastman observed that Hemingway seemed to have "a continual sense of the obligation to put forth evidences of red-blooded masculinity." All the swing of his shoulders and the strutting of his prose cannot mask the stench of "wearing false hair on the chest."

Some of Hemingway's most famous men and women merge their genders. The lovers in **A Farewell to Arms** grow their hair "the same," speak of getting "all mixed up," and have sex with the man in the "female position." The look-alike lovers in **For Whom the Bell Tolls** are so close they feel as if they've merged. "I am thee and thou art me and all of one is the other," one says. "If thou should ever wish to change, I would be glad to change."

All this latency burst into view in **The Garden of Eden.**

At the beginning of the book, newlyweds David and Catherine are in paradise. "When they had made love they would eat and drink and make love again. It was a very simple world and he had never been truly happy in any other." But as in the Alphabet of Ben Sira, the story soon takes a wicked turn. One evening Catherine comes back with a boyish haircut and that night in bed undergoes a werewolflike transfor-

mation into a sexually aggressive man named
Peter who claims David as his female lover. "I'm
a girl. But now I'm a boy too and I can do anything and anything and anything," she/he says.
"I'm going to make love to you forever."

Catherine is on top, in every way imaginable,
and initially, at least, David submits. He even
cuts and dyes his hair to match his suddenly
sexually assertive wife/husband.

"Dave, you don't mind if we've gone to the
devil, do you?" she asks.

"No, girl," he says.

"Don't call me girl."

"Where I'm holding you you are a girl."

Hemingway was familiar with the Lilith
story, his biographers say, from the 1869 poem
"Eden Bower" by Dante Gabriel Rossetti. Plus,
he was drawing on androgynous imagery that
goes back thousands of years, to Plato's **Symposium** and, of course, to the opening chapter of
the Bible. But that was not widely appreciated at
the time. Critics have speculated that Hemingway's gender-bending narrative would have been
so scandalous in 1946 that fear over the reaction
may have been the reason he never published
the novel.

Still, for all the sexual experimentation in the

book, tradition triumphs in the end. As in the underlying story, light prevails over dark. No sooner does Catherine turn herself into Peter and begin leading David toward the wild side, then along comes a more suitable woman to keep him on track. Hemingway, a convert to Catholicism, calls this more conventional heroine Marita, Little Mary.

And what a perfect helpmeet she is. Marita is pliant; she's agreeable; she even reads his work and gives him positive feedback, something Catherine, whom he calls "Devil," never does. (Memo to lovers of writers: They, er, we, like positive feedback!)

Eventually Catherine, like Lilith, flees to pursue her devilish ways. At the end of the novel, she returns one last time to Eden and takes up residence in the bedroom she once shared with David. That night, he goes to visit her.

"Can we start again?" Catherine asks.

"I don't think so," David says.

"Then why did you come in here?"

"This is where I belong," he says.

"No other reason."

"I thought you might be lonely."

"I was."

"Everybody's lonely," David says.

Sexual whims may twist and change, but the real message of Eden never dies.

THERE'S ONE MORE IRONY to Hemingway's reluctance to publish **The Garden of Eden** in his lifetime: At least as far as the demon temptress was concerned, Hemingway was only a few years ahead of his time. In the decades after his death, Lilith went through a remarkable resuscitation. Long a source of revulsion, she suddenly became a source of pride.

To understand that part of the story, I headed to northern Connecticut to spend a weekend with a small group of students who were part of the larger movement to bring renewed respect to the tradition of outsider women. On an unseasonably chilly summer Friday morning, about four dozen women, ranging in age from twenty-five to seventy, crammed into a yurt on the grounds of the Isabella Freedman Jewish Retreat Center.

The women represented a remarkably diverse array of backgrounds, including doulas, dancers, poets, environmentalists, and entrepreneurs, and an equally wide range of gender and sexual identifications, including gay, straight, trans-

gender, bisexual, and asexual. I learned this because everyone introduced herself and described
what had brought her here. When the time came
for me to speak, there was an awkward pause. I
was quite clearly the only male.

"I'm a cisgender, heteronormative, circum-
cised, bar mitzvahed, fifth-generation Jew from
the American South," I said.

To my utter relief, there was laughter.

Rabbi Jill Hammer opened the morning session. She was seated cross-legged in front of a
small altar. "Today I want to talk about one of
the most notorious demons in history," she said.
"Her name is Lilith, and she embodies the aspects of darkness, terror, and escapism that all
of us carry around within us. She also represents
all of us who don't want to be 'good girls.'"

Jill is a slight woman, with superlong, slightly
graying brown hair, on top of which she wears a
crocheted skullcap. She looks like the kind of
ethereal figure you might see illustrated on the
cover of a girl's young adult fantasy novel. She's
also deeply learned, with a PhD in social psychology, an ordination from the Jewish Theological Seminary, and a day job teaching finely
tuned distinctions in religious law at the Academy for Jewish Religion, a pluralistic rabbinical
seminary in Yonkers, New York.

In her spare time, Jill has spent more than a decade preparing women to lead religious rituals, from baby namings to funerals. The catch: She doesn't train her students to be clerics, rabbis, or prelates. She trains them to be priestesses. Specifically she grooms them to mix traditional religious practices with natural spiritual rituals like reverence for the seasons, worship of the moon, and celebrations of the monthly fertility cycle.

"Three weeks ago I officiated my friend's wedding in the desert of California," one of the priestesses explained to me. "The couple wanted an intergalactic high-desert affair that would also appeal to the groom's Midwest, middle-of-America parents along with CEOs and crystal healers. I said, 'Sounds like a job for a priestess!'"

In all the years I've been traveling in the footsteps of biblical stories, one thing has struck me more than anything else: the Bible's remarkable powers of regeneration. No matter what's going on in the world, these stories, the youngest of them thousands of years old, have the uncanny ability to reinvent themselves to become utterly urgent today. A huge part of this is because the text attracts a never-ending cast of devotees and enthusiasts who embed themselves in its characters and find meaning in its themes.

Jill Hammer is a perfect example. Though she comes from a different theological, spiritual, and cultural tradition than John Mark Comer, in many ways she's attempting something similar. She's trying to take followers who might otherwise drift away from organized religion and find a way to keep them engaged. In her case, the constituency she's appealing to would be ideal candidates for the nondenominational, free-form spirituality currently in vogue. **I'm not religious; I'm spiritual.** Her message: Don't give up on tradition; don't give up on rigor; don't give up on the Bible.

Jill had what she calls a bourgeois Jewish upbringing in rural New York, where her father was a dentist and her mother a German war refugee. Unable to have children, they adopted Jill. "My adoption had a deep impact on my desire to look for mother figures," she told me.

After marrying and earning her PhD, Jill became involved in traditional religious practice, but with a feminist twist. "I began leading services using feminine pronouns for God and the feminine name for God, **Shekhinah**," she said. One day a visiting professor gave a lecture in which she said that it was immoral to use this kind of language. Jill confronted her, but the woman refused to back down. That night Jill had a dream.

"I was at a cocktail party, and everyone crowded around waiting for the guest of honor," Jill explained. "The guest of honor turned out to be God, who was an enormously radiant, glowing pregnant woman. She had long, honey-colored hair, breasts, belly, the whole thing."

Jill was ecstatic. "I jostled to sit next to her and began telling her all I think about God and gender. She thought it was all very funny. Then she picks up an unlit, wrought-iron lantern, gives it to me, and . . . I wake up." Jill turned to her husband next to her in bed. "God gave me a lantern, and I don't know what to do with it!"

"Boy, are you in trouble," he said.

The next day she applied to rabbinical school.

In the seminary, Jill excelled at the most eso-teric aspects of Jewish law but was horrified by its male-centeredness. During a study year in Is-rael, she grew attached to the legacy of honoring the land, building altars, and using other forms of worship that had been squeezed out of daily practice. She also got divorced and began dating a female drummer named Shoshana.

"For a gift, Shoshana bought me a Web site and said, 'Go figure this out,'" Jill said. She organized an experimental weekend gathering of women to explore their spirituality. On the last day, everyone gathered in a cave with a river running through it. Candles were everywhere.

"Shoshana was drumming," Jill said. "I climbed down the ladder and felt, 'My God, this is what our ancestors meant by ritual.'"

Along with a colleague, Taya Shere, Jill started a priestess institute called Kohenet, using the feminine variation of **kohen**, or priest. The two designed an intensive three-year curriculum that prepares students to fulfill any number of spiritual roles women have played over the centuries, from midwife to storyteller to wisewoman.

"And let me tell you," Jill said. "We succeeded beyond our wildest dreams." The forty women who had graduated so far had led prayer, facilitated marriages, written books, delivered babies, and generally helped others embrace the sacred feminine in their lives.

"These women testify to a reality only partly revealed in the Bible and other sacred texts," Jill said. "Priestesses are part of our history. Now they are part of our future as well."

Tonight was the graduation ceremony for the fourth class, and this morning was the final session. A number of alumnae were also in attendance. Jill passed around a few medieval texts, along with photographs of silver amulets. Jill drew special attention to one that said, "ADAM AND EVE: OUT LILITH."

"What this shows," she said, "is that there has always been a threatening aspect of women's sexuality. Adam and Eve were 'in'; Lilith was 'out.' We have to speak more openly about our eagerness to conceal our power."

The women responded with a chorus of "Hmm," "Uh-huh," and "You said it."

At the end of the discussion, Jill brought forward a dozen wooden bowls filled with stones and beads. There was malachite representing hope and pregnancy, jasper for willpower and sexual energy, and so on.

"This would be a good time for you to make a personal amulet in response to our conversation," Jill said.

THE IDEA THAT LILITH, a maligned figure for centuries, could somehow go in the course of just one century from being "out" to "in," is a remarkable turnabout and represents an enormous shift in how the story of Adam and Eve resonates. The single most common question I was asked when I told people I was writing about Adam and Eve is whether I was also writing about Lilith.

Hollywood played a critical role in this. From the early years of film, the names "Lilith," "Lil," or "Lola" have been given to women of unbridled sexuality. Mae West had her biggest Broadway hit with 1928's **Diamond Lil**, which became a film in 1933. The following year Jean Harlow played Lil in **Red-Headed Woman**, a movie so controversial it was pulled from circulation. In **Damn Yankees!** (1958), Lola is an employee of the Devil who sings "Whatever Lola Wants, Lola Gets"; Lil runs a brothel in **Gaily, Gaily** (1969), is a hooker in **Islands in the Stream** (1977), and owns a bar in **Coyote Ugly** (2000). In the long-running sitcoms **Cheers** and **Frasier**, Lilith is the icy psychiatrist who first dates, then marries, and later cheats on fellow shrink Frasier Crane. Even the children's cartoon series **Rugrats** (1991–2004) has a Lil who eats worms and drinks from the toilet.

Two of Hollywood's biggest stars addressed the story directly. In **The Private Lives of Adam and Eve** (1960), Mickey Rooney plays the devilish Nick, who's bickering with his wife, Lil. When the couple find themselves on a bus to

Vegas with another feuding pair, Ad and Evie, the two couples switch partners. An elaborate dream sequence ensues that replays the story of the Garden of Eden, which jolts everyone back to their senses. The film ends with Ad and Evie reunited and expecting a baby.

In the 1964 film **Lilith**, Warren Beatty plays Vincent, a returning soldier who takes a job in a mental institution, where he falls in love with Lilith, a schizophrenic played by Jean Seberg. The sexually omnivorous Lilith sleeps with a female patient, fondles a boy, and confesses to trying to seduce her brother. After a doctor warns that mental illness can lead people to act as predatory spiders, Lilith weaves her own hair into a blanket for Vincent. Lilith is a figure of such sexual wantonness she can out-wanton Warren Beatty!

A far more consequential moment in the resuscitation of Lilith occurred in a far less storied place. In 1972, the Grailville retreat in Loveland, Ohio, hosted one of the earliest conferences of women in theology. Among the speakers was Judith Plaskow, a Long Island native who was a graduate student in theology at Yale.

"Every single teacher in my program was male," Judith told me over lunch near Manhattan College, where she's a professor of religious studies. "Every single book and every single article was written by men."

Judith joined with a smattering of peers to start the first-ever women's caucus at the American Academy of Religion. They also began hosting conferences like the one in Loveland, where they discussed how to introduce women's lived experience into the study of religion.

"Consciousness-raising is really how we experienced the world," she said. "The exercise was built around what we called the 'yeah, yeah experience,' from the Beatles song. Someone would say they read an article by a woman and saw their life reflected on the page, and everyone would mutter approvingly, 'Yeah, yeah.' Someone else would say they attended a lecture and suddenly a piece of their life fit together in a new way, and everyone would say, 'Yeah, yeah.' The 'yeah, yeah' moment is how we became sisters."

On the final day of the conference, Judith retreated to her room and wrote a story she hoped could tie together the myriad themes of the conference. "It's the only thing I've ever written where I feel like I was a channel for it," she told me.

What she wrote was an 850-word retelling of the Lilith story. It begins conventionally enough, with God forming Adam and Lilith equally from the earth. But Adam, looking for ways to make Lilith subservient, says, "I'll have my figs now." Lilith has no interest in being Adam's manservant. She utters God's name and flies away.

When Adam complains to God about that "uppity woman," God attempts to sooth his loneliness by creating Eve. Adam and Eve get along nicely for a time, until Lilith threatens their peacefulness. The outcast woman tries to breach the walls of the garden. Adam hurriedly strengthens the barricades and tells Eve there's a fearsome demon living on the other side who threatens pregnant women and absconds with their children.

The next time Lilith makes a failed assault, however, Eve catches sight of her. **She doesn't look like a demon**, Eve thinks. **She looks like me.** "The very idea attracted Eve," the story says. "Sensing capacities in herself that remained undeveloped," Eve goes in search of this other woman. She spots an apple tree at the edge of the garden, climbs it, and swings over the fence.

Lilith is waiting for her. "What is your story?" the two ask each other. They talk, laugh, listen, and cry, "till the bond of sisterhood grew between them." Back in the garden, Adam and God are worried by Eve's absence. They're even more befuddled when she returns with her newfound lady friend, "bursting with possibilities, ready to rebuild the world."

That night, at the closing dinner, Judith read what she had written. "People were ecstatic," she recalled. "One person asked to reprint it in a book the following year. Others invited me to give speeches. I delivered the story at the first conference on feminism and religion and got a standing ovation. People totally recognized their own experience in the story. In today's terms, it went viral."

Judith Plaskow's Lilith story is now widely regarded as the signature moment in what we might call the second coming of the longtime demon outcast. Overnight, Lilith as a symbol of female strength became an icon to the feminist movement. Magazines were named after her. Operas were composed in her honor. And in her most unlikely glorification in her four-thousand-year-old history, the fiendish succubus who first entered history in whispered incantations by the rivers of Babylon became the public face of a traveling music festival founded by Canadian singer-songwriter Sarah McLachlan.

"Lilith Fair" featured female artists like Shawn Colvin, Queen Latifah, Emmylou Harris, and the Indigo Girls. Organizers chose the name, they said, because Lilith was a woman who sought equality and independence. Not everyone appreciated the reference. The editor of Jerry Falwell's newspaper denounced the fair for linking itself to what he considered to be Devil culture.

"Lilith mated with demons and had a demonic brood of children," he told the **Washington Post**. "That is dangerous, and parents need to know."

The charge of Devil worship had the opposite effect, of course. It helped stir up publicity. The fair grossed $16 million in its first outing, the highest of any touring festival that year.

So what does Judith think today of this frenzy she initiated?

"It feels very funny to me," she said. "Initially I thought it was because the story captured the power of consciousness-raising. Today I think it's more about rewriting the creation story."

People care deeply about Adam and Eve, she went on, and this story caused people to view them differently.

"Lilith is not a demon; she's a self-confident woman who was named a demon by a tradition that doesn't know what to do with strong women. Being strong used to be threatening. I guess we helped make it appealing again."

SIX HOURS AFTER their class on Lilith, the nine women of the fourth class of Kohenet priestesses marched into a tent on the grounds of the retreat center to attend their ordination. They were dressed in floor-length white gowns and flowing outer garments: turquoise vests, earth-hued scarves, iridescent coats. Their hair was braided, dreadlocked, tucked into buns, or left to hang naturally. A few were barefoot, some wore heels, one sported bedazzled high-top tennis shoes with blinking lights. They looked like a cross between debutantes and an a cappella singing group at Burning Man.

The first graduate to step before the wooden and stone altar gave a history of the class. The next led the audience in a prayer to the four elements—fire, earth, air, and water. Another paid homage to the ancestors.

Finally the time came for the formal ordination. One by one, Jill called the graduates to the altar and rubbed dirt on their feet. "From before," she said. Taya spread anointing oil on their foreheads. "From above." Shoshana lay hands on her stomach. "From below." And the scores of loved ones gathered in the tent cried in unison, "And from this moment on. You. Are. A. Kohenet!!"

Afterward, as everyone gathered around hummus, cantaloupe, and green tea, Jill relaxed in the corner, playing with her eight-year-old daughter. I asked her to reflect on the long journey that had finally brought Lilith and Eve together.

"The whole idea that Lilith doesn't belong in the garden is a split many of us are no longer prepared to live with," she said. "Lilith and Eve are really the same person. They belong together. That's one of the things we're doing here. We're reuniting women with their shadows."

"So those negative aspects of her have gone away?" I asked.

"No, they haven't gone away. We've embraced them. Look, I have an Eve in me. I'm a mother who worries about who gets fed and who takes a bath. And I have a Lilith in me who wants to run away and write poetry and hang out with these women.

"Literally, on this campus, I've been running back and forth between the two," she continued. "The question is when do I listen to my

Lilith and push myself to play more, and when do I listen to my Eve and say, 'You know what, you need to be the responsible one. Sit this one out.'"

I asked what she would say to others who wrestle with similar tensions.

"That everyone shares your struggle," she said. "We all have this part of us that we can't live out or don't want to live without. We all have a piece of us that wants to run off to Paris, or never have become a parent, or doesn't like the job we're in, or the relationship we're in. That's why we need Lilith. To remind ourselves of what it would have meant to do those things. Lilith is our way of feeding our fantasies. She's fun, she's sexy, she's rebellious. If we didn't have her, we'd be boring."

I left Jill to enjoy her daughter and walked outside the tent. Part of my conviction that Adam and Eve have something to say to modern relationships is based on Lilith. These days, most everyone has a lost love by the time they settle down. The idea that virginal, barely mature children are set up by their parents and live happily ever after in Eden-like relationships might have been fine for earlier centuries, but it hardly applies to today. These days, heartbreak has become indelible to narratives of the heart. As psychologists, friends, barkeeps, and horoscopes remind us, sometimes stumbling miserably at love is a precondition for later succeeding in love.

To me, Lilith represents that part of us that has tried and failed at love, that's been wounded, shamed, or embarrassed, was immature, unready, or just the victim of bad timing. Whatever the reason, we all have past loves that even though long gone still call to us when we least expect it, inviting us to remember them in our darkest moments of doubt, as our current lovers, partners, or spouses lie next to us in the bed, wondering who is calling.

And those voices from the past become part of our ongoing relationships, the shadows that bring meaning and light to the pairings that have succeeded them. If we're lucky, those memories might even make us appreciate what we have today even more.

In my favorite Garth Brooks song, a man on a date with his wife runs into his high school flame. "God, how I prayed nightly to make her mine," he recalls. Within minutes, after talking to his old girlfriend, he concludes that time has changed both him and her and that he prefers his wife. "Some of God's greatest gifts are unanswered prayers," he sings.

The lesson of Lilith is that love can have fissures and still be strong. We can have fantasies that pull us away from our partners but still accept the benefits that tug us back toward them. We can be like Adam and Eve, each holding on to our memories, our indiscretions, and our past loves, while still choosing to hold on to each other.

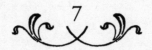

FAMILY AFFAIR

Are We Our Children's Keepers?

I N D ECEMBER 1821, Lord Byron, already one of the more flamboyant and daring Romantic poets, asked his publisher to forward an unsolicited version of his latest manuscript to his friend, the novelist Sir Walter Scott. Byron chose the author of **Ivanhoe** because of his well-known reputation as a defender of the faith. The purpose of the solicitation was to ask Scott if he would mind if Byron dedicated his new work to him. The work was a medieval-style play entitled **Cain, A Mystery**, and Byron, who was living in Ravenna at the time, was worried about a backlash over his depiction of the first family—Cain, Abel, Adam, and Eve. In effect, Byron wanted a blurb from Scott to give him cover.

Scott replied promptly, and enthusiastically.

"I accept, with feelings of great obligation the flattering proposal of Lord Byron to prefix my name to the very grand and tremendous drama of 'Cain.'" He went on to say of his younger friend's work, "I do not know that his Muse has ever taken so lofty a flight," then added, "He has certainly matched Milton on his own ground."

Byron was actually part of a miniboomlet in writing about Cain and Abel in early nineteenth-century England. Samuel Taylor Coleridge, Percy Bysshe Shelley, and William Blake all undertook important works about the first sons, their rivalry, and the unsettling relationship between violence and faith. The writings, all of them considered responses in some way to **Paradise Lost**, were both inventive and, in a world where religion still maintained a strong grip on public discourse, controversial.

Byron was considered the biggest offender. His play opens with Cain refusing to offer prayers to God because of the way his parents were treated in Eden. Seeing an opening, Lucifer steps in and offers to show the disgruntled Cain the future, which is filled with death and destruction. Depressed by what he sees, Cain takes out his frustration on his pious brother, accidentally striking him dead. Comforted by his wife, Cain comes to realize that he is his brother's keeper and must bring his brother's sensitive spirit back into the world.

Byron's play was lambasted for an array of sins, from leaving out God to glorifying a murderer. But the criticism overshadowed what was truly beautiful, even heartbreaking, about the work: the way he brought to life the pain of Cain's parents in response to their sons' dispute.

"Who, or what hath done this deed?" Adam asks upon discovering his slain child. "Speak, Cain! and say it was not thou!"

"It was," cries Eve. "I see it now—he hangs his guilty head, and covers his ferocious eye with hands incarnadine."

Furious, Eve disowns her own son, "I curse him from my sight for evermore!" Then, in an exclamation anyone with a child can relate to, she moans, "Oh death! death! Why didst thou not take **me**? . . . Why dost thou not so now?"

One often overlooked aspect of Adam and Eve is that they weren't just partners, lovers, sinners, and seekers. They were also parents. The first parents—tasked before anyone else with learning to love their children as they learned to love each other. But in a story that would become all too familiar among their descendants, their children turn out to be not all barrels of laughs and bundles of joy. They're also rivalrous, irascible, abominable, and adorable all at the same time. In other words, they are human beings with minds and instincts all their own.

How Adam and Eve learn to accept that, cope with that, even overcome that, especially in the face of the most horrific outcome a parent can imagine, is a central part of their story. That they were able to do all those things while also maintaining, even deepening, their relationship with each other may be their greatest accomplishment of all.

AFTER LOOKING AT COUNTLESS iterations of Adam and Eve over the years, I would say one thing saddened me more than any other: how little attention is given to what happens to them after they leave Eden. That includes the Bible, which covers the remaining nine hundred years of their combined lives in fewer than a hundred words.

Some commentators make a few passing observations about their having children, others a phrase or two about their demise, but generally, that's about it. No discussion of how they survived in the wilderness, no thoughts on their parenting, no exploration of how they managed to stay together during all those years in exile. It's as if the collected literature about Adam and Eve is the earliest example of age bias: We care about you only when you're young.

In one sense, this is understandable. Adam and Eve have served their primary function in the narrative by now, and the text is eager to move on to the scores of characters, stories, and lessons that follow. The Bible isn't a biography, it's a moral anthology. But there's a consequence to this lacuna: By turning away from Adam and Eve as soon as they exit paradise, the text leaves us with a tainted view. We are tempted to see only their faults, not their grit and resilience, and certainly not the ongoing commitment they display toward each other.

What Adam and Eve achieve during these years is a revelation. The time after the couple exits the garden is the most affecting, the most emotional, and ultimately the most illustrative about what it means to sustain an enduring relationship. Leaving Eden may have pushed Adam and Eve further away from God, but evidence suggests it pushed them closer to each other—which may have been God's intent all along.

Before considering what happened to the first couple during these years, we have to go back to what got them expelled in the first place. Eating the fruit brought them closer in many ways— remember all that language about their becoming "two"—but it still alienated God. No sooner do Adam and Eve cover themselves with fig leaves than they hear the sound of their creator "walking in the garden in the cool of day." On the surface, the language is innocent enough. God, who up to now has only demonstrated hands, suddenly manifests feet and a hankering for pleasant strolls at favorable times of day. Who could begrudge a deity who wants to admire his creations?

Yet the implication for Adam and Eve is ominous. It's as if a **Jaws**-like sound track is echoing through the trees. God knows he's been disobeyed, and he's angling for a reckoning. Adam and Eve are clearly afraid. They hide "among the trees." **Not there,** one wants to shout, **surrounded by all the evidence!** Adam and Eve are like children (or dieting adults, for that matter), who, caught with a hand in the cookie jar, duck for cover behind the Oreo shelf.

"Where are you?" God calls.

The text says he speaks only to the man, which is curious considering the woman is the one who ate first. Maybe he's not angry after all and this is merely a social visit. Adam and Eve are under no such illusion. One can almost see their wan smiles as they step from behind the trees, specks of fruit flesh still stuck in their teeth, drops of fruit juice still dribbling down their cheeks.

"Oh, hi! What a pleasant surprise. We were just talking about you."

Adam, his hands lamely covering his crotch, quickly babbles an excuse. "I heard you in the garden, and I was afraid because I was naked; so I hid."

Startled to hear that Adam is suddenly self-conscious about his appearance, God replies, "Who told you that you were naked? Have you eaten from the tree that I commanded you not to?"

If you've been following this far, you can guess what happens next: Does Adam man up, accept responsibility for his misdeeds, and do everything in his power to protect his true love? Not a chance. Adam blames Eve. "The woman you put here with me—she gave me some fruit from the tree, and I ate it." Worse than just fingering Eve, Adam also partly blames God, implicating him for putting the woman by his side in the first place.

God then turns to Eve and asks her what happened. Having learned to pass the buck from Adam, she promptly passes it on to the snake. "The serpent deceived me, and I ate." she says. Unlike Adam, who merely describes what happened, she tries to justify it by explaining that there was a sound reason for what she did.

Neither Adam nor Eve lies to God; nor do they entirely tell the truth. They didn't eat just because they were forced to; they ate because they wanted to. And they enjoyed it when they did.

What follows is among the most challenging parts of the entire story. God doles out three pronouncements, first to the serpent, then to the woman, then to the man. Some observers view these as punishments; others as actions somehow beneficial to the recipients, at least the humans. The serpent's statement alone is called a "curse." The snake is informed it will be damned above all species, obliged to crawl on its belly, and forced to eat dust. Also, God says he will create enmity between the serpent's offspring and those of the woman. Because Eve and the snake once trusted each other, their descendants will distrust each other forever.

Adam is told the ground will be hardened by what he's done, and he'll have to work hard to get food from it. "By the sweat of your brow you will eat your food," God says, "until you return to the ground." Then comes the iconic line that brings the human back to the place from whence he came and that sounds at funerals still today. "For dust you are and to dust you will return."

Eve gets by far the shortest pronouncement, but it's the one that has generated the longest debate.

I will greatly multiply your pain in childbearing;
in pain you shall bring forth children,
yet your desire shall be for your husband,
and he shall rule over you."

These lines were used for so long to justify women's oppression that it's hard to read them not through that lens. Contemporary critics have tried, though, with some success. The first half of this sentence, for example, is often considered as referring to labor pains, but some scholars believe it more accurately reads "I will increase your labor," as in work of any kind, and your "childbirths," as in pregnancies. In other words, you will work hard in your life and you will have many children, not you will work hard **to** have children.

The second half, about your husband "ruling" over you, has been harder to explain away. One feminist scholar calls it the greatest challenge to equality in the entire Hebrew Bible, though she does add that the scope is limited to sexual activity and not a blanket statement referring to all aspects of life.

Despite this seemingly harsh parade of declarations, it's worth noting what's missing from these statements: In no way does God follow through on his original threat. Adam and Eve do not die. Even more striking, directly after God issues his decrees, Eve is reborn. The woman who up to now has been called "the woman" finally gets a name. The text says, "Adam named his wife Eve, because she would become the mother of all the living."

Threatened with death, Eve becomes the source of life. Tarnished with spoiling humanity, Eve becomes the wellspring of humanity. This characterization is the pinnacle depiction of women in the book of Genesis, and it comes via Adam. Their relationship, at least, has survived their sentencing.

The final thing God does before banishing Adam and Eve from the garden may be the most touching of all. In a clear indication he does not intend to abandon his creations once they leave his sacred home, God fashions "garments of skins" for Adam and Eve and clothes them. Fresh off censuring his first creations, he sends them into the world with his blessing so they can fulfill his mandate to "be fruitful and multiply."

And they do. The immediate next line, the first in Genesis 4, begins a radically new story. As in chapter 3, this story uses sexuality as a source of togetherness. The Hebrew says Adam "knows" his wife; the New International Version is more romantic: Adam "makes love" to his wife. This milestone is worth celebrating. Once outside the garden, they face together what Adam inside the garden had faced by himself: loneliness.

And they respond with intimacy. Instead of being rent apart by the wilderness; Adam and Eve are drawn together by it. Wrapped in protective skins, they remove those skins and wrap themselves in each other's skin. The contemporary poet Irene Zimmerman imagines Adam apologizing to Eve in this moment: "I'm sorry. Forgive me," he says. Confused by these unfamiliar words, Eve understands "when she touched his tears."

This interpersonal breakthrough in the face of existential dread is the first in what will become a series of similar occasions throughout the Hebrew Bible: Exile, instead of being a dead end of human life, is a source of renewal. The same will happen later to Abraham when he leaves his native land and goes into the Promised Land, to Jacob when he leaves the Promised Land and goes into the land of Egypt, to the Israelites when they leave the land of Egypt and go into the land of the Sinai, and to the Jerusalemites when they leave the land of Judah and go to the land of Babylon.

"Be patient and tough," Ovid said. "Someday this pain will be useful to you."

Sure enough, Adam and Eve's pain is rewarded: Eve soon gives birth to a son. Actually, it's two sons! Wait, are they twins?

The language the Bible uses to describe the brothers' births is unusual. After Adam and Eve make love but before Cain appears, Eve declares, "With the help of the Lord I have brought forth a man." Is Eve suggesting God is the father?

Many commentators believed so. Others, trying to protect Adam from being the source of Cain's iniquity, said the Devil must be the father. Still more, trying to protect Eve, said Cain grew out of a hookup between Adam and Lilith.

It's the next sentence, though, that introduces the ambiguity about the siblings. Speaking of Eve, the text says, "Later she gave birth to his brother Abel." Cain's birth is preceded by lovemaking between the first couple; Abel's is not. Since no conception is mentioned, many believed Abel must be Cain's twin.

Whatever their lineage, the brothers' relationship is the first of many in the Bible that turns sour fast. Cain becomes a farmer, Abel a shepherd. Both brothers make sacrifices to God. Cain offers fruit, Abel his choicest sheep. When God prefers Abel's sacrifice, Cain is incensed. He summons his brother to a field, rises up, and slays him. When God asks the firstborn son what happened to Abel, Cain issues one of the Bible's top ten most quoted lines, "Am I my brother's keeper?"

Perhaps the first thing to say about this story is how perceptive it is. We're not even a paragraph into the life of the first family and already we have the first family dysfunction. And not just the mild Thanksgiving table variety, but the salacious made-for-TV-miniseries variety. And not without reason. Statistics show that about a quarter of all murders are family murders, split roughly evenly among murders of spouses, murders of children, and murders of one family member by another. Eight in ten of these murderers are men. While the presence of fratricide in the opening of Genesis may not be cause for celebration, the Bible once again gets it right.

But what exactly is Cain's motive? There are two prevailing theories. The first is that the dispute is over their livelihoods. Abel is born second, but his profession, herding sheep, is mentioned first, suggesting God prefers wanderers to farmers. This preference can be seen throughout the Bible.

The second theory is that Cain and Abel were fighting over a girl. This taps into one of the most peculiar and enduring of biblical puzzles: Who was the mother of Cain's children? After Cain kills Abel, he, like his parents, is sent into exile, where he has children of his own. Considering that the Bible mentions no women being born, who is their mom?

Commentators from the earliest days of the Bible hotly debated this point. The most popular answer is that Adam and Eve had a daughter; in some versions she's actually Abel's twin. Genesis Rabbah, from around the fifth century, includes the story that this sister was the subject of a love triangle. Cain announces, "I will have her, because I am the firstborn"; Abel responds, "I must have her because she was born with me." The advantage of this theory is that it deflects blame from God for playing favorites and places responsibility for the dustup squarely on the boys.

But while everyone from priests to poets loved to speculate about what transpired between Cain and Abel, virtually none seems to have taken much interest in what transpired between their parents when they heard the bloodcurdling news. When you do take up that question what you find is both surprising and profound—and worthy of a biblical parable all its own.

FROM THE BEGINNING of Lord Byron's play **Cain**, the relationship between Adam and Eve and their elder son is strained. Cain looks down on his parents, believing they have forgiven God too easily for evicting them from Eden. "My father is tamed down," he says. "My mother has forgot the mind which made her thirst for knowledge at the risk of an eternal curse."

Adam and Eve, meanwhile, are concerned that Cain is moody and selfish. When all the members of the family pay homage to God at the start of the play, Cain abstains. "Wherefore art thou silent?" Adam asks. "Why should I speak?" Cain replies. You've got nothing to be thankful for? his father asks. "No," Cain answers.

The fractured relationship between parents and son becomes the driving force of the entire drama and, in effect, the reason the family ends up destroyed. Like the best interpreters, Byron mines an often overlooked vein in the biblical story to draw attention to a larger truth: Having children is hard.

"Becoming a parent is one of the most sudden and dramatic changes in adult life," writes Jennifer Senior in **All Joy and No Fun: The Paradox of Modern Parenthood**. Prospective parents tend to think having a child will bring them unchecked glee and eternal bliss, but the reality is often the opposite. One of the more persistent findings of social science is that having children is surprisingly harmful to parents, to their sense of happiness and self-worth, and to their relationship with each other.

That begins with childbirth. Decades of research shows that babies weaken rather than strengthen relationships. They zap resources, decimate sleep, and reduce sex. Parents come to hate minding their children so much that Nobel Prize-winning economist Daniel Kahneman found that childcare ranked sixteen out of nineteen on a list of things parents enjoy, behind even housework. Eighty-three percent of new mothers and fathers experience "severe crisis"; ninety percent suffer a decline in marital satisfaction.

These numbers do level off after several years, as parents begin to enjoy many of the intangible benefits of having children. Being a parent weakens happiness, but it does strengthen meaning and purpose. Yet the numbers plunge again when children reach adolescence. Nearly half of parents of teens experience low self-esteem, increased distress, and more insomnia.

If those young people grow up to become adults who somehow fall short of their parents' expectations, either by not finding career success or not settling into healthy relationships, the damage to those parents can be chronic. Fathers tend to express their frustration through anger and guilt, mothers through disappointment and worry. Dads grow more disturbed over failures in career, moms over failures in relationships.

So what does all this suggest about Adam and Eve?

First, while having two boys in rapid succession may have been a source of joy for the couple, it may also have been a source of stress.

Second, any rivalry between those sons would surely have stoked anxiety for their parents.

Third, Mom and Dad might have registered those feelings differently, thereby creating an additional layer of tension between the two of them.

Byron perfectly captures this fraught domestic stew. When Adam and Eve discover Cain with blood on his hands, it's Eve who has the more militant reaction. "Drive him forth o'er the wilderness, like us from Eden," she cries. "All bonds I break between us." Adam originally tries to placate her, but, as happened with the fruit, soon joins her. "Cain! get thee forth: we dwell no more together," he says. "Henceforth alone—we never must meet more." Adam turns so severely on his son he's even prepared to return to the state he never hoped to revisit, aloneness.

Still, as illuminating as Byron's portrait is, the greatest insight I gained into what it must have been like to be parents of a murderer came from a most unlikely source.

SUE KLEBOLD was in her office in downtown Denver at a few minutes after noon on April 20, 1999, when she received a call from her husband, Tom. "Look at the television!" he shouted. Sue panicked, unable to comprehend. "Whatever is happening is big enough to be on TV?" she thought. And yet, deep down, she understood. "I knew just from the sound of his voice that something had happened to one of our boys."

Tom reported that gunmen were shooting at people at Columbine High School, where their son Dylan was a senior. The gunmen were wearing black trench coats, like the one Sue and Tom had bought Dylan at his request the previous year. Dylan's best friend, Nate, had just called Tom and said, "I don't want to alarm you. But I know all the kids who wear black coats, and the only ones I can't find are Dylan and Eric." Tom went tearing through the house, looking for the trench coat, convinced that if he located it Dylan would be okay. He couldn't find the coat, he told Sue.

Sue hung up without saying good-bye. She ran to her car and began the twenty-six-mile drive to their home in the comfortable suburb of Littleton, Colorado. She remembered her son leaving home that morning without saying where he was going. "Dyl?" she called as he opened the door to leave. He responded with a sharp, decisive, "Bye."

"They say your life flashes before you when you die," she later recalled. "But on that car ride home, it was my son's life flashing before me."

Once she got home her disquiet only deepened. A SWAT team arrived and escorted Tom and Sue from their house so they could search it. The frightened couple huddled on the driveway as neighbors gathered and news helicopters circled. Tom's lawyer called to say he had spoken with the sheriff's office and their worst fears were confirmed: "Dylan was one of the gunmen."

"Like all mothers in Littleton, I had been praying for my son's safety," Sue said. "But in that instant I knew the greatest mercy I could pray for was not my son's safety, but for his death."

I was not a parent when the Columbine massacre happened; nor was I even married. I was just beginning what would become a decades-long passion of trying to relate biblical stories to the present. And for most of that time, if you had told me something so horrific and seemingly modern as Sue and Tom Klebold's experience with their son could illuminate something so bygone and archetypal as Adam and Eve's experience with their son, I would have scoffed. Unike Cain, Dylan Klebold was a mass murderer; he used semiautomatic weapons; he had mental health issues. He also had, in Eric Harris, a brother-in-arms who was a psychopath.

And yet, from the moment I heard Sue's story, initially in interviews, then in her remarkably candid memoir, **A Mother's Reckoning**, and finally in an exchange of e-mails, I was so profoundly moved by how universal her experience felt, how vividly it captured every parent's fears, and how much more it taught me about the first couple's possible reaction than anything else I'd seen. By telling her story in all its raw horror, Sue inadvertently created a remarkable midrash on one of the least understood stories of the Bible.

One of the first issues Sue confronts, beginning that very night, must surely have been one of the first issues Adam and Eve confronted: Were they at fault? Are parents to blame for the crimes of their children? Our society tends to say yes. Bad children are bad because of the deficiencies of their upbringing. The Klebolds defy this. Sue worked with disadvantaged children; Tom was a work-at-home dad who took his son to ball games. They were deeply committed parents.

The writer Andrew Solomon, the first to interview the Klebolds, said he didn't want to like them, "because the cost of liking them would be an acknowledgment that what happened wasn't their fault." Alas, he liked them very much. Of the hundreds of families he's interviewed, Solomon said, he'd want to join theirs the most. Adam and Eve might have been neglectful as parents, but Cain's murder of Abel doesn't prove it.

The next question Sue elucidates is the one that Byron builds his play around: Would Adam and Eve turn their backs on Cain? Byron says yes, though the Bible is less clear. One curiosity of the Genesis account is that the killer gets off easy. Cain is forced into exile, but like his parents, he goes with God's blessing. God gives him a mark that will prevent others from harming him. Cain may not be his brother's keeper, but God appears to be his. The text is silent on Adam and Eve's reaction, but that silence at least suggests they don't object. How could this be?

Sue offers a hint. In the first days after the shooting, she was startled to discover she kept finding excuses to explain away Dylan's actions. Whatever he had done, Sue wrote, Dylan was still "my son." She was furious with him for some time, but soon her motherly instinct took over. "Anger blocks the feeling of love," she wrote, but "the love kept winning."

Finally, perhaps the most haunting connection between the Klebolds and Adam and Eve is what turns out to be Dylan's real motivation. Months after the crimes, Sue and Tom, along with Eric's parents, were given access to journals the boys had kept. Sue was stunned. The most common images in Eric's pages were decapitated heads, bodies on fire, girls being raped. The most common image in Dylan's pages: huge, hand-drawn hearts. The word Dylan used most frequently in his writing was "love."

"Dylan writes heartbreakingly and sometimes eloquently, about his unfulfilled, excruciating desire for romantic love," Sue recalls.

Dylan, in other words, was lonely. And while none of this justifies his violence, it does shed new light on it. Only when Sue felt alone and cut off in the wake of his crime, she said, did she have "insight into what it must have felt like for my son to be marginalized."

All these connections lead to perhaps the biggest question of all: What impact did having a child murderer have on the relationship between Adam and Eve? Here the Klebolds provide a more sobering example. Married almost thirty years, Sue and Tom had different reactions to their plight. Though "we had always been strongly attracted to each other," Sue said, "it was becoming increasingly clear Tom and I were going in different directions with our pain." She wanted to be with others and discuss what happened; he preferred being alone. "I wanted to throw open the doors, and Tom wanted to circle the wagons," she said.

Worse, they focused on different aspects of their suffering. Sue looked backward, incessantly reviewing memories of Dylan as a boy; Tom looked forward, thinking of everything Dylan would never be able to do. Ultimately these differences proved insurmountable. Fifteen years after the incident, Sue and Tom divorced.

"We ended our marriage to save our friendship," she said.

So what insight might this suggest for Adam and Eve? Sue insists she doesn't want to be a messenger. "Who wants advice from the mother of a murderer?" she says. And yet she carries a message nonetheless. First, the love of a child can easily prevail over fury toward that child. Second, the different reactions men and women have can doom a relationship. Finally, the key to survival is discovering a safe space within yourself.

In her memoir, Sue cites a quote about cancer patients that gives her inspiration. "The people who do well create a place in their mind and their spirit where they are well, and they live from that place." This is what it's like to survive the unsurvivable, she says. You dwell in that small place where you can function, even if it means giving up your lover who wants to live someplace else.

As DREADFUL as it is to be the parents of a child killer, Adam and Eve also face an additional burden: Their second son is dead. To understand how they might have responded to that, I drove two hours east from my home to central

Long Island to attend a special meeting of the Compassionate Friends of Rockville Centre.

The Compassionate Friends is one of several national groups dedicated to offering support and understanding to bereaved parents. The organization has found that if you add together stillbirths, the death of children under twenty-one, and the death of adult children, one in five parents experiences the loss of a child. This chapter was started by Elaine Stillwell, a vivacious Catholic schoolteacher and mother of three, whose two older children, twenty-one-year-old Dennis and nineteen-year-old Peggy, died in a car accident on August 2, 1986. Feeling she had no place to turn, Elaine created her own support group. She still holds meetings every month at a local college.

"The grief books say that when we share our sorrow we divide the pain," she said. "That's why our motto is 'No need to walk alone.'"

Elaine convened a special session one Saturday afternoon to explore some of the bereavement issues facing Adam and Eve. After we settled in a circle, she began, per custom, by having everyone introduce themselves. The statements were both matter-of-fact and thunderous.

"Hi, my name is Diane. My husband, John,

and I lost our middle child, Mark, in 1998. He took his own life."

"Hi, my name is Denise. My husband and I lost our only son, Noah, on September 2, 2003. He died from a reaction to an herbal supplement."

"Hi, my name is Carol. I lost my son Darin one month ago today."

"Hi, my name is Cecille. My daughter Marianne was thirty-five years old when she passed from cancer. I also lost two babies prematurely."

"Hi, my name is Helene, and this is my husband, Tim. We lost our only son, Ryan, on July 23, 2007. He fell off the back of a truck while he was working his summer job."

"Hi, my name is Barbara. I lost my son Eric thirteen years ago from substance abuse. His father and brother are left to grieve with me."

While there aren't tons of commentaries about how Adam and Eve reacted to Abel's death, there are some. The themes are remarkably similar to the stories I heard that afternoon. The fifth-century Byzantine monk Ephrem the Syrian wrote about Eve's mystified reaction upon discovering her slaughtered son. It was, after all, the first instance of death. "What is this strange, undendurable sight? Abel, you are silent and don't speak to your mother."

The parents in the Compassionate Friends were similarly so stunned by their child's death they didn't know how to function—sometimes for years. Cecille, an elegant retiree whose daughter had cancer, said she felt so aggrieved she considered suicide. "The depression was so immense I could understand, for the first time, how someone could take their own life."

"Every day is hard, especially in the beginning," said Diane, who worked in real estate. "The loneliness and emptiness are just intense. Going to sleep and waking up is beyond impossible that first year, but the second year, believe it or not, is harder. The first year you're just in shock, but the second year you realize your child is not coming home."

Denise, a homemaker, said she finds happy occasions the hardest—Mother's Days, birthdays, holidays. "The anticipation is just so painful," she said. "You see the date circled on the calendar and it looms. One minute you're fine, and the next minute you start crying."

One common sentiment I heard is that losing a child is deeply unusual, so the experience demands learning an entirely new language that's harder to master than losing a parent. A legend from the early centuries of Judaism captures this feeling. When Adam and Eve find Abel's body, it's being watched over by a dog who's protecting it from wild beasts. Unsure what to do, the parents sit and weep, until a raven alights at their feet. "I will teach this couple what to do," the raven thinks. It takes a dead bird from nearby, digs a grave, and buries the corpse. "Like this raven I will act," Adam says. He then does the same for his son, thereby inventing the tradition of interment.

The bereaved parents I met with spoke of insecurity over how much or how little to memorialize their deceased children. Barbara, whose favored son died of substance abuse and who wore multiple buttons and ribbons bearing his picture, said at the funeral she kept uttering, "Who took my baby, my baby?" After that, anything Eric had touched was sacred to her.

"It's been thirteen years since Eric passed," she said, "and his room is unchanged. Throwing away anything is like throwing away a memory." She took a large teddy bear she had given him as a boy, propped it on the bed, and dressed it in one of Eric's sweaters and caps. "It helps me keep in touch," she said.

This desire to remain in contact with a dead child is intense. In William Blake's poem "The

Ghost of Abel," a distraught Eve sees what she calls a "visionary Phantasm" of her lost son. "I see Him plainly with my Mind's Eye," she says. Nearly all the parents I met had a similar experience. Cecille was so disillusioned with her Catholic faith that she went to visit a medium. "I went to Mass every morning and still couldn't pray," she said. "One day I came home and my husband, Joe, said, 'I saw her.' I looked at him, baffled. 'I was sitting on the edge of the bed, and she kissed me on the forehead,' he said."

Cecille and Bob sought out a medium, too, and the first thing he told them was, "You've had a visit. She wants you to know she's okay." "Now he had no way of knowing that!" Cecille announced. The whole experience strengthened her faith, she said. "It gave me a peek at what we've been told—that there's life after death."

Everyone in the circle agreed that losing a child stunted their marriage—at least for a time. This dovetails with biblical tradition. In the most well-known commentary about Genesis 4, the rabbis said that after Abel's death Adam abstained from sexual relations with Eve for 130 years. During this time, he fraternized with various female spirits, including Lilith. The daughters he is believed to have had with Eve are said to have persuaded him to return to their mother.

"Losing my son almost cost me my marriage," Diane said. "The first few months, my husband couldn't mention Mark's name. He tried to pretend everything was okay. We talked about everything—except Mark. Finally I said to him, 'I don't get it. You were an amazing father.' He said, 'I don't bring him up because I don't want to upset you.'" We had already lost Mark, she said. The challenge was not to lose each other.

So what do these couples believe it takes to stay together through such a tragedy? Their answer, to a person, was that there came a moment in which they faced a do-or-die choice. As the Bible suggests, there was a period of separation, then each party had to make an affirmative decision to recommit to the relationship. They had to give love a second chance.

"My life was a fairy tale before Eric died," Barbara said. "Then it became a nightmare. My husband was closer to my older son; I was much closer to Eric. So I built a memorial garden. I had his picture in every room. It was all too much for my husband. Finally, I said to him, 'You'd be better off without me.' He thought for a second and said, 'I'll take you any way I can get you.'"

Tim and Helene, whose son, Ryan, was studying to be a youth minister, spoke of how alienated they felt from each other. What saved them,

Tim said, was rethinking their understanding of love. "I used to think love was the opposite of hurt, in the same way that joy is the opposite of sadness," he said. "Now I realize you can't have one without the other. If you truly love the person you're with, you'll accept everything that happens to you." That includes money problems, illness, even the loss of a child.

"There's a reason Adam and Eve had to experience the death of a child," he went on, "and that all of us have to keep repeating the pattern. It's a way to teach us what relationships are for. I would never wish what happened to us on anybody, but I do think it made us realize that our love can withstand it. And the same goes for them."

Their fellow grieving parents applauded.

So is Tim right? Can what transpired between Adam and Eve regarding their children somehow teach us something larger about love? Did the first couple learn—or even intuit—some valuable insight about relationships that the rest of us could benefit from when we face our own crises, big or small?

The answer, I believe, is yes—and there is data to prove it.

Shirley Murphy was a PhD student in nursing at the University of Oregon in 1980 when she submitted a proposal for her dissertation. Her advisor folded it into a paper airplane and sailed it across the room. "Certainly you can do better than this," he said.

A few weeks later Mount St. Helens erupted, killing fifty-seven people and injuring dozens more. Overnight, Shirley was thrust into the role of bereavement counselor, especially for the many families who lost children. There was little research and lots of misinformation, she told me. She had found her subject. With a $1 million grant from the National Institutes of Health, Shirley went on to redefine the field of parental response to trauma.

Shirley's research explodes the most persistent myth of parental loss: Divorce is more common among bereaved parents. This oft-repeated assertion is simply not true, she said. Of the 271 families she tracked for over thirty-five years, only a handful broke up. Eighteen other studies found similar results. Traumatized couples face problems—from displaced anger to reduced intimacy—but they manage to work through them. How?

Shirley's answer is that they write a new story about their lives. In a study of 138 parents over five years, Shirley found that only 12 percent had found new meaning after a year. That number was unchanged after two years. At five years, though, the number ballooned to almost 60 percent. What happens between years three and five that allows sufferers to begin making meaning out of their lives?

First, they finally begin to accept the finality of their situation.

Second, they begin to do the necessary emotional work. This includes at least one thing Adam and Eve could not do—attend support groups—and one thing they could have—engage in "self-talk." "You have to do a lot of saying, 'Okay, I'm going to get through this. I need distractions, I need obligations, but I can do this,'" she said.

Third, they tend to revert to their pretrauma selves. "If you're outspoken you might go to court, change laws, or start advocacy groups," she said. "If you're quieter, you might build memorials, light candles, or lay flowers at the grave." The single most effective thing trauma survivors do, she said, is write about their experience. "There's something about expressing your feelings in that way that helps you believe you can manage the pain. You go from ruminating to coping," she said.

What all these have in common is crafting a new life narrative that accepts your changed circumstances. Only when you fix your own story can you reconnect with those you love. "What happens," Shirley said, "is after a person goes through their own healing process, they look up and realize their spouse sitting across from them is struggling, too, and they reach out. That opens the door to reconciliation and, in some cases, a strengthened relationship."

The famed rabbi Harold Kushner, who lost his fourteen-year-old son to the premature aging disease progeria, illuminates this turn from degeneration to regeneration in his book **When Bad Things Happen to Good People**. Tragedies, illnesses, and natural disasters are all part of life, he writes, though we should not call them "acts of God." The real act of God is the courage to rebuild your life after such an occasion, he says.

"All we can do is try to rise beyond the question 'Why did it happen?'" Kushner writes, "and begin to ask the question 'What do I do now that it has happened.'"

For those in relationships that means making an affirmative decision to continue. "We do not have to love," the psychiatrist and author M. Scott Peck said. "We choose to love." To choose to love after the death of a child is even more fearless than to do it the first time because you already know the suffering you'll have to endure.

And yet this is the choice Adam and Eve make. Genesis 4:25 reports that following Cain's murder of Abel, the first couple elects to become a couple again and have another child. "Adam knew his wife again, and she bore a son." This son, Seth, will go on to populate humanity.

"Love does not consist in gazing at each other," Antoine de Saint-Exupéry said, "but in looking outward together in the same direction." In Eden, Adam and Eve gazed at each other. That was love, I believe, but this is something richer. In exile, they look outward together in the same direction, while still managing to hold on to what they left behind.

Lin-Manuel Miranda captures a similar harrowing transition in his Pulitzer Prize-winning masterwork **Hamilton**. Alexander Hamilton and his wife, Eliza, are estranged after his ruinous affair. Only one thing is strong enough to bring the two of them back together: the death of their nineteen-year-old son, Philip, in a duel. "There are moments that the words don't reach," Eliza's sister sings of the grief that mother and father share. "There is suffering too terrible to name. You hold your child as tight as you can."

And yet the onetime lovers—bitter, broken, unspeaking—try to do the unimaginable: They try to forgive each other. They take long walks. They move uptown. They pray. And finally, in a silence, a sorrow, and a need so deep only the other aggrieved person can understand, Eliza takes Alexander's hand.

They rewrite their story.

It is this lesson of recommitment in the face of loneliness that is sitting in plain sight for all of us to see in the lives of Adam and Eve. And while it may not be spelled out in the opening chapters of Genesis, it is made clear in the final chapters of Deuteronomy. In the last few verses of the Pentateuch, Moses has led the Israelites through forty years in the desert. He has put up with their rebellions, their kvetching, their golden cows, and he has just learned that he will be denied entry into the Promised Land. The one thing Moses most wants to achieve he will not achieve. He, like Adam and Eve, will not have the perfect ending. The grace note of the Five Books of Moses echoes back to the grace note that opens them.

So what does Moses do? He doesn't buckle,

or fight, or complain. He gathers the Israelites on Mount Nebo and delivers a passionate valediction. His words have come down as among the most powerful in the Hebrew Bible. Life will not always be easy, Moses says. There will be pain, heartbreak, unimaginable misery. But you have something that no other of God's creatures has. You have choice.

"I have put before you life and death, blessing and curse," Moses says. "Choose life."

Adam and Eve, at yet another critical juncture in their lives following the collapse of their family, choose life. They choose togetherness over aloneness. They choose each other.

They choose love.

And in so doing they give the rest of us that choice forever.

THE LOVE YOU MAKE

Bless the Broken Road

S USAN B. ANTHONY WAS RUNNING LATE. Lucretia Mott was darting around the yard trying to ascertain the delay. Elizabeth Cady Stanton was inside the living room speaking with visitors. It was a few minutes after 9 A.M. on a Saturday in late July, and about four dozen guests had gathered on the still-damp lawn of the Elizabeth Cady Stanton House just across the lake from downtown Seneca Falls, New York. The occasion was the start of Convention Days, a three-day annual event in the "historic gateway to the Finger Lakes" that commemorates the Seneca Falls Convention of 1848, the gathering that is widely regarded as the start of the women's rights movement in America.

By now, the crowd was expected to have

begun parading to a reconstructed chapel in the center of town that was the site of the original convention. "I don't know what's keeping Ms. Anthony," said Ms. Mott, or, more accurately, the reenactor playing Ms. Mott. "I think she couldn't find her red cloak. And you know she won't go anywhere without that cloak."

Meanwhile, one of the guests in the living room was asking Mrs. Stanton a question. "What was it like for you as a woman to be so intelligent?"

Stanton, a native of upstate New York and the most voluble of the first generation of women's rights leaders, was being portrayed this morning by another local daughter done good, Melinda Grube. A professor of nineteenth-century women's religion at a nearby college, Melinda was wearing a floor-length cobalt blue Victorian dress, black fingerless gloves, and a white bonnet.

"Being an intelligent woman in the 1830s was almost like starving," Melinda answered as Mrs. Stanton. "When you're hungry, you need food. The intellect also hungers for stimulation." She had books, she went on, but very few people were willing to spend the time to engage in the deep conversations she craved. There were men around, but they didn't realize she had the ability.

"That's why when I met Ms. Anthony we clung to each other," she continued. The two developed a lifelong partnership, helped by the fact they had different skills.

"Ms. Anthony would write and say, 'We have a terrible problem, Mrs. Stanton, and we need your help!' I would say, 'My soul is with you, but my hands are occupied.' I had seven children, after all, and she had none. So Ms. Anthony would say, 'Well I'll take care of your children. I'll play with the toddler, I'll hold the baby, and I'll stir the pudding, while you write the speeches.' We worked like this for fifty years."

Until, in the 1890s, with the two aging activists in their seventies, and with women's suffrage on the precipice of becoming reality, the two diverged, their friendship soured, and the organization they'd built together voted to boot Stanton from its ranks. The lingering stench of this incident ran so deep that it is said by historians to have been the reason Stanton was all but erased from women's history for the next seven decades, leaving Anthony to become the public face of women's rights, her portrait on the dollar coin.

The episode that caused this rift is little remembered today, yet it's among the most telling examples of the challenges women faced in the nineteenth century. It's also among the more remarkable stories in the long history of Adam and Eve and a potent illustration of the stubborn role the first couple continued to hold on male-female relations.

After fighting for women's rights for half a century, Stanton decided that equal standing in law, politics, and work were not enough. In order to be truly free, women needed equal standing before God. To achieve that, she had to rethink the most important story ever told. She had to reimagine the story of inequality that had undermined women for three thousand years.

In a flamboyant publication in 1895 called **The Woman's Bible**, Stanton created one of the most original documents in the history of biblical criticism—and one of the most destructive to its creator. In the process, she reaffirmed a core conviction of Western thought going back thirty centuries: that every relationship today is shadowed in one way or another by the earliest relationship ever recorded. To be in dialogue with a sexual partner today is to be in dialogue with Adam and Eve.

The only problem: The rest of the world wasn't ready for this message, so the world did what the world had long done in such situations. It slew the messenger. What the world didn't foresee is that the message would still prevail, because what Stanton had to say about Adam and Eve constitutes one of the most trenchant and farsighted readings ever made.

AFER THE MURDER OF ABEL, which occurs about halfway through Genesis 4, the narrative shifts its attention to Cain. Once Cain is expelled from his birth family, he sets out to birth a family of his own. He makes love to his (unnamed) wife, and she gives birth to Enoch, who in turn begets Irad, who in turns conceives Mehujael, and on down the line until Lamech, who like his great-great-great-grandfather, commits murder. The long tail of bad character in the Bible is chilling.

But the same goes for good character. Suddenly, in the last verses of chapter 4, after this sad recitation of degeneration, the story turns to some upbeat news. A baby announcement! "Adam knew his wife again," the text says, "and she bore a son and named him Seth, meaning, 'God has provided me another offspring in place of Abel, since Cain killed Abel.'"

The parallels with the birth of Cain at the start of chapter 4 are striking. In both cases, there's been a dramatic upheaval for Adam and Eve, followed by the restorative act of lovemaking, followed by the uplifting occasion of Eve giving birth to a son. Repeatedly the possibility of rupture between the first man and first woman is trumped and softened by the reality of their coming back together.

In the case of the latter birth, there is some lingering distance between the couple. Eve is not named in the second sequence; she's again referred to merely as "the wife." But though she doesn't have the stature of being called by her name, she does have the stature to give the baby its name. The balance of power here is both delicate and deeply relatable. Eve is subdued by her lack of identity, yet she's strong enough to bestow identity on their son. Adam is subdued in that Eve takes the lead in producing the child, yet he takes the lead in conceiving the child. By this point in their relationship they seem to understand that each must step back on occasion to let the other lead, while stepping forward on occasion to take the lead themselves. Who among us who has been in a relationship cannot relate to that?

This subtle give and take in the twilight of Adam and Eve's life together feels stunningly modern. In one of their final appearances on the biblical stage, Adam and Eve are portrayed as a couple who have endured repeated blows of hardship and shown remarkable qualities of reconciliation. And they did this all without role models, self-help books, or group therapy. At this point in the human story, they alone know the gloom of banishment; they alone know the isolation of loss; they alone know the despair of a long, challenged life. And yet they commit to writing a final chapter to their lives together. With Cain banished, there is no history unless they create Seth. There is no future unless they overcome their wounds.

It's seems both fitting and heartening that the earliest love story ever told introduces what will become a major theme of love stories to follow: the essentialness of hurt to human relationships. "I must choose, either to cease from suffering, or to cease from loving," says the narrator of Proust's **Remembrance of Things Past**. We say love never dies, but sometimes it almost kills us along the way. One reason: it's subject to the wild swings of emotion and periodic upheavals. As seismic as these fluctuations seem when we're young, they become more bearable as we age. A love that endures repeated disruptions learns to endure them more effectively, if not more easily. Real conflicts between two people are not destructive, writes Erich Fromm in **The Art of Loving**. "They lead to clarification, they produce catharsis from which both persons emerge with more knowledge and more strength."

While it may seem anathema to the messages about romance that our youth-obsessed culture regurgitates daily, this idea of learning to love more meaningfully over time has deep roots. It's the principal reason Plato suggested the old have a thing or two to teach the young about love. "Not wild glorification," in May's summation, "but discerning surrender; not unconditional but inescapably conditional; not deluded but knowing."

What Fromm and Plato have in common is the idea that this enlightened form of love is built around knowledge. Sure enough, it's the same word the Bible chooses in describing when Adam and Eve conceive Cain and again when they conceive Seth. Adam "knows" Eve. The root the Bible uses for "knowing," **yada**, is also the root the Bible uses for "reason." This overlap is not accidental. It implies that marital love contains a deep knowledge of your partner that is neither rose tinted nor rainbow hued but battle tested and well earned. This type of love is not wide-eyed; it's open-eyed. It's not irrational; it's rational.

Frank Sinatra captured this sentiment in the Oscar-nominated song, "The Second Time Around." "Love is lovelier the second time around," the song begins. "Just as wonderful with both feet on the ground." There's a particular satisfaction, it goes on, in knowing that your type of love song has finally been sung and that your type of love would be wasted on the young.

I'm partial to this message, I suppose, because I experienced it myself. Linda and I dated for a year and a half; then didn't date for a year a half (during which time we each dated other people); then got back together and were married a year and a half later. Linda has always referred to this time in our lives as Round 1 and Round 2, broken up by the "interregnum." The first song we danced to at our wedding was "Bless the Broken Road."

Even after we were married, we continued to face extended moments of disruption of the kind every relationship faces. You might call them "intraregnums." In our case, there was the glorious but tumultuous upheaval of newborn identical twins, followed by the far more harrowing ordeal of my facing life-threatening cancer. Our story, like every story, is pocked with endurance, separation, unrest, and just plain gutting it out when it doesn't feel particularly worthy of Sinatra.

The story of Adam and Eve has a similar oscillating quality. Especially in the chords of the birth of their third child, their lives contain a particular quality of love that's rarely sung out loud: duration. Students of infatuation, that period of intense awareness and obsessive immersion that often characterizes the initial phase of a relationship, say it lasts a matter of months.

Dorothy Tennov, the groundbreaking psychologist who spent decades studying how people fall in love, concluded that this period, which she called "limerence" because of its poetic qualities, lasts an average of eighteen months to three years. During this euphoric time, a distinct cocktail of chemicals are juicing through our bodies—dopamine, norepinephrine, serotonin. Together they help create what Homer called "the pulsing rush of Longing."

While this pulsing rush is fun, it quickly gives way to other feelings. For some it's hostility, disappointment, and a deep-seated boredom; for other's it's empathy, contentment, and a deep-running affection. These feelings turn out to be equally chemically rich. While limerence involves regions of the brain sizzling with dopamine and associated with happiness (the caudate nucleus), long-term relationships ignite regions of the brain brimming with oxytocin and vasopressin and associated with emotions, memory, and attention (the insular cortex).

Helen Fisher, whose brain scans helped shape this young field, suggests this change in the neurological regions involved in enduring love shows that as we age, we begin to collect and evaluate data about our partners' feelings, their reactions to social situations, and their emotional states. When it works, we don't just want to shag our lovers all the time; we want to sustain them as well. (When it doesn't work, we no longer want to knock them up; we want to knock them off.)

Fisher identifies three stages of love. Lust, which motivates people to seek sexual union with almost any partner; romance, which encourages people to focus their attention on more appropriate, potentially lifelong partners; and attachment, which allows us to live with one partner at least long enough to raise children to maturity. Each of these stages of love travels along different pathways of the brain, she says; each produces different behaviors, hopes and dreams; each is associated with different neuro-chemicals.

For Adam and Eve, the lustful stage was their initial meeting after she was formed from his body. That was the moment Adam exclaimed, "At last!" and gushed about "bone of my bones" and "flesh of my flesh." The romantic stage was their union, their clinging to each other to create a family, their being naked and feeling no shame. The attachment phase was what followed after they were exiled from the garden and had to find a new way to coexist, including having children.

For some, the attachment phase may seem like a pale comparison to the real thing, a tepid echo of the bright colors of passion. But the history of humankind suggests it's actually something greater, a rich, varied palette that includes understanding, compassion, and sometimes acceptance. "Love is not breathlessness, it is not excitement, it is not the promulgation of promises of eternal passions," writes Louis de Bernières in **Captain Corelli's Mandolin.** "That is just being 'in love,' which any fool can do." Love, he goes on, "is what is left over when being in love has burned away, and this is both an art and a fortunate accident."

Adam and Eve, in pushing back against the pain, the distrust, and maybe even the boredom; in pushing through the interruptions and the interregnums; in returning to their conjugal bed to both know each other again and embrace the unknowingness of having another child, obstinately maintain the same fierce commitment to the art and accident of human love. That they make such a decision without the benefit of a millennia of poetry, philosophy, and functional brain scans to come, makes their achievement all the more singular.

They asserted by their very actions that love is not just union; it is re-union. It includes, by its very endurance, some element of choice. And it encompasses, by its very survival, the necessity of progress.

There is no love without time.

And there is no love without respect for the other. To have that, you must see the other not as higher or as lower. You must see the other as your equal. It was that essential goal—rare even in the history of love—that inspired Elizabeth Cady Stanton and her allies from the start.

Statues by Ted Aub depicting Susan B. Anthony
(left), Amelia Bloomer (center), and Elizabeth
Cady Stanton (right) overlook the Seneca River
in downtown Seneca Falls.

· · ·

SUSAN B. ANTHONY eventually showed up, and the bright red cloak seemed worth the wait. Lucretia Mott made a few opening remarks, and soon the parade was off. There were about fifty people in total walking along the sidewalk. These included college students with a banner calling for transgender rights, what looked like a bridge club with T-shirts labeled "Granny Brigade"; and a cluster of adolescent girls carrying signs that read "GIRL SCOUTS ENCOURAGE MORE STEM ACTIVITIES."

As the star of the proceedings, Melinda Grube—Elizabeth Cady Stanton—was walking with her husband, teen daughter, and ten-year-old son, all of whom were dressed in period clothes. "I'm an extremely introverted person," she explained, "so in order to talk to people, I put myself in character."

Melinda's interest in religion dates to when she was thirteen. Her father, a minister, was kicked out of his church for performing a same-sex marriage. Melinda attended divinity school and considered becoming a preacher, but shifted to academic work instead. She came alive when she discovered the central role women played in the abundant religious revivals of nineteenth-century America. Her PhD is on how women used religious language to help fight for equality. "Women had not been allowed to use the Bible," she said, "and they knew that in order to be equal they had to make it their own."

After less than an hour's marching, the procession reached the Women's Rights National Historical Park downtown. At the original convention in 1848, the women arrived at the Methodist chapel on the morning of July 19 to find they had forgotten the key. A young boy climbed through a window to let them in. To commemorate that moment, Melinda's son climbed through a window of the rebuilt chapel and let the marchers inside.

At 11 A.M., Melinda rose to the podium to read the founding document, the Declaration of Sentiments, with its signature line: "We hold these truths to be self-evident: that all men and women are created equal."

Born in 1815, Elizabeth was the eighth of eleven children of Daniel and Margaret Livingston Cady. Daniel was a wealthy attorney, a strict Presbyterian, and a member of Congress. Five of Elizabeth's siblings died in infancy. A sixth, her older brother and the only surviving

male, Eleazar, died at twenty. In a searing incident on the day of Eleazar's funeral, ten-year-old
Elizabeth crawled into her father's lap to comfort him. Her grieving father put his arm around
her and said, "Oh, my daughter, I wish you were
a boy!"

"At the heart of every story lies a kernel of
pain," Melinda told me. "This was Elizabeth's
pain. Her entire life she was told she was never
good enough, so she went into the world determined to prove to her father that she could be
everything her brother could have been."

Spurred by this pain yet with the generous
financial support of her father, Elizabeth got a
formal education and was married to the lawyer
and abolitionist Henry Stanton. On the day of
their wedding, she removed the line about
"obeying" him from their vows. "I obstinately
refused to obey one with whom I supposed I
was entering into an equal relation," she said.
With Henry traveling for work, the two spent
most of their lives apart, leaving Elizabeth to
rear their children alone.

Stanton was made for activism. She was feisty,
opinionated, and scathingly polemical. One
biographer describes her as "brilliant, self-
righteous, charismatic, self-indulgent, mischie-

vous, intimidating, and charming." Compared to Anthony, who was tall and lean, Stanton was the opposite. One friend characterized her, in print no less, as having a figure that "suggests a preference for short walks over long."

But as much as she could out-argue anyone on either side of the Atlantic and was a tireless agitator for women's rights, abolition, and temperance, she had a natural distaste for organizations, meetings, and conferences, and the compromises that inevitably came with them. "I would rather be burned at the stake than attend another," she wrote Anthony.

Stanton's groundbreaking efforts for women's rights were full throated and broad based. She attacked discrimination against women in property rights, voting rights, wages, divorce laws, and custody restrictions. She went to the polls and demanded the right to vote; in 1866 she declared herself a candidate for the House of Representatives, the first woman to do so. Stanton was also partly responsible for a schism in the women's rights movement when she and Anthony refused to back the Fourteenth Amendment, which granted African-American men the right to vote. Her argument was that it would provide more male votes to block women from getting the same right.

But after waging this battle for women's equality for over fifty years, Stanton had a revelation. In some ways she returned to her deepest instincts growing up with a father who based his views on women on the laws of an unforgiving God. Attacking women's inequality in the courts, in the streets, and at the ballot box could only get her so far, she realized. She needed to attack it at its core—the pulpit, the pew, the prayer circle. Politicians were not her biggest obstacle; preachers were.

"Religious superstitions of women perpetuate their bondage more than all other adverse influences," Stanton wrote. The time had come for women to demand "justice, liberty, and equality in the Church as well as in the State." The time had come to take on the Bible.

Why go after such a cherished target?

"Because it's the mother of all sacred cows," Melinda said. "Whenever she brought up voting rights, someone said, 'The Bible says . . .' Whenever she brought up marital rights, someone said, 'The Bible says . . .' Whenever she brought up the rights of women to love whom they wanted, someone said, 'The Bible says . . .' With women, it always comes back to the Bible, to Eve being created from Adam's rib, to Eve being Adam's helpmeet, to Eve bringing sin into the world. If Elizabeth wanted to help women, she had to go back to Adam and Eve."

Beginning around 1890, seventy-five-year-old Stanton began reaching out to dozens of women to help her rewrite the Bible in "plain English," elevating the stories of women, who made up only 10 percent of the whole. Her quixotic effort called to mind a similar exercise by Thomas Jefferson seventy years earlier in which he compiled a Bible without all those pesky miracles. Most of the women turned Stanton down, warning her that it was a bridge too far. She'd bring ridicule on herself and ruin to the movement. Even the twenty-six who accepted ultimately did very little. If Stanton wanted a new Bible she'd have to write it herself.

So she did. The first volume of **The Woman's Bible** was published in 1895, the same year Stanton turned eighty. (Guess she didn't need those long walks after all.) The book consists of selected passages from the Five Books of Moses, chosen because they involve female characters, followed by extensive commentary designed to undermine the prevailing interpretive tradition that emphasized women's inferiority to men.

After a brief introduction, the first chapter gets to work immediately. Stanton leaves out the entire story of God creating the world, and quotes only three verses of Genesis 1. The hundred or so words she cites include the climactic lines, "Let us make humanity in our image after our likeness." She then writes two thousand words of commentary that hammer the message that women are created contemporaneously with men and with God's complete blessing.

"Here is the sacred historian's first account of the advent of woman," she writes, "a simultaneous creation of both sexes, in the image of God. It is evident from the language that there was consultation in the Godhead, and that the masculine and feminine elements were equally represented." All those theories based on the assumption that man was created prior to woman "have no foundation in scripture," she writes.

Moving on to Adam and Eve in the next chapter, Stanton eviscerates the hierarchical interpretation that was still commonplace. "It is evident that some wily writer, seeing the perfect equality of man and woman in the first chapter, felt it important for the dignity and dominion of man to effect woman's subordination in some way," she writes. Drawing on everyone from Plato to Darwin, she debunks the idea that being made from Adam's rib diminished Eve and reframes the eating of the forbidden fruit (which she identifies as a quince) as an act of courage and dignity.

"Compared with Adam she appears to great advantage through the entire drama," Stanton writes in an observation that anticipates a century of egalitarian commentary to come.

The Woman's Bible is a landmark document, an aggressive, in-your-face broadside against the most cherished myths of Western thought. The fact that Stanton begins with Adam and Eve and continues through every major biblical story, climaxing in a second volume published three years later with the story of Jesus Christ himself, is even more breathtaking. It's one thing for writing like this to appear in monkish commentaries or obscure corners of academic thinking; it's something else entirely for it to appear in a major publication from one of the highest-profile women in America. As Stanton writes, "We have made a fetish of the Bible long enough. The time has come to read it as we do all other books, accepting the good and rejecting the evil it teaches."

In some ways, the publication worked. The book went through seven printings in six months and became a best seller. But in almost every other way it was a disaster for Stanton. She was denounced from pulpits, public gatherings, and editorial pages. The book was called a frontal assault on the integrity of women and an insult to the moral integrity of the country.

Worse, it undermined the causes she had fought for her entire life. Opponents of women's suffrage cited **The Woman's Bible** as Exhibit A of all that could grow wrong if women had more power. "Every one who believes that the word of God is divinely inspired," thundered one opponent, "who believes in the purity of the family and the sanctity of marriage," must stop the assault. One historian called **The Woman's Bible** "the most devastating weapon in the antisuffrage arsenal."

Worst of all, the organization that Stanton and Anthony started, the National American Woman Suffrage Association, was rent by the publication. At its annual meeting in January 1896, which Stanton per usual did not attend, Anthony gave the opening remarks and tried to quell the rising anger. It didn't work. A resolution was introduced, pushed by delegates from the South, saying the group was nonsectarian, focused only on women's right to vote, and "has no connection with the so-called **Woman's Bible** or any other theological publication."

A heated debate followed, and on January 28 a vote was taken on the resolution. It passed 53 to 41. Stanton was expelled from the group. She had taken on the sacredest of sacred cows and had been flattened. It would take the better part of a century, until the second wave of feminism in the 1960s, for her reputation to recover. A towering figure had gone head-to-head with Adam and Eve and emerged damaged goods.

I asked Melinda if she thought Stanton regretted the book.

"No," she said. "Because the major point of feminism has always been going after the idea that man is primary and woman is secondary." Stanton understood that in order to do that, you had to convince people—especially women— that the prevailing narrative of Eve's inferiority was no longer relevant.

"It all goes back to the moment when her brother was lying in the casket," Melinda continued. "Elizabeth climbs into her father's lap and listens to his broken heart. What does he say to her? 'Oh, my daughter, I wish you were a boy!'" Everything she does from that moment on is determined to fix that problem. How to be a boy.

"But it's never enough," Melinda said. "When Elizabeth speaks before the New York State Assembly, as her father would have wanted his son to do, he's disgusted. When she runs for Congress, he's angry. She lives with the exquisite pain that the one person in life she wants to say 'You're a fully worthy human being' can't say this. Why? Because he's deeply religious, and because the Bible says that at the heart of every relationship is the idea that men are primary, women are secondary, and women are created to serve men."

"So you think that passage in **The Woman's Bible** about men and women being created in God's image is not just her speaking to the world, it's her speaking to her father?"

"Absolutely. It's her saying what we all want to say to our parents, our spouses, or whomever we most love. 'Look at me. Embrace me as fully human. Love me for who I am.' That's the heart of feminism and that's the insight Stanton found in Adam and Eve."

IN THE LATE SPRING OF 1816, around the time Elizabeth Cady Stanton was turning six months old, eighteen-year-old Mary Wollstonecraft Godwin was traveling to the Swiss Alps. The daughter of the famed women's rights advocate Mary Wollstonecraft and her novelist husband,

Mary was already the mother of two children herself (one of whom died in infancy). She was accompanied by her married lover and soon-to-be husband, the poet Percy Bysshe Shelley. The two, along with several others, settled in a modest house outside of Geneva. Nearby, in more luxurious surroundings, were Lord Byron and his companion, Dr. John Polidori. The two parties quickly merged and enjoyed several weeks of boating, dining, and sharing horror stories.

One stormy night, Byron proposed a ghost-story writing competition. The rules were lax—the story had only to involve the supernatural—and most of the participants did not finish what they started. But Mary went all in, writing an entire novel that would be published nineteen months later anonymously. Most reviewers assumed it was by Shelley or Byron. The name of the novel was **Frankenstein**, and the inspiration for it could be found in the epigraph, a quotation from **Paradise Lost** in which a fallen Adam supplicates himself to God:

> Did I request thee, Maker, from my clay
> To mold me Man? Did I solicit thee
> From darkness to promote me . . . ?

In all the retellings of Adam and Eve that I came upon, none surprised me more than Mary Shelley's **Frankenstein**. Perhaps I was the last to know that this ubiquitous story of man playing God and science gone wrong was modeled on the oldest story of them all—and the love story part of it at that. Indeed, the way Shelley updated the biblical themes, particularly the plight of loneliness and the desperate need of all human beings for intimacy, affection, and love, shows how deeply those ideas still resonated at the dawn of the industrial age.

Everybody in Shelley's novel is looking for a connection. That includes the seafarer Robert Walton, who rescues the bedraggled Victor Frankenstein at the outset of the novel; the starry-eyed doctor himself; even the monster. Time and again, words like "solitude," "solitary," and "alone" reverberate through the text. Frankenstein's desire to play God is made clear from the beginning when he declares his intention to make a creature "like myself." "A new species would bless me as its creator," Frankenstein says. In a move straight out of Genesis, when the doctor first eyes his creation he declares it good.

But also like the Bible, soon that wonderful partnership turns sour. Repulsed by his creation,

Frankenstein bolts his laboratory, leaving the wretch to fend for himself. The fiend, frustrated and estranged, murders Frankenstein's brother, then flees into the wilderness. Here the story takes an unexpected turn toward the Garden of Eden. While squatting alongside a cottage, the monster grows attached to a family who lives inside. He even learns to speak by eavesdropping on them. One day the creature comes across a satchel of books, from which he teaches himself how to read. One of those books: **Paradise Lost**. Right away, the monster sees the connection. "I am Adam!" he realizes.

When Frankenstein himself wanders into the wilderness, he comes upon his creation in his hideaway. The wretch, now steeped in biblical typology, pleads his case. "Like Adam, I was created apparently united by no link to any other being in existence," he says. Adam was "a perfect creature, happy and prosperous," but I am horrid, helpless, too "hideous" for love. "No Eve soothed my sorrows, or shared my thoughts," he says. "I was alone."

There is only one solution, the monster pleads. "You must create a female for me." He even promises to take his love and disappear into the antipodes. They will return to Eden, in other words, and leave humanity alone.

The rest of the novel involves an increasingly bleak standoff between creator and created. The doctor refuses to create a companion; the monster murders the doctor's wife; Frankenstein begins forming a female then abandons the effort; doctor and murderous beast chase each other to the ends of the earth.

At the start of the industrial age, Mary Shelley created an iconic reimagining of the most primal domestic story ever told. She also produced a stark reminder that all the chemistry, metallurgy, and technology of our time can do little to diminish our deep craving for companionship. For all our advances, our chief afflictions are still the ones faced by Milton, Michelangelo, Augustine, and all of humanity back to Adam and Eve: the need for intimacy, for connection, for love.

The fact that this story was written by a woman, especially one whose mother was known for her trailblazing works **Thoughts on the Education of Daughters** and **A Vindication of the Rights of Woman**, shows how the themes of human emotion and intimacy, once confined to the "women's sphere" of home, would soon become elevated once women had their chance to retell the creation story. That God himself appears nowhere in **Frankenstein** also portends a time when the creator is in retreat but humans still re-create the same archetypal stories with the same ageless desires. For many, love was beginning to replace the divine as the ultimate goal worth seeking.

AND SHELLEY WAS NOT ALONE. Beginning in the 1800s, as religion began retreating from public life, the number of explorations of Adam and Eve did not diminish, as one might have expected; it exploded.

Romantic novelists especially loved portraying women as emerging from confined environs and tiptoeing into the world. **Jane Eyre** opens with the protagonist staring through a window into the garden and ends with her in love as the mistress of an estate. **Les Misérables** has Marius first eyeing Cosette in one walled garden, then courting her in another, where the two "melt and merge" into a "sublime and sacred unity," the "infinity of Eden." Only later do the two venture into the open to "live in the sun."

A consistent theme in these depictions is the Eve-like figure stepping out from Adam's shadow to claim the light herself. Charlotte Brontë in **Shirley** creates a heroine who is a giant, "like what

Eve was when she and Adam stood alone on earth," a "woman-Titan" who dares to "contend with Omnipotence." The heroine has strength that could withstand a thousand years of bondage, vitality that could endure through uncounted ages, and a vast heart whence gushes the wellspring of nations. "That Eve is Jehovah's daughter," rhapsodizes Shirley, "as Adam was his son."

We've come a long way from the weak-kneed domestic helpmeet of the Middle Ages.

These portrayals are part of a larger trend. Love in the modern world takes its next massive leap forward from a state of reverence men exhibited toward women, slowly, fitfully, inexorably toward a state of greater equality between the sexes. This evolution was not speedy or universal, but it was widespread and persistent. One historian wrote that the modern Western marriage emerged in the decades after the American Revolution. "During these fifty years, love became the most celebrated criterion for choosing a spouse, even if property, family, and social status continued to weigh heavily in the decision." As Jane Austen wrote, "Men of sense . . . do not want silly wives."

All this happened in part because women like Shelley, Stanton, the Brontës, and Austen were not content to hold their tongues. Erich Fromm observed that the greatest impact of women's equality on love is that it put women on the path to becoming individuals—to telling their own stories. This allowed each party in a relationship to retain their own identity while voluntarily entering into a coidentity with their partner.

"Mature love is union under the condition of preserving one's integrity, one's individuality," Fromm wrote. Each side gets to overcome the sense of loneliness and isolation, he went on, yet is permitted to retain the feeling of freedom. "In love the paradox occurs that two beings become one and yet remain two."

Not everyone embraced this change, of course. Some powerful women, like Virginia Woolf, derided romance as a fool's errand, a "pleasant illusion," she said. Others argued that even companionate marriage made women too dependent on men. Love has become "a religion" for women, wrote Simone de Beauvoir in **The Second Sex**. "The woman in love tries to see with his eyes." She reads the books he reads, prefers the music he prefers; cares only about the ideas that come from him.

Still, more and more women—and men, too—came to embrace this new equality in love, at least as an ideal worth aspiring to. The activist Emma Goldman wrote a century ago that despite its limitations, love is still "life's greatest treasure." "The demand for equal rights in every vocation of life is just and fair," she wrote. "But, after all, the most vital right is the right to love and be loved." For women's emancipation to be complete, she continued, it will have to do away with the ridiculous notion that to be loved, to be sweetheart and mother, is synonymous with being a slave. It must replace it with the idea that to give of one's self is to find one's self richer, deeper, better. "That alone can fill the emptiness, and transform the tragedy of women's emancipation into joy, limitless joy."

Inevitably, advocates of sexual equality realized that to be most effective, they needed to recover these values in Adam and Eve. In remarkably short order, they did just that. In a rarely told story, beginning in the 1970s, a group of interpreters swiftly picked up the work of **The Woman's Bible** and revived it. Mary Daly, a self-described radical lesbian feminist at Boston College, said a perversion of Adam and Eve used across time "projected a malignant image of the male-female relationship."

"Elizabeth Cady Stanton was indeed accurate," Daly wrote. "In a real sense the projection of guilt upon women **is** Patriarchy's Fall, the primordial lie."

The most influential rereading came from Phyllis Trible, a Virginia-born PhD in biblical studies who was among the first female faculty members at the esteemed Union Theological Seminary in New York. Trible's masterstroke was to undermine the most iconic moments of Eve's alleged inferiority, starting with her secondary creation. Trible loved to ask her students why Adam was superior to Eve.

"Because he was created first!" they would cry.

"Then why aren't the animals superior to humans when they're created first?" In the Bible, she pointed out, what's last is often first. Just as God's six days of creation build toward its climax in human beings, so his human creation builds toward its climax in Eve. The woman is "not an afterthought," Trible insists. "She is the culmination."

What's most stunning to me about this effort is how recently it all happened. The Adam and Eve story has been around for more than thirty centuries; only in the last thirty years or so has it finally been widely discussed not as de facto dis-

criminatory against women but as a more nuanced back and forth between two people
struggling to figure out how to live in relation to
each other. Similar reinterpretations happened
to other biblical figures during this time. The
"Jesus is a Jew" movement helped reconnect the
Messiah with his Hebraic roots. Abraham came
to be seen not just as the father of Jews but also
the father of Christians and Muslims.

Still, these changes pale next to the impact of
seeing Adam and Eve no longer as examples of
hierarchy between the sexes but as examples
of the sexes standing side by side, striving both
for independence and integration. That change
affects nearly every family, every relationship,
and every romantic interaction in the West today.
Eve may have stepped out from Adam's shadow,
but the rest of us still live in theirs.

So what do the women who pulled off this
transformation think of their effort? And what
do they think are the lessons the rest of us might
learn from a rehabilitated Adam and Eve? To
find out, I drove deep into the Bronx not long
after Convention Days to meet one of the more
surprising public faces of that movement and
the one who bears perhaps the most visible
bruises.

Elizabeth Johnson welcomed me into her ascetic office at Fordham University. With a cherubic face, short salt-and-pepper hair, and quick wit, she could be cast as a judge in one of those daytime reality shows where people go to adjudicate their romantic entanglements. She is, in fact, quite wise about relationships, though she's never technically been in one herself.

Born into an all-Catholic neighborhood in Bay Ridge, Brooklyn, in the 1940s, Elizabeth was entranced by the theatrics of the Church— the candles, the incense, the processionals where everyone would strew rose petals in front of the Virgin Mary. "The idea that God was everywhere and you could live your life around the idea that love should flow to all your neighbors was very beautiful to me." Immediately after graduating from high school she entered the convent.

I asked her if she felt like she was marrying Jesus.

"No, but everyone else apparently did!" she said with an easy chuckle. "After one year of being a novice, we dressed as brides in white and came down the aisle with a candle to make our vows to be Jesus's spouse. At the end of the ceremony, we went downstairs, had our hair cut off, put on a black habit, and came back in to the sobs of all our families, who felt as though they had lost us. It was so dramatic."

After becoming a nun in 1959, Elizabeth continued her education and eventually got caught up in the protest movements of the 1960s, from Vietnam to women's rights. In the 1970s, she became the first woman to get a PhD at Catholic University. In the 1980s, she was poised to become the first female tenured professor, until the Vatican balked, saying her views were not consistent with traditional teaching. When she refused to back down, her case became a global cause célèbre, her male colleagues in her department rallied, and Elizabeth became the symbol of a generational divide in the Church.

"So what was this really about?" I asked.

"Need you ask?" she said, putting her hands on her hips like the scolding Catholic school nun she once was. "I'm a woman! There was absolutely nothing wrong with what I had done, but it made them soooo nervous."

Though it took the better part of two decades, Elizabeth eventually prevailed. And today the tenured professor and celebrity nun (at least in certain circles) prays every day that the new era of acceptance in the Church will continue into the future.

But what about the past? I asked if she considered Elizabeth Cady Stanton a role model when she started speaking out for women's rights.

"Not at the time," she said, "but now I do. I love what she did. She tried to make the Bible more accessible, and she paid the price, especially among other women. Every one of us who went down this road has tried to use our gifts toward the same end, equal rights for all."

"Does that include Adam and Eve?"

"It begins with Adam and Eve!" she said. "The main thing my generation of scholars did was to reclaim the essential equality at the heart of the story. We took the focus that had been on Genesis 2 and all the hierarchical questions and returned it to Genesis 1, where men and women are jointly made in the likeness of God. We spent thousands of years discussing the maleness of God. Now it's time to return the favor and discuss the femaleness.

"When you do that," she continued, "you begin to see that these old distinctions we made between men and women don't hold up anymore. I've lived too long with women in religious orders to believe women are somehow morally superior. We are equal in sin and grace.

And I know men who are beautiful people! What I see in Adam and Eve is two people who equally reflect that glory of God in different ways."

They each sin, she said; they each betray the other.

"That moment in front of God when he blames her for eating the fruit," Elizabeth said. "Ooh! She could have left him right there. And yet, despite these feelings, they remain faithful. They maintain a relationship. I think they understood before the rest of us that it takes wisdom from each side in order to get through a long life together."

This sense that each side in a healthy relationship contributes something to the whole may be the single greatest accomplishment of the rewriting of the rules of love that grew out of women's liberation. "The notion that man and woman face each other as equals in love is, of course, a hard-earned historical victory," writes Robert Solomon. It emerged only when women began to have more choice about their lives. He cites Milton as the earliest example, when he depicts Adam asking God not for a playmate or helpmeet but a mirror of himself, an equal, for among unequals "what harmony or true delight?"

Just because lovers are equals doesn't mean there's always harmony between them. If anything, there's greater disharmony, which leads to the perpetual negotiating and shifting of terms, the giving and taking of control that's apparent at the end of Adam and Eve's life as they negotiate the convulsive fates of their children. "One cannot and should not deny one lover's superiorities," Solomon says. One person may be more articulate; better at expressing emotions; more facile in the garden, the boardroom; quicker at repairing breaches. No, the equality love demands is not the equality of skills, Solomon says. It's the equality of status—and the shared ownership that comes from working through these struggles.

I asked Elizabeth whether she believed that love could grow stronger with this kind of strife.

"I don't know anyone who would say no," she said. "I believe love comes from God. And one thing about God is no matter how much trouble we cause him, he doesn't give up on us. There's a line in Isaiah that I keep coming back to. 'I have been with you since you were born, and now that you are old and gray, I will still carry you.' To me, that's the idea of love that God models, and he challenges us to find it in each other. It's not just woman's responsibility to find it in man; it's also man's responsibility to find it in woman.

"And I have to tell you," she continued. "When I look at my students, most of them cannot conceive of the type of patriarchal, male-female relationships we had for thousands of years. The facts on the ground have gone far beyond what we all dreamed of. They look at what all those commentators said about Adam and Eve all those centuries and it embarrasses them. They laugh. They look at the first couple and see themselves."

"So you've won!" I said.

She chuckled in her friendly way again. "We're still at the very beginning."

CONCLUSION

AFTERLIFE

What Adam and Eve Can Teach Us
About Relationships

THEY MADE IT HARD to come see the pope in Philadelphia. The "they," in this case, was the fifty government agencies that oversaw security for the historic visit of Pope Francis to the nation's fifth-largest city. The agencies included the FBI, Secret Service, Border Patrol, Coast Guard, Department of Homeland Security, and anybody else with a gun, a badge, and an eavesdropping device. A four-mile traffic box was cordoned off downtown, which led to the towing of 1,500 cars. One thousand state troopers filled the streets, along with 500 soldiers from the National Guard, dozens of armored vehicles, and hundreds of metal detectors. The over-the-top security was compared, unfavorably, with Orwell, the Berlin Wall, and every other trip taken by the pontiff.

"If Rio was excessive," said one Francis biographer, "this was pathological."

It was also, on occasion, amusing. When I went through the first of three checkpoints at 7 A.M. on the last Saturday in September on my way to the Benjamin Franklin Parkway where that night the pope would address the crowd on the meaning of love, relationships, and family, one of the volunteers who searched my bag confiscated an apple.

"I can't take an apple to see the pope?" I asked.

"It could be a bomb," she said, as if this were obvious. Or true.

"Now that's what I call payback for Adam and Eve," I replied.

She didn't seem to get the joke.

Despite the three-hour security lines, up to a million of the faithful and the not-so-faithful crowded onto the mile-long parkway between the Philadelphia Museum of Art and City Hall. By 10 P.M., the interfaith Festival of Families was nearing its climax. Mark Wahlberg had made enough awkward jokes. Sister Sledge had performed "We Are Family." And the Queen of Soul, Aretha Franklin, had managed to walk onstage, sing "Amazing Grace," and exit, all without acknowledging the pope sitting immediately behind her. (She later issued an apology, saying she hadn't known he was on stage.)

Finally the pope took to the podium to deliver his remarks. Only he never delivered them.

I was sitting a few steps away during all this, crowded into a small television booth alongside Chris Cuomo, Poppy Harlow, and Father James Martin. We were broadcasting the event live on CNN. I had been part of CNN's small team of commentators traveling with the pope since he arrived in the United States. Francis's carefully choreographed visit was controversial, exhausting, and for anyone who cares about religion, exhilarating. What other world figure could seize the media spotlight so completely from misbehaving athletes, demagoguing politicians, and feuding real housewives? Who else could force us to ask, What is the meaning of love?

Still, none of this prepared us for what happened that night. Members of the media had been given advanced copies of Francis's remarks. But the legendary people's pope from the barrios of Buenos Aires enjoys surprises more than anything. So when he arrived at the podium, he ditched his carefully argued speech about families and spoke—extemporaneously, ebulliently, brilliantly—about what he believes is a central message of the Bible.

He spoke about Adam and Eve.

FOLLOWING THE BIRTH of Seth at the end of Genesis 4, Adam and Eve make no more appearances together in the Hebrew Bible. Adam does appear alone. Genesis 5 opens with a brief recapitulation of human origins. This rendition, a bookend to chapter 1, is technically a third version of the formation of human beings. "When God created humankind, he made them in the likeness of God. He created them male and female and blessed them." What started in equality ends with equality.

The story goes on to mention the birth of Seth, which occurs "when Adam had lived 130 years," and then adds two seemingly simple sentences. "After Seth was born, Adam lived 800 years and had other sons and daughters. Altogether, Adam lived a total of 930 years, and then he died."

These lines have drawn intense interest over the years. Commentators focused on who these "other sons and daughters" were. Answers included: (a) those were the daughters who became the spouses of Cain and Seth, and (b) Adam and Eve wanted three sons, the ideal number, but they knew they had to have extras in case some died. The famed first-century Roman writer Josephus, for instance, said the first parents, "according to the old tradition," had thirty-three sons and twenty-three daughters.

Other interpreters fixated on how it is that Adam lives to be 930. Various explanations were offered, including that numbers had different meanings in primordial times; time was calculated in nontraditional ways before the Flood; age was a sign of godliness, and who was closer to God than Adam?

Early Christians focused on a different aspect. Beginning in the second century, Church Fathers drew a direct line from the death of Adam to the death of Jesus. In a widely retold story, Adam, on his deathbed, dispatches Seth to the Garden of Eden to retrieve the oil of mercy that he believes will heal him. Seth and Eve return to the gates of paradise and plead with St. Michael to let them in. Michael refuses, but gives them an olive branch from the garden. Michael tells Seth to plant the tree on Adam's grave, and when it bears fruit, Adam will be redeemed.

Seth and Eve do as they're told, but no fruit

appears. Initially disappointed, they eventually realize the words are prophetic. The olive tree produces the wood that becomes the cross on which Jesus is crucified. Christ, the "Second Adam," is the fruit that redeems the "First Adam." To this day you can see depictions of Adam's skull at the Church of the Holy Sepulchre in Jerusalem, under the spot where Jesus is said to have been crucified.

What's missing from all these commentaries, as well as the story itself, is the more human question: How does Eve react to Adam's death? On one level this is surprising. Given how much scrutiny has attended this story, how could commentators simply ignore the sudden widowhood of the first woman and the sudden demise of the first couple? On another level, the absence of focus on Eve's feelings is entirely consistent with the way she was shunned and looked down on for centuries.

But just because Eve's grief is not explicitly addressed does not mean there are no clues. The first place to look for insight is the Bible itself. Death and mourning are frequent topics in Hebrew Scripture. There's often an initial outpouring of grief, as when Abraham "mourns" for Sarah and "weeps" for her. Many biblical figures tear their clothes in response to death. When Jacob see's Joseph's bloodstained coat of many colors he rends his garments, as does David when he learns of the death of Saul, and Job when he suffers the loss of his children.

But that outburst of grief is usually worked through fairly efficiently. Hebrew ritual calls for a week of sitting shiva, or receiving visitors in the home, and an entire month of giving up social conventions. When the deceased is a parent, there's a full year of curtailed activity. One Talmudic formula states: three days for weeping, seven days for lamenting, and thirty days for wearing mourning garments and not cutting hair. The expectation is that the bereaved, comforted by God, will move in a timely way toward acceptance. As Psalm 23 puts it, "Even though I walk through the valley of the shadow of death. I will fear no evil, for you are with me."

Contemporary social science largely endorses this timeline. Unlike losing a child, losing a spouse turns out to be less crippling than we imagine. The most well-known model, Elizabeth Kubler-Ross's five stages of grief, which says we experience waves of denial, anger, bargaining, depression, and acceptance, has been undermined by subsequent research. The leading scholar of mourning today, Columbia's George Bonanno, has found that most widows find grief neither overwhelming nor unending. Three quarters bounce back within six months. "As frightening as the pain of loss can be," Bonanno writes, "most of us are **resilient**." We may feel shocked and sad, "but we still manage to regain our equilibrium and move on."

Perhaps that happened for Eve, but her case does seem special. First, she's known Adam since the moment she was born. Second, they once shared body parts. Third, she has no widows to learn from. Already the first mom to experience the death of a child, now she's the first wife to experience the death of a husband.

Literature offers its own perspective, and it's quite different from this portrait of easy acceptance. In **Romeo and Juliet**, when Romeo thinks Juliet is dead, he kills himself to join her—and is ecstatic about it. "O my love! my wife!" he cries. "How oft when men are at the point of death / Have they been merry!" When she awakens from sleep and sees him poisoned, she decides to join him. She kisses his still-warm, poisoned lips, then stabs herself. "O happy dagger!" she wails. "This is thy sheath; there rust, and let me die."

In Emily Brontë's **Wuthering Heights**, Heathcliff similarly dreams of reuniting with his deceased lover, Cathy. The night Cathy is buried, Heathcliff digs up her grave and pines for her. He bribes the sexton to remove the side of Cathy's coffin and later, after he's buried next to her, to do the same with his coffin, so the two lovers can lie forever side by side, dissolving into the earth.

Given that Adam and Eve began life side by side, it's tempting to imagine her craving a similar ending, especially as they were told when leaving Eden, "for dust you are and to dust you will return."

The most telling insight into Eve's state of mind comes from two of the most celebrated modern chroniclers of widowhood. Joan Didion, in **The Year of Magical Thinking**, writes that losing a husband is disorienting. "Life changes fast. Life changes in the instant. You sit down to dinner and life as you know it ends." Joyce Carol Oates, in **A Widow's Story**, described the experience as making her "utterly crazy." "It's clear—**widow** trumps all other identities, including **rational individual**," she wrote. But above all, they agree, losing a husband makes you feel one all-encompassing thing. Alone.

Didion: "What I remember about the apartment the night I came home alone from New York Hospital was its silence." Didion: "I remember thinking I needed to discuss this with John. There was nothing I did not discuss with John." Didion: "The unending absence that follows, the void, the very opposite of meaning, the relentless succession of moments during which we will confront the experience of meaninglessness itself."

Oates: "Never have I been alone so much, so **starkly unmitigatedly alone.**" Oates: "There is a terror in **aloneness.** Beyond even **loneliness.**" Oates: "**This house is so lonely! It's almost unbearable!**" Oates: "**There are bouts of utter loneliness and a sense of purposelessness.**" Oates: "**I am the lone person who is alone.**"

Here is something that brings us closer to Eve and allows us to hypothesize about her feelings. The first widow surely feels upon Adam's death what Adam was feeling before she was born. Eve now feels the one thing that God says it's not good for humans to feel. Eve feels alone. And maybe, in that instant, she feels closer to Adam. Maybe she's reminded what it means to really need somebody. Maybe she understands what might have gotten somewhat lost in all those years they spent together: that she loves him.

But what now?

As the accounts of Didion, Oates, and countless others make clear, the literature on loss suggests a period of meaninglessness. Maybe with
Eve it lasts a week, a month, or, given her lon-
gevity, a century. But then there is a turning,
something that jolts the mourner into reclaim-
ing life. For the narrator of bell hooks's "The
Woman's Mourning Song," it's the mundane
task of kneading dough: "the warrior in me returns / to slay sorrow / to make the bread." For
Oates it's when she ventures into her husband's
garden in spring and recalls Whitman, "The
smallest sprout shows there is really no death."
For Didion it's when, riding an escalator, she recalls the last trip to Paris with her husband. "If
we are to live ourselves there comes a point at
which we must relinquish the dead, let them go,
keep them dead," she says.

To endure, we must no longer try to reverse
time, she says. We must live it along its forward
trajectory.

"Of the widow's countless death-duties there
is really just one that matters," Oates writes.
"On the first anniversary of her husband's death
the widow should think **I kept myself alive.**"

Eve certainly achieves that—and a whole lot
more. One rarely discussed curiosity of Adam

and Eve's story is that Adam dies in the biblical account, while Eve does not. It's possible this is an oversight or another indication of Eve's inferior status. Maybe the compilers of the Bible simply don't care enough about the first woman—or women in general—to mention her passing.

But a look at other famous figures in the story suggests a different reading. The deaths of all three patriarchs—Abraham, Isaac, and Jacob—are mentioned in the Bible, as are the deaths of all three of their wives—Sarah, Rebecca, and Rachel. Even Leah, Jacob's unloved first wife, is honored in her death. The same goes for Noah, Joseph, Moses, Moses' brother, Aaron, even Moses' sister, Miriam.

Alone among major figures of the Five Books, Eve is never described as dying. "The mother of all the living" just goes on living and living and living. Given the evident care given to every syllable in the text, this elision would appear to be intentional. Eve's immortality, it seems safe to presume, is a sign that something in her life cannot be allowed to die. But what?

For some it might be the negative example of her story. See, this is what happens when you disobey the rules, overstep your bounds, and disrespect your partner. Her immortality would thus be her final slight. Yet this harshness is hardly consistent with how both God and Adam conduct themselves toward Eve after she leaves Eden.

I prefer an alternative view—that Eve is allowed to go on living because of the positive example of her life. Her immortality, far from being an insult, is a reward. See, this is what happens when you forge your own identity, overcome hardships, persevere with your partner. "The half-life of love is forever," wrote Junot Díaz in his Pulitzer Prize-winning novel **The Brief Wondrous Life of Oscar Wao.** He might as well have been speaking of Eve. By continuing to live, Eve guarantees that her story continues. By never dying, she guarantees that her love never dies.

ALMOST FROM THE DAY he became pope in 2013, the former Cardinal Jorge Mario Bergoglio made love a central feature of his papacy. We live in a time of "crisis in the family," Francis said. "The family is one of the most precious assets of humanity. But is it not perhaps the most vulnerable?"

Yet in trying to convert his vision into a working philosophy that could guide and comfort hundreds of millions of families around the world, the first pope from the Americas got buffeted by crosswinds. On the one hand he advocated a strict theology of the family that has its roots in Adam and Eve. God created man and woman equal in their "essential dignity," he argued, but "complementary" in their roles. "Complementarity," the idea that God intends different roles for men and women, has been used for decades to justify male superiority and exclude women from leadership positions. The pope also argued that marriage between a man and a woman, which began with Adam and Eve, is an inviolable sacrament. Anyone known to violate these norms—including homosexuals, adulterers, and divorcées—is often barred from many Church activities.

On the other hand, Francis had been a hands-on priest in the slums of Buenos Aires, and he approached many decisions less with a theologian's legalism and more with a pastor's heart. He called for a more merciful, less judgmental Church, and offered olive branches to the divorced and remarried, as well as to those who had abortions. And he famously said of homosexuals, "Who am I to judge?"

"A faith that does not know how to root itself in the life of people remains arid and, rather than oases, creates other deserts," Francis said. The moments of greatest suffering, he added, are "precisely the occasions for God to show mercy."

Religion, since its earliest days, has struggled with the tension between walls and bridges. You can build enclosures of law, tradition, belief, or any other standard, and insist the world either come in or stay out. Or you can build bridges of compassion, charity, and forgiveness, and invite the world to come in or out as they wish. In the first instance you get purity but may suffer contraction; in the second you get flexibility but may suffer indifference. I know of no religious institution that doesn't struggle with this question and no spiritual leader who doesn't anguish over this trade-off.

It won't surprise you that Adam and Eve, in order to have survived as long as they have, embody this tension. They may even have initiated it. The Garden of Eden is the original walled enclave. When Adam and Eve don't comply with its regulations, God evicts them. Yet once Adam and Eve are outside those walls, God continually builds bridges of compassion with them.

He wraps them in clothes, helps them conceive children, comforts them after loss.

As has been the case for centuries, you can read Adam and Eve as blunt messengers of the consequences of disobedience. Or you can read them as ambassadors of equality, transgression, forgiveness, and reconciliation. As Francis made clear that night in Philadelphia, he takes the latter view.

When I first read the pope's prepared remarks to the Festival of Families, they took my breath away. The pope laid out almost exactly the reading of Adam and Eve I had been piecing together since I visited the Vatican with my daughters. One of the exquisite mysteries of the Bible, Francis began, is that "God did not want to come into the world other than through a family. God did not want to draw near to humanity other than through a home." This is why God, from the very beginning, said, "It is not good for man to be alone." "We can add," the pope wrote, "it is not good for woman to be alone, it is not good for children, the elderly or the young. It is not good."

The families God wants us to create, he went on, are built on love. He quoted Erich Fromm: "To love someone is not just a strong feeling—

it is a decision, it is a judgment, it is a promise." The speech ended with a call to return to God's original vision for a loving family in Eden. "Stake everything on love," he said. "We cannot call any society healthy when it does not leave real room for family life."

This was the passionate, well-reasoned cri de coeur that Pope Francis planned to deliver to the million or so or celebrants on Franklin Parkway. Except he never did. The ceremony was, to be charitable, running late. Six families from around the world stood before the pope and gave detailed testimonials. The Hollywood performers added an extra frill. The brief remarks of the various dignitaries turned into slogs. CNN, which was supposed to have been off the air hours earlier, was still broadcasting.

Even the pope, who had been going virtually nonstop since dawn and was suffering from sciatica, was slumping in his chair. Behind him, on the storied art museum steps Sylvester Stallone ran up in **Rocky**, was a temporary installation of Robert Indiana's famed LOVE statue in which the English letters had been recast with the Spanish, **AMOR**.

The upshot of all this was that by the time the pope finally shuttled to the podium, everyone was exhausted, including him. So the seat-of-the-pants populist did what he does best, he went rogue. He realized that no one in the crowd (except me!) wanted to hear his dissertation. So he spoke off the cuff.

He began with an anecdote. "Once a boy asked me, 'Father, what did God do before he created the world?' I can tell you it was hard for me to come up with an answer." Finally, the pontiff told the boy, "Before creating the world God loved, because God is love."

God went on to create many things in this "marvel in which we live," the pope went on, but the most beautiful thing he created was the family. "He created man and woman, and he gave them everything," Francis said. He asked them to grow, to cultivate the earth, to make it bloom, he said. And he gave them his love.

And we are destroying it, Francis said. "Obviously, this earthly paradise is no longer here," he said. "Life has problems." This began when Adam and Eve turned their backs on God; it continued when one of their sons murdered the other. It continues to this day.

"Sure, one of you could say to me, 'Father, you speak this way because you're single.' In families, we argue; in families, sometimes the

plates fly; in families, the children give us head-
aches. And I'm not even going to mention the
mother-in-law."

Yes, the world's most famous bachelor made a
mother-in-law joke.

But the family is still a factory of hope, he
said. Hatred is not capable of overcoming these
difficulties. Division of hearts is not capable of
overcoming these difficulties. Only love can do
it. "Love is a festival," he said. "Love is joy. Love
is to keep moving forward." He concluded, "Let
us care for the family, because it's there, there,
that our future is at play."

The crowd erupted. Chris Cuomo, sitting in
the anchor chair beside me, said, "That was the
legendary Cardinal Bergoglio." I thought it was
the highlight of the week. But reflecting on it
later, I actually think it's more. Francis's speech
was hardly a breakthrough in thought. The prepared remarks were more nuanced. But what
Francis captured under the stars that night was
how the role of the first couple has changed over
the centuries.

For most of their history, Adam and Eve represented the stern message of religion. "Do as
you're told; be grateful for what you have; love
the Lord your God with all your heart, with all

your soul, and with all your strength." In short, "You live in a walled world. Follow the rules or get out."

But today, that message is less effective in the world of religion. "Oughts" are being pushed aside in favor of "perhaps you should considers." Commandments are being replaced with recommendations. Obligations with invitations.

Walls are tumbling down.

Bridges are springing up.

Sure, not everyone is building bridges these days. There are plenty of traditionalists in all faiths who are erecting higher and higher barricades and, in some cases, taking violent actions to impose their strictures on others. But for the vast majority of people who were lining the streets of Philadelphia that night, who were watching clips on their mobile phones, or who were just going about their lives but still care about matters of spirituality, walls are no longer the best way to inspire them. Most seekers don't want mandates anymore, they want guidance. They don't want restriction, they want direction. They don't want antiheroes; they want heroes.

What Francis showed that night is that Adam and Eve, by being created by God and formed into a family that endures hardship and difficulties, still have a role to play in this new world of do-it-yourself spirituality. Their story is not just about sin, disobedience, ingratitude, squandering their inheritance, and ruining life for the rest of us. Their story is also about originality, forgiveness, bouncing back from calamity, and modeling resilience.

Their story is about love, in all its messy, carnal, hopeful, resurgent glory.

The sooner we recognize that, the sooner we might be able to hear what they've been trying to say to us all along.

SO WHAT IS THAT? What is the message of the Love Song of Adam and Eve?

When I took my daughters to the Vatican before Francis became pope, I was feeling an unease not dissimilar from the one he's made the centerpiece of his papacy. It's the same discomfort moms and dads, husbands and wives, politicians and poets have been worried about for some time: How do we find meaning in a fast-changing world? How do we hold together as a society and not succumb to hate? How do we cultivate love, how do we maintain it if we do discover it, and how do we bring it back if we lose it for a while?

These questions were on my mind as I reached the end of my journey. To help answer them, I assembled some of the sager voices I knew, my own conclave of love, if you will. Members included Rabbi Lord Jonathan Sacks, the star speaker at Francis's first Synod on the Family. Simon May, whose two books on love have reshaped the field. And Helen Fisher, the anthropologist whose many books and TED Talks have made her a go-to voice on the biology of love.

I began asking how they define the current problem in the world that their work in love helps address. All three gave similar answers: the growing sense of isolation, separation, and disconnection in our always-on society, the problem I had been summing up with the term "loneliness."

Here's what Sacks had to say: "Today we have the most individualistic culture in all of human history. Beginning with de Tocqueville, who invented the word 'individualism' in 1835, you can trace the rise in three book titles. David Riesman, 1950, **The Lonely Crowd**; Robert Putnam, 1996, **Bowling Alone**; Sherry Turkle,

2011, **Alone Together**. We are the lonely crowd, and that is the problem that threatens our happiness."

May: "**The** topic of the modern age is alienation. We are separated and isolated from the ones we love. That begins with God. Human beings have an imperishable need for the sacred, and since we've lost contact with the sacred, we have a giant hole in our lives. Love has filled that hole, and we have this belief that it's the answer to life's problems."

Fisher: "Love is hardly new. It's the oldest, most adaptable human drive. What's new is how important it's become to society, and that's because of one movement, women piling into the workplace. Once women were no longer stuck at home making the socks and the candles, they gained financial freedom. That freedom gave them the power to walk out of a bad relationship, which in turn gave them the ability to define what a good relationship is. I've asked people in dozens of countries what they most want in a relationship, and the number one answer is always love for your partner."

All three agree, in other words, that love is the antidote to the atomization and harshness in modern society. They also agree that if we're going to put so much emphasis on love, we have to define what we're talking about. "You can't have a successful relationship if you don't know what that relationship is aimed at," Simon May said.

Fair enough. I asked my conclave to help me come up with a definition. So herewith my list of the six elements of romantic love, or, in the vernacular of the moment, What Adam and Eve Taught Me About Relationships.

1. **Covenant.** In his speech before the Vatican's Synod on the Family, Sacks said that the revolutionary breakthrough in Genesis is that every human being, regardless of class, color, or creed, is made in the image of God. "We know that in the ancient world it was rulers, kings, emperors and pharaohs who were held to be in the image of God," Sacks said. "So what Genesis was saying was that we are all royalty."

What's critical about this framework is that our one-on-one relationship with God becomes the model for our one-on-one relationships with other people, especially our lovers. "There is a deep connection between monotheism and monogamy," Sacks said. Both are about "the all-embracing relationship between I and Thou, myself and one other."

Throughout Hebrew Scripture, one concept is used to characterize this relationship: covenant. Modeled on ancient legal treaties, a covenant is an agreement between two parties, in which each side has rights as well as obligations. God's relationship with humans is called a covenant, as is a husband's relationship with his wife, and vice versa. Two hundred and eighty times the word appears in the Hebrew Bible.

At first blush, the notion that something as old-fashioned and seemingly anachronistic as a covenant has any relevance in the era of Snapchat and Ashley Madison seems laughable. Can you imagine young lovers on Valentine's Day using #covenant? On the other hand, the idea captures the gravity and timelessness of the love relationship, which is exactly what we're missing these days. It certainly embodies the significance that the Bible places on such an alliance.

"Seven times the word 'good' appears in the story of creation," Sacks told me, "culminating in the creation of humans, which God calls 'very good.' But then there's a break. It's almost like a bit of bar talk in the midst of a Bach harpsichord sonata. Adam is alone, and it's **not good**."

Long before we had computer searches, Sacks continued, he went through the whole of the Mosaic books and discovered the phrase "not good" appears only one other time, when Moses is told it's not good to lead alone.

"The Bible makes it clear that we are not meant to be alone," Sacks said. "And yet many of us feel alone. The fundamental message of Adam and Eve is that we have to find a way to bridge that loneliness. We have to find a way, as the poet John O'Donohue said, to 'bless the space between us.' Love is the narrow bridge across the abyss between soul and soul."

To me that's the first lesson of Adam and Eve. We must resacralize that narrow bridge between soul and soul. We must recapture the specialness of what contemporary life has turned into a commodity, the loving relationship between two individuals. We must restore the idea of covenant, with all its heaviness and old-fashionedness. If we do, maybe we'll treat relationships with a little more humility and awe.

Fortunately, in the first man and woman of the Bible, we have a good example of how to do that. In the traditional Jewish marriage ceremony, the bride and groom are blessed with seven benedictions. The sixth blessing says, "Make these beloved companions as happy as were the first human couple in the Garden of Eden." That Adam and Eve are the model loving couple has been held out before us all this time, it turns out. Adam and Eve kept covenant with each other. It's time we keep covenant with them.

2. **Connectedness**. The single most underappreciated aspect of Adam and Eve is how they continually return to each other after periods of separation. They start life united, then Eve separates and goes off alone. Eve could remain separate at this point; instead she returns to Adam. Adam could separate himself from her when she returns; instead he joins her. They could depart Eden separately after being expelled; instead they go together. They could separate forever after losing their son; instead they reunite and have another child.

This togetherness in the face of repeated separateness is the singular achievement of Adam and Eve. It's also an expression of the second central quality of romantic love: connectedness. Adam and Eve clearly feel a strong, even overwhelming sense of belonging with each other. They exhibit the deepest and most reassuring human feeling of all, attachment.

"Love is about finding a home in the world," Simon May told me. "It's about experiencing the other person's mere presence as grounding. It's a form of rapture in which you believe that you're heading into the world alongside a person with whom you achieve your vision of the promised land."

May's term for this feeling is "ontological rootedness," a term even he concedes only a philosopher could love. He believes this feeling has become predominant in the last century as a direct consequence of the retreat of religion. As he writes in his book **Love: A History**, human love is "widely tasked with achieving what once only divine love was thought capable of: to be our ultimate source of meaning and happiness." "God is love" became "love is God," he writes, "so that it is now the West's undeclared religion."

While I wouldn't go that far—I know plenty of people who value romantic love but who also still love God—I do find the formula instructive. The feelings of groundedness and purpose we once exclusively attached to God are now feelings we also attribute to the one we love. Love, writes philosopher Robert Nozick, is when your own well-being is tied up with that of someone you love. When a bad thing happens to a friend, you feel bad for your friend, he says. "When something bad happens to one you love, though, something bad also happens **to you**."

The reason: A central quality of being in love is being physically, emotionally, and, yes, onto-logically connected to another person. "Only connect," E. M. Forster selected as the epigraph to **Howards End**. The injunction still holds. Sure enough, it's another quality first exhibited by Adam and Eve.

3. **Counterbalance.** One of the many insights Milton had into Adam and Eve is that their re-lationship involves a give-and-take, a seesawing of power in which first one party, then the other, takes the lead. Eve is made from Adam's body, but Adam clings to her. Adam gives Eve leeway to go into the garden alone; Eve gives Adam the option of whether to eat the fruit. Adam initi-ates the lovemaking that produces their chil-dren; Eve delivers the children and chooses their names. Anyone in a relationship can recognize this back and forth. You take care of the garden, I'll iron the fig leaves; we'll meet by the fruit tree at noon.

We have this fantasy of love that equality is somehow the destination. "Where love does not find equals, it creates them," Stendhal said. Think of Cinderella and Prince Charming, Beauty and the Beast, King Edward VIII and Wallis Simpson, the billionaire and the hooker in **Pretty Woman**. Love is the one thing that's said to be stronger than class, power, or beauty.

But this idea is misleading. The central dynamic in most modern relationships is not equality, it's equilibrium. "Everyone wants to believe in equality," Helen Fisher said. "But there are many relationships that are unequal. He's rich and ugly; she's beautiful and dumb. She's successful and hard-driving; he works with his hands and rides a motorcycle." Even in relationships that appear to be equal, she said, somebody's going to have more power in the kitchen, somebody's going to make more money, somebody's going to be better with the kids.

"The bottom line is you don't need equality to have a good relationship," she said. "You need balance. Both sides need to feel that they're getting what they need. You need cooperation."

The best way to achieve that, Fisher said, is to ensure that each party in a relationship has autonomy as well as intimacy, independence along with interdependence. "Mature love," writes Fromm in **The Art of Loving**, allows both parties to "overcome the sense of isolation," while allowing them to "retain" the "sense of integrity."

One of the main endeavors of love is to maintain this equilibrium, which is both absolutely necessary and nearly impossible. The pleasure comes in trying to weigh walking side by side with your partner while occasionally walking alone. Two lovers strolling "hand in hand," as Milton put it, while also going their "solitary way."

"Let there be spaces in your togetherness," Kahlil Gibran writes in **The Prophet**. "And let the winds of the heavens dance between you." Gibran goes on:

Fill each other's cup but drink not from one cup.
Give one another of your bread but eat not from the same loaf.
Sing and dance together and be joyous, but let each one of you be alone.

Love is the answer to loneliness, as long as there's aloneness within it.

4. **Constancy.** If there's one thing everyone agrees Adam and Eve taught the rest of us it's that all relationships have problems. You think your wife is difficult? Adam's wife brought death into the world. You think your husband is a letdown? Eve's husband blamed her for original sin.

A short list of the hardships Adam and Eve faced includes: losing their home, losing their source of food, losing their child. An accounting of the interpersonal offenses includes: infidelity, inattention, incrimination. Any one of these would have been grist for couples counseling or even divorce court.

Only there were no counselors or divorce lawyers. Adam and Eve had to figure it out for themselves. And what thanks do they get from the rest of us?

None. They get universal scorn, eternal damnation, and lots of naked pictures of them at their weakest moment.

What a shame.

Instead of censuring them, we should be celebrating them. Instead of excoriating their weakness, we should be extolling their constancy.

"People have misunderstood the role of love in life," Rainer Maria Rilke said. "They have made it into play and pleasure because they thought that play and pleasure were more blissful than work," he said. But they're wrong. "There is nothing happier than work," he went on, "and love, just because it is the extreme happiness, can be nothing else but work."

At the end of his speech at the Vatican, Jonathan Sacks homed in on what he called an overlooked moment in the story of Adam and Eve. It's their hour of greatest vulnerability, yet it's the time they show great tenderness toward each other. At the end of Genesis 3, just as Adam and Eve are leaving Eden, God says, "By the sweat of your brow you will eat your food." Adam's response is to officially give his wife her name, **Chavah**, Eve, "the mother of all the living." God's reaction is to make "garments of skins" for them and send them on their way.

Why did God telling the man he is mortal lead to his giving Eve her name? Sacks asked. And why did these acts lead God to clothe Adam and Eve? The answer, he said, is that only when Adam realizes he's mortal does he finally realize he needs Eve.

At the moment they are poised to enter the real world, what Sacks calls "a place of darkness," Adam gives his wife "the first gift of love, a personal name." And God, in turn, responds to them both "in love," and makes them garments to clothe their nakedness, or as the second-century sage Rabbi Meir put it, "garments of light.'"

In the grip of peril, they reaffirm their love.

In the face of darkness, God bathes them in light.

This is the fourth great love lesson of Adam and Eve. Love is not about avoiding conflict; it's about overcoming it. Love is not about pushing problems away; it's about pushing through them. "Love is not love / Which alters when it alteration finds," Shakespeare writes in Sonnet CXVI. "O, no; it is an ever-fixed mark." Love, he concludes, "bears it out even to the edge of doom."

Who knows the edge of doom better than Adam and Eve? Nobody. Which is why their constancy deserves our constant acclaim.

5. **Care**. Not everything Adam and Eve can teach us about love is positive. Thinking of all the love stories that follow theirs, one can easily identify a number of weaknesses in theirs.

First, Adam and Eve show very little affection for each other. There are no rose petals, back rubs, doing the 4 A.M. feeding to let the other sleep in. Also, they never express their commitment to each other: The closest we get is Adam effusing, "At last! This one is bone of my bones, and flesh of my flesh." Finally, they don't seem to be having a lot of fun. Missing are the nicknames, the inside jokes, the playful routines that sustain even the shakiest connections. Adam and Eve love each other, but do they like each other?

Still, there's yet another void in their relationship that's even more disappointing, and that's the fifth great characteristic of love: care. Part of loving is the willingness to diminish yourself in the service of upholding the other. "Attention is the rarest and purest form of generosity," wrote Simone Weil. "Taken to its highest degree, [it] is the same thing as prayer." Do Adam and Eve pay attention to each other?

The idea of selflessly giving to the other has roots in the Bible, so it's possible to imagine Adam and Eve having exposure to this idea. Christians sanctified the idea of kenosis, a hollowing out of oneself in the service of God, which Christ embodied on the cross. More recent writers use other ways to capture this idea. Simon May adopts the term "attentiveness"—"the practiced, almost meditative, open attentiveness to the other"—and says it's the fundamental quality of interpersonal love.

John Gottman, one of the leading psychologists of contemporary relationships, uses the term "attunement." Gottman pioneered the practice of videotaping couples in simulated living situations and analyzing their behavior. He dubbed his facility the "Love Lab." One powerful predictor of a couple's success, he found, is how well the couple repairs arguments, meaning one side takes affirmative steps to address the concerns of the other.

Gottman calls this gesture attunement, which he defines as "the desire and the ability to understand and respect your partner's inner world." Couples who are high in attunement spend less time in the "nasty box" during disputes, and more time in the "nice box." Adam and Eve certainly spend time in the "nasty box"—"the woman" ate first, Adam bitterly tells God. It would be nice to see them spend time in the "nice box," too.

The common attribute of all these descriptions is a willingness to turn away from the self and turn toward the other. "Love is to be identified with curiosity," writes Avivah Zornberg. It's committing yourself to first learning about, then inhabiting, the self-made world of the other, and attempting to make it a better place to be.

It would be gratifying to know that Adam and Eve make this commitment to each other.

And maybe they do. Their story, alas, shows little evidence of it. Attunement, attentiveness, kenosis, curiosity, there are many names for this idea. I prefer the plainspoken "care."

Care for your lovers. What could be more straightforward than that?

6. **Co-narration**. William James remarked that the great "unbridgeable chasm" in nature is that between two minds. It has long been the role of romantic love "to cross that abyss," wrote novelist William Gass, "to create a new creature made of mingled intimacies, to fill one soul with another."

The most effective way to do that is to have the lovers create a new story—a shared story—of their life together. This new story is not a one story. It's a two story. It has two protagonists, two people whose needs must be fulfilled, two individuals whose fears must be surmounted. This shared story does not replace the individual stories each lover tells. It rests on top of them. It's the second story in each person's imagination. The first story is love of self; the second is love of other. The second cannot survive unless the first is well built.

The process of cocreating this shared story—

what psychologists call "co-narration"—is the last great quality of romantic love, and it's the one Adam and Eve are most responsible for introducing. Theirs is the first joint byline.

Perhaps the most salient characteristic of joint storytelling is that it's more challenging than solo storytelling. The word "acrobatic" comes to mind. This sense of physicality gets at the inherent difficulty of relationships: They take coordination. The most common metaphors we use about love miss this point. We speak of being struck by lightning, punched in the gut, hit by a truck. These are all passive.

Love is active. Fromm liked to say that our primary metaphor of romance, that we "fall" in love, is misleading. Falling is easy; standing is hard. Falling is reactive; it just happens to you. Standing takes work. Yet that long-term state is what we're after. We say we want to fall in love, but what we really want is to stand in love.

That process of standing in love is built on a number of things, including the shared exchange of ideas, deeds, and bodily fluids. But most of all it's built on words. The great Swiss child psychologist Jean Piaget coined a phrase to describe how preschoolers play. Children he said, engage in "collective monologue," meaning they gather together but talk only to themselves. Love is the inverse of this. It's "collective dialogue," meaning the two sides construct a shared version of reality. This coordination doesn't preclude both parties from having their own version of reality; that happens, too, of course. But it's the version they assemble together that represents their intermingled union.

And this story is not just abstract; it's concrete, too. Helen Fisher has found evidence of long-term attachment in the human brain. She put individuals who had been married an average of twenty-one years into brain scanners. Most had grown children. Then she looked at the regions of their brain that were most active. Those who scored highest on marriage satisfaction questionnaires showed increased engagement in three areas of their brains.

"The first has to do with empathy," she said. "The second has to do with controlling your emotions. The third has to do with positive illusions, specifically the ability to overlook what you don't like about a person and focus on what you do." It's like that old song, she said, "Accentuate the positive, eliminate the negative."

"Can you actually teach your brain to learn that skill?" I asked.

"Absolutely. The brain is very malleable. That's why we call this type of thinking positive illusions. You can learn to focus on the positive aspects of the relationship and not focus on the negative." It all comes down to storytelling, she said. "To be in a healthy relationship, you don't have to agree on everything, but you have to agree on enough things so you have a good story to tell."

This to me is the most exciting thing I learned about Adam and Eve. Love is a story. But not just any story. A love story has a number of qualities that set it apart from other stories.

First, it's a story we construct with another person. We can't be the sole author of our own love story; we can't impose our will or demand the last word. We must, by definition, share credit, share ownership, share creation. Tales of pinings and yearnings and unrequited love are oft-told phenomena, but they're not love stories. They're stories with only one teller. A love story, by definition, has two.

That's why Adam and Eve aren't a love story when Adam alone feels lonely or even when he gushes that Eve is the "one"! They don't become a love story until she begins to feel the same way. When "the two of them" are naked and feel no shame; when "the two of them" open their eyes and discover they are naked; when "the two of them" lie face-to-face and conceive.

Second, a love story takes time. The most common definition of love is that it's that remarkable period of tingles, infatuation, novelty, and lust one often feels at the start of a relationship. That can be part of love, of course, but it's not a requirement, and it's not the whole story. Love is also the long-term stew of reinvention, reconciliation, hardiness, and appreciation.

To me, this is the essential mistake in how we talk about our most central obsession. We define love in a way that guarantees we can't succeed at it. We describe love as something passive and fleeting, then are surprised when it goes away. We glorify love as effervescent, then are disappointed when it evaporates.

Love is not eternal and unchanging; it's ever-changing and ever-evolving. Love is not a moment in time; it's the passage of time. It was this way for Adam and Eve, and it's the same for us.

Finally, a love story is one we tell along the way. We experience the passion, the pain, the jocularity of love while we're trying to craft the narrative of that love. We're living the story while we're telling it. Indeed, we can never escape our story, which is one reason we find love stories so escapist. We work through our own issues by comparing them to the issues of those we read about, watch, and talk about.

That's one reason Adam and Eve have endured for so long. Every generation compares its problems to theirs. And yet we don't respect them for what they achieve: their willingness to keep walking, keep talking, keep coming back to each other, keep working it through.

We are resistant to the idea that Adam and Eve are a love story, I believe, not because they don't exhibit the attributes of love, but because we've misidentified what those attributes are. "Love is not an initial conquest followed by a relationship, much less 'happily ever after,'" Robert Solomon writes, any more than a good novel climaxes in the second chapter, five hundred pages from the end. Love is "the continuing story of self-definition, in which plots, themes, characters, beginnings, middles and ends are very much up to the authorship of the indeterminate selves engaged in love."

We get disappointed when we don't have a storybook romance, he adds, but the truth is that we have to create our own story, our own romance.

This is what I took from Adam and Eve: Love is a story we tell with another person. And, as it is with them, the telling never ends.

ON DECEMBER 13, 1867, Mark Twain was touring Jerusalem when he visited a room in the Church of the Holy Sepulchre identified as "Adam's Tomb." He was overcome with emotion. "The fountain of my filial affection was stirred to its profoundest depths," he wrote. "I leaned upon a pillar and burst into tears." How touching it was that "here in a land of strangers, far away from home, & friends, & all who cared for me, thus to discover the grave of a blood relation. True, a distant one, but still a relation."

Twain became obsessed with the forefather he never met. He jokingly proposed a statue of Adam be built in his wife's hometown, Elmira, New York. When the public unexpectedly embraced the idea, he commissioned Congress to pay for it. They turned him down. Next he contributed to the Statue of Liberty but urged organizers to replace the woman with a monument to Adam. They never responded to his letter. Twain even adopted as one of his pen names "A Son of Adam."

Twain went on to write half a dozen little-known but extraordinary pieces about the first couple, including "Extracts from Adam's Diary" and an unfinished "Autobiography of Eve." Taken together, one historian wrote, "they are perhaps the most personal of Mark Twain's writing."

Adam, in Twain's telling, is at first uncomfortable with Eve. She eats too much, goes out all the time, and talks a lot. "It used to be so pleasant and quiet here," he says. Adam gets anxious when she takes up with the snake. "I advised her to keep away from the tree. She said she wouldn't. I foresee trouble. Will emigrate."

Eve is equally unimpressed with Adam. "He talks very little. Perhaps it is because he is not bright, and is sensitive about it."

But slowly the two come around. "I see I should be lonesome and depressed without her," Adam says. "Blessed be the sorrow that brought us near together and taught me to know the goodness of her heart and the sweetness of her spirit." A similar transition happens to Eve. "I love him with all the strength of my passionate nature," she says. "It is my prayer, it is my longing, that we shall pass from this life together."

Twain completed the last of these writings,

"Eve's Diary," soon after the death of his beloved wife, Livy, in 1904. "I am a man without a country," Twain wrote a friend. "Wherever Livy was, that was my country." In a one-sentence epilogue to "Eve's Diary," which was originally titled "Eve's Love-Story," Twain adds a similar panegyric from the mouth of Adam. Standing beside Eve's grave, the original lonesome man laments, "Wheresoever she was, **there** was Eden."

Twain's touching eulogy to his wife, placed in the mouth of his "blood relation," captures everything I admire about Adam and Eve: Their ability to speak to us, to give us the message we most need to hear in our most vulnerable hour. That message, in its simplest form, is that there is an ideal of undying love. There is a promise of eternal happiness in the Bible just as powerful as the promise of eternal peace.

There is promised love as well as promised land.

Today, we need that promise more than ever. In a time of dislocation and disconnection, we need to be reminded we're not meant to be alone. In a time of crumbling commitments and disposable pleasure, we need to rehear that the first relationship lasted forever. In a time of "work-life balance" and "Can we have it all?" we need to recollect that even the first couple struggled to find individuality in their togetherness. In a time when we all let ourselves and our lovers down, we need to recall that the first man and first woman found a way to heal their wounds and forgive their wrongs.

We need, above all, to remember that the relationship at the foundation of our civilization was a success, not a failure.

We need Adam and Eve as our role models.

And they've earned it. In a world dominated by **I**, Adam and Eve were the first **we**. They were the first to say **we** are better off as an **us** than either of **us** is as a **me**.

Adam and Eve are the first love story.

That doesn't mean they are the best love story, any more than the first game of baseball was the best game of baseball, the first novel was the best novel, or the first orange soufflé was the best orange soufflé. It doesn't mean they are the first lovers to have their story told. There may have been hunter-gatherer sonneteers on the savannas of Africa or an Egyptian Jackie Collins in the court of King Tut.

But Adam and Eve are the first love story in the sense of the first to exemplify the conscious decision to elevate human-human love to the

plane of god-god love or god-human love. They
are the first to have survived, been retold, been
sampled, been reimagined. They are the first
that every other love story gets compared to, fa-
vorably or not.

Just look at how we remember them. They
are Adam and Eve.

Not Adam.

Not Eve.

Adam and Eve. One name is rarely mentioned
without the other.

In 1956, the poet Philip Larkin visited Chich-
ester Cathedral in southern England, where he
came upon two stone effigies in Lewes Priory.
The figures were the 10th Earl of Arundel,
Richard FitzAlan, and his second wife, Eleanor
of Lancaster. The two were lying on their backs,
carved in marble, holding hands.

"Side by side, their faces blurred / The earl
and countess lie in stone," Larkin wrote in "An
Arundel Tomb."

> Our almost-instinct almost true:
> What will survive of us is love.

I am struck that what Larkin saw in these figures is what Twain saw in Adam and Eve. It

echoes some of what Mary Shelley, John Milton, Lord Byron, Michelangelo, Ernest Hemingway, Elizabeth Cady Stanton, Pope Francis, and so many others saw in the first couple as well.

And it's what I choose to see, too.

I see in Adam and Eve what I believe they saw in themselves: that what will endure of their union is their togetherness.

What will survive of them is love.

ACKNOWLEDGMENTS

I'd like to thank the dozens of people who appear by name in this book, all of whom gave up their time, invited me to their homes and workplaces, and answered my often probing and personal questions with aplomb, insight, and good cheer. You are testament to the ability of Adam and Eve to continue to shape the world thousands of years after they first entered it. Thank you for your guidance, your wisdom, and, in many cases, your friendship.

Avner Goren walked the early steps of this journey with me in Jerusalem, as he has done on nearly every journey I've taken since our first meeting nearly two decades ago that led to **Walking the Bible**. In Israel, I am profoundly grateful for Susan Silverman, Anat Hoffman, Avital Hochstein, Nama Goren, and Michal Govrin. For help with the Sistine Chapel, Geraldine Torney and the wonderful team at Italy With Us, Enrico Bruschini, Gregory Waldrop, Jeremy Zipple, and Ian Caldwell. For their companionship in the Galápagos, the Pan-Stier family: Max, Florence, Zachary, and Noah.

At the Fashion Institute of Design & Merchandising Museum, Kevin Jones and Shirley Wilson. Also in Los Angeles, David Wolpe. The many women of Kohenet, and the team at Hazon. On Long Island, the entire community of the Compassionate Friends. In Seneca Falls, Coline Jenkins, Ami Ghazala, and Rev. Allison Stokes. To everyone at CNN who invited me to cover the pope, Jeff Zucker, Charlie Moore, Kerry Rubin, Rebecca Kutler, and especially Anderson Cooper. At the **New York Times**, Stuart Emmrich and Laura Marmor.

For their support in keeping this project and my life running smoothly, Chadwick Moore and Jerimee Bloemeke. Also, Tim Hawkins and Tyler Gwinn.

David Black handled the genesis of this book with deftness and skill and continued to be its champion for its entire life. Scott Moyers embraced this idea with enthusiasm, steered it to completion with both generosity and acumen, and published it with gusto and grace. Thank you for welcoming me into your family. I am deeply grateful for Ann Godoff's support, commitment, and leadership. Christopher Richards improved the manuscript immeasurably with his detailed, thoughtful eye and collaborative spirit. I have been wowed at every turn by the professionalism and creativity at Penguin Press. Special appreciation to Matt Boyd, Sarah Hutson, Yamil Anglada, and so many more.

Thank you to fellow travelers who help make the creative fields a challenge still worth pursuing: Ben

Sherwood, Joshua Ramo, Craig Jacobson, Alan Berger; to those who travel along wherever we go: Justin Castillo, David Kramer, Jeff Shumlin; and to my traveling sisterhood: Cari Bender, Lauren Schneider, Karen Lehrman Bloch, Sunny Bates. And a personal shout-out to the many people who engage these passions with me on the page, in person, and on social media.

I am deeply fortunate (most of the time!) to have two joyous, hands-on extended families to indulge my passions and share my life with. Such rarities don't happen by accident. In my case, they're entirely made possible by the dedication and stewardship of Jane and Ed Feiler and Debbie and Alan Rottenberg.

Linda Rottenberg is surely the most indulgent person alive of my crazy ideas—and she's a certified expert, having written her own book, **Crazy Is a Compliment.** It's a profound compliment to her love and patience that she nurtured this dream of mine, improved every draft, helped tug the book back on course a few times, and came out smiling her legendary smile. After almost two decades together, I can at least say this: Honey, I may not be paradise to live with, but at least with me you never get lost!

It is a source of utter joy for me that this book began with our daughters, Tybee and Eden, noticing something I hadn't seen in one of the most famous pieces of art ever made. From when they were very young, I urged them to be good "noticers." This book also embodies our family mission statement, "May your first word be adventure, and your last word love." Girls, every word on these pages in infused with my dream that you live out these twin gifts just as you teach us every day the gifts of being twins.

My brother, Andrew, has been at my side, red pen in hand, for this book as he has for every book I've written. During the life of this project he found, with Laura Adams, the fulfilling, artful, nurturing relationship he has been seeking for so long. In the spirit of the first love story, this book is dedicated to them.

SELECT BIBLIOGRAPHY

Ackerman, Diane. **A Natural History of Love**. New York: Vintage, 1995.

Almond, Philip C. **Adam and Eve in Seventeenth-Century Thought**. Cambridge: Cambridge University Press, 1999.

Alter, Robert. **The Art of Biblical Narrative**. New York: Basic Books, 1981.

_____. **Genesis**. New York: W. W. Norton, 1996.

Anderson, Gary A. **The Genesis of Perfection: Adam and Eve in Jewish and Christian Imagination**. Louisville, KY: Westminster John Knox, 2001.

Armstrong, Karen. **In the Beginning: A New Interpretation of Genesis**. New York: Ballantine, 1997.

Aschkenasy, Nehama. **Eve's Journey: Feminine Images in Hebraic Literary Tradition**. Detroit, MI: Wayne State University Press, 1994.

Augustine. **The Confessions**. Translated by Maria Boulding. New York: Vintage, 1998.

_____. **The City of God**. Garden City, NY: Image, 1958.

Badiou, Alain, Nicolas Truong, and Peter R. Bush. **In Praise of Love**. London: Serpent's Tail, 2012.

Bal, Mieke. **Lethal Love: Feminist Literary Readings of Biblical Love Stories**. Bloomington: Indiana University Press, 1987.

Barna, George. **Revolution**. Wheaton, IL: Tyndale House, 2005.

Barthes, Roland, Richard Howard, and Wayne Koestenbaum. **A Lover's Discourse: Fragments**. New York: Hill and Wang, 2010.

Becker, Ernest. **The Denial of Death**. New York: Free Press, 1997.

Berger, Peter L. **The Desecularization of the World: Resurgent Religion and World Politics**. Washington, DC: Ethics and Public Policy Center, 1999.

Blanning, T. C. W. **The Romantic Revolution: A History**. New York: Modern Library, 2012.

Blech, Benjamin, and Roy Doliner. **The Sistine Secrets: Michelangelo's Forbidden Messages in the Heart of the Vatican**. New York: HarperOne, 2009.

Borg, Marcus J. **The God We Never Knew: Beyond Dogmatic Religion to a More Authentic Contemporary Faith**. San Francisco: HarperSan Francisco, 1997.

Bouteneff, Peter. **Beginnings: Ancient Christian Readings of the Biblical Creation Narratives**. Grand Rapids, MI: Baker Academic, 2008.

Brogaard, Berit. **On Romantic Love: Simple Truths about a Complex Emotion**. New York: Oxford University Press, 2015.

Brontë, Charlotte. **Jane Eyre: An Authoritative Text, Context, Criticism**. Edited by Richard J. Dunn. New York: Norton, 2001.

Browne, Janet. **Charles Darwin: The Power of Place**. Princeton, NJ: Princeton University Press, 2002.

_____. **Voyaging**. Princeton, NJ: Princeton University Press, 1996.

Bruschini, Enrico. **In the Footsteps of Popes: A Spirited Guide to the Treasures of the Vatican**. New York: William Morrow, 2001.

Buber, Martin. **I and Thou**. Translated by Walter Kaufmann. New York: Charles Scribner's Sons, 1970.

Buscaglia, Leo F. **Love**. New York: Fawcett, 1996.

Byron, John. **Cain and Abel in Text and Tradition: Jewish and Christian Interpretations of the First Sibling Rivalry**. Leiden, Netherlands: Brill, 2011.

Cacioppo, John T., and William Patrick. **Loneliness: Human Nature and the Need for Social Connection**. New York: Norton, 2009.

Campbell, Gordon, and Thomas N. Corns. **John Milton: Life, Work, and Thought**. Oxford: Oxford University Press, 2008.

Capellanus, Andreas. **The Art of Courtly Love**. Translated by John Jay Parry. New York: Norton, 1969.

Christ, Carol P., and Judith Plaskow. **Womanspirit**

Rising: A Feminist Reader in Religion. San Francisco: HarperSan Francisco, 1992.

Collins, John J. **Between Athens and Jerusalem: Jewish Identity in the Hellenistic Diaspora.** Grand Rapids, MI: William B. Eerdmans, 2000.

Comer, John Mark. **Loveology: God, Love, Sex, Marriage, and the Never-ending Story of Male and Female.** Grand Rapids, MI: Zondervan, 2013.

Coogan, Michael David. **God and Sex: What the Bible Really Says.** New York: Twelve, 2010.

Crowther, Kathleen M. **Adam and Eve in the Protestant Reformation.** Cambridge: Cambridge University Press, 2010.

de Botton, Alain. **How to Think More about Sex.** New York: Picador, 2013.

_____. **On Love.** New York: Grove, 1993.

de Waal, F. B. M. **Our Inner Ape: A Leading Primatologist Explains Why We Are Who We Are.** New York: Riverhead, 2006.

Delumeau, Jean. **The History of Paradise: The Garden of Eden in Myth and Tradition.** Urbana: University of Illinois, 2000.

Diamond, Jared M. **Why Is Sex Fun?: The Evolution of Human Sexuality.** New York: HarperCollins, 1997.

Díaz, Junot. **This Is How You Lose Her.** New York: Riverhead, 2012.

Didion, Joan. **The Year of Magical Thinking.** New York: Vintage International, 2007.

Edgell, Penny. **Religion and Family in a Changing Society.** Princeton, NJ: Princeton University Press, 2006.

Eliade, Mircea. **The Sacred and the Profane: The Nature of Religion.** Translated by Willard R. Trask. New York: Harcourt, Brace & World, 1959.

Enns, Peter. **The Evolution of Adam: What the Bible Does and Doesn't Say about Human Origins.** Grand Rapids, MI: Brazos, 2012.

Erskine, John. **Adam and Eve: Though He Knew Better.** Indianapolis, IN: Bobbs-Merrill, 1927.

Evans, J. Martin. **Paradise Lost and the Genesis Tradition.** Oxford: Clarendon Press, 1968.

Fara, Patricia. **Erasmus Darwin: Sex, Science, and Serendipity.** Oxford: Oxford University Press, 2012.

Fisher, Helen E. **Why We Love: The Nature and Chemistry of Romantic Love.** New York: Henry Holt, 2004.

Fox, Everett. **The Five Books of Moses: Genesis, Exodus, Leviticus, Numbers, Deuteronomy; A New Translation with Introductions, Commentary, and Notes.** New York: Schocken, 1995.

Frankel, Estelle. **Sacred Therapy: Jewish Spiritual Teachings on Emotional Healing and Inner Wholeness.** Boston: Shambhala, 2003.

Frankl, Viktor E. **Man's Search for Meaning.** Boston: Beacon Press, 2006.

Fredrickson, Barbara. **Love 2.0: Creating Happiness**

and Health in Moments of Connection. New York: Plume, 2014.

Fredriksen, Paula. Augustine and the Jews: A Christian Defense of Jews and Judaism. New York: Doubleday, 2008.

Fromm, Erich. The Art of Loving. Translated by Marion Hausner Pauck. New York: Harper Perennial Modern Classics, 2006.

Frymer-Kensky, Tikva. Reading the Women of the Bible: A New Interpretation of Their Stories. New York: Fawcett Columbine, 2004.

_____. In the Wake of the Goddesses: Women, Culture, and the Biblical Transformation of Pagan Myth. New York: Fawcett Columbine, 1993.

Gibran, Kahlil. The Prophet. London: Heinemann, 1926.

Gilbert, Creighton. Michelangelo: On and Off the Sistine Ceiling. New York: George Braziller, 1994.

Ginzberg, Lori D. Elizabeth Cady Stanton: An American Life. New York: Hill and Wang, 2009.

Ginzberg, Louis. The Legends of the Jews, vol. 1, From the Creation to Jacob. Translated by Henrietta Szold and Paul Radin. Baltimore, MD: Johns Hopkins University Press, 1998.

Goff, Bob. Love Does: Discover a Secretly Incredible Life in an Ordinary World. Nashville, TN: Thomas Nelson, 2012.

Gottman, John Mordechai, and Nan Silver. What Makes Love Last?: How to Build Trust and

Avoid Betrayal. New York: Simon & Schuster, 2012.

Grant, Adam M. **Originals: How Non-Conformists Move the World.** New York: Viking, 2016.

Hammer, Jill. **Sisters at Sinai: New Tales of Biblical Women.** Philadelphia, PA: Jewish Publication Society, 2004.

Hammer, Jill, and Taya Shere. **The Hebrew Priestess: Ancient and New Visions of Jewish Women's Spiritual Leadership.** Teaneck, NJ: Ben Yehuda, 2015.

Hammer, Jill, and Holly Taya Shere. **Siddur HaKohanot: A Hebrew Priestess Prayerbook.** N.p.: Lulu.com, 2007.

Hammer, Jill, with Shir Yaakov Feit. **Omer Calendar of Biblical Women.** Falls Village, CT: Kohenet Institute, 2012.

Hanh, Nhất. **Cultivating the Mind of Love.** Berkeley, CA: Parallax, 2008.

_____. **How to Love.** Berkeley, CA: Parallax, 2015.

Harari, Yuval N. **Sapiens: A Brief History of Humankind.** London: Harvill Secker, 2014.

Haught, John F. **Deeper than Darwin: The Prospect for Religion in the Age of Evolution.** Boulder, CO: Westview, 2003.

Hauser, Marc D. **Moral Minds: The Nature of Right and Wrong.** New York: Harper Perennial, 2007.

Heidegger, Martin, John Macquarrie, and Edward S. Robinson. **Being and Time.** New York: HarperPerennial/Modern Thought, 2008.

Hemingway, Ernest. **The Garden of Eden.** New York: Scribner, 1986.

Heschel, Abraham Joshua. **Man's Quest for God: Studies in Prayer and Symbolism.** Santa Fe, NM: Aurora, 1998.

Hickman, John, and Julian Fitter. **Galápagos: The Enchanted Islands through Writers' Eyes.** London: Eland Pub, 2009.

Hill, Christopher. **The English Bible and the Seventeenth-Century Revolution.** London: Penguin, 1994.

Hollis, James. **The Eden Project: In Search of the Magical Other.** Toronto: Inner City, 1998.

Holmes, Richard. **The Age of Wonder: How the Romantic Generation Discovered the Beauty and Terror of Science.** New York: Vintage, 2010.

Holmes, Richard. **Footsteps: Adventures of a Romantic Biographer.** New York: Vintage, 1996.

Holy Bible: New Revised Standard Version with Apocrypha: Reference Edition, Burgundy Bonded. New York and Oxford: Cambridge University Press, 1998.

hooks, bell. **All about Love: New Visions.** New York: Perennial, 2001.

Hugo, Victor, and Norman Denny. **Les Misérables.** London: Penguin, 1982.

Hurwitz, Siegmund. **Lilith, the First Eve: Historical and Psychological Aspects of the Dark Feminine.** Edited by Robert Hinshaw. Einsiedeln, Switzerland: Daimon Verlag, 2009.

Illouz, Eva. **Why Love Hurts: A Sociological Explanation**. Malden, MA: Polity, 2015.

Jankowiak, William R. **Intimacies: Love and Sex across Cultures**. New York: Columbia University Press, 2008.

Johnson, Elizabeth A. **She Who Is: The Mystery of God in Feminist Theological Discourse**. New York: Crossroad, 1992.

Jung, C. G. **The Essential Jung**. Introduction by Anthony Storr. Princeton, NJ: Princeton University Press, 1997.

Keller, Timothy, and Kathy Keller. **The Meaning of Marriage: Facing the Complexities of Commitment with the Wisdom of God**. New York: Dutton, 2011.

Kern, Kathi. **Mrs. Stanton's Bible**. Ithaca, NY: Cornell University Press, 2001.

Kern, Stephen. **The Culture of Love: Victorians to Moderns**. Cambridge, MA: Harvard University Press, 1994.

Kimball, Dan. **They Like Jesus but Not the Church: Insights from Emerging Generations**. Grand Rapids, MI: Zondervan, 2007.

King, Ross. **Leonardo and the Last Supper**. New York: Bloomsbury, 2013.

————. **Michelangelo and the Pope's Ceiling**. New York: Penguin, 2003.

Kinnaman, David, and Aly Hawkins. **You Lost Me: Why Young Christians Are Leaving Church . . . and Rethinking Faith**. Grand Rapids, MI: Baker Books, 2011.

Kinnaman, David, and Gabe Lyons. **Unchristian: What a New Generation Really Thinks about Christianity . . . and Why It Matters.** Grand Rapids, MI: Baker Books, 2007.

Kipnis, Laura. **Against Love: A Polemic.** New York: Vintage, 2004.

Klitsner, Judy. **Subversive Sequels in the Bible: How Biblical Stories Mine and Undermine Each Other.** New Milford, CT: Maggid, 2011.

Knust, Jennifer Wright. **Unprotected Texts: The Bible's Surprising Contradictions about Sex and Desire.** New York: HarperOne, 2011.

Koltun, Elizabeth. **The Jewish Women: New Perspectives.** New York: Schocken Books, 1976.

Konner, Melvin. **The Evolution of Childhood: Relationships, Emotion, Mind.** Cambridge, MA: Belknap Press of Harvard University Press, 2010.

———. **The Jewish Body.** New York: Nextbook, 2009.

———. **Unsettled: An Anthropology of the Jews.** New York: Viking Compass, 2003.

———. **Women After All: Sex, Evolution, and the End of Male Supremacy.** New York: Norton, 2015.

Krauss, Nicole. **The History of Love.** New York: Norton, 2005.

Kushner, Harold S. **How Good Do We Have to Be?: A New Understanding of Guilt and Forgiveness.** Boston: Little, Brown, 1997.

Kvam, Kristen E., Linda S. Schearing, and Valarie H. Ziegler. **Eve and Adam: Jewish, Christian, and**

Muslim Readings on Genesis and Gender. Bloomington: Indiana University Press, 1999.

Lamm, Maurice. The Jewish Way in Love and Marriage. Middle Village, NY: Jonathan David, 1991.

Lawrence, D. H. Women in Love. Mineola, NY: Dover Publications, 2002.

Leibowitz, Nehama, and Aryeh Newman. Studies in Bereshit (Genesis): In the Context of Ancient and Modern Jewish Bible Commentary. Jerusalem: Eliner Library, Joint Authority for Jewish Zionist Education, Department for Torah Education and Culture in the Diaspora, 1995.

Leider, Emily Wortis. Becoming Mae West. New York: Farrar, Straus, Giroux, 1997.

Lerner, Anne Lapidus. Eternally Eve: Images of Eve in the Hebrew Bible, Midrash, and Modern Jewish Poetry. Waltham, MA: Brandeis University Press, 2007.

Lerner, Gerda. The Creation of Patriarchy. New York: Oxford University Press, 1986.

Levenson, Jon Douglas. Creation and the Persistence of Evil: The Jewish Drama of Divine Omnipotence. Princeton, NJ: Princeton University Press, 1994.

Lewalski, Barbara Kiefer. The Life of John Milton: A Critical Biography. Oxford: Blackwell, 2000.

Lewis, Anthony J. The Love Story in Shakespearean Comedy. Lexington: University of Kentucky Press, 1992.

Lewis, Thomas, Fari Amini, and Richard Lannon. **A General Theory of Love**. New York: Vintage, 2001.

Luttikhuizen, Gerard P. **Eve's Children: The Biblical Stories Retold and Interpreted in Jewish and Christian Traditions**. Leiden, Netherlands: Brill, 2003.

MacDonald, George. **Lilith: A Romance**. Seaside, OR: Watchmaker, 2009.

Mack, Cheryl Birkner, Vivian Singer, Natalie Lastreger, Avigail Antman, Rachel Cohen Yeshurun, and Tammy Gottlieb, eds. **Women of the Wall: Prayers for Rosh Hodesh and Weekday Mornings**. 4th ed. Chesterland, OH: CustomSiddur, 2014.

Makiya, Kanan. **The Rock: A Tale of Seventh-Century Jerusalem**. New York: Pantheon, 2001.

May, Simon. **Love: A History**. New Haven, CT: Yale University Press, 2012.

Merton, Thomas. **Love and Living**. Edited by Naomi Burton Stone and Patrick Hart. San Diego: Harcourt Brace Jovanovich, 1985.

Miles, Jack. **God: A Biography**. New York: Vintage, 1996.

Miller, Geoffrey F. **The Mating Mind: How Sexual Choice Shaped the Evolution of Human Nature**. New York: Anchor, 2001.

Miller, Henry. **The World of Sex**. Harmondsworth, UK: Penguin Classics, 2015.

Miller, Shannon. **Engendering the Fall: John Milton**

and Seventeenth-Century Women Writers. Philadelphia: University of Pennsylvania Press, 2008.

Milton, John. **Paradise Lost: Authoritative Text, Sources and Backgrounds, Criticism.** Edited by Gordon Teskey. New York: Norton, 2005.

Mitchell, Stephen A. **Can Love Last?: The Fate of Romance over Time.** New York: Norton, 2002.

Moyers, Bill D. **Genesis: A Living Conversation.** New York: Doubleday, 1996.

Murphy, Cullen. **The Word According to Eve: Women and the Bible in Ancient Times and Our Own.** Boston: Houghton Mifflin, 1998.

Neumann, Erich. **Amor and Psyche: The Psychic Development of the Feminine: A Commentary on the Tale by Apuleius.** Princeton, NJ: Princeton University Press, 1971.

Oates, Joyce Carol. **A Widow's Story: A Memoir.** New York: Ecco, 2012.

Pagels, Elaine H. **Adam, Eve, and the Serpent.** New York: Vintage, 1988.

Pardes, Ilana. **Countertraditions in the Bible: A Feminist Approach.** Cambridge, MA: Harvard University Press, 1992.

Patai, Raphael. **The Hebrew Goddess.** Detroit, MI: Wayne State University Press, 1990.

Paz, Octavio. **The Double Flame: Love and Eroticism.** San Diego: Harcourt Brace, 1996.

Pelikan, Jaroslav. **Mary Through the Centuries: Her**

Place in the History of Culture. New Haven, CT: Yale University Press, 1996.

Phillips, John A. **Eve, the History of an Idea**. San Francisco: Harper & Row, 1985.

Pierce, Ronald W., Rebecca Merrill Groothuis, and Gordon D. Fee. **Discovering Biblical Equality: Complementarity without Hierarchy**. Downers Grove, IL: InterVarsity, 2005.

Plato. **Symposium**. Translated by Robin Waterfield. Oxford: Oxford University Press, 2008.

Pogrebin, Letty Cottin. **Deborah, Golda, and Me: Being Female and Jewish in America**. New York: Crown, 1991.

Potts, Malcolm, and Roger Short. **Ever since Adam and Eve: The Evolution of Human Sexuality**. Cambridge: Cambridge University Press, 1999.

Putnam, Robert D., and David E. Campbell. **American Grace: How Religion Divides and Unites Us**. New York: Simon & Schuster, 2010.

Raver, Miki. **Listen to Her Voice**. San Francisco: Chronicle, 2005.

Ridley, Matt. **The Red Queen: Sex and the Evolution of Human Nature**. New York: Perennial, 2003.

Rilke, Rainer Maria. **Rilke on Love and Other Difficulties**. Translation and Considerations by John J. L. Mood. New York: Norton, 2004.

Rougemont, Denis de. **Love in the Western World**. Princeton, NJ: Princeton University Press, 1983.

Ruether, Rosemary Radford. **Religion and Sexism:**

Images of Woman in the Jewish and Christian Traditions. New York: Simon and Schuster, 1974.

Rūmī, Jalāl Al-Dīn. **Rumi: The Book of Love: Poems of Ecstasy and Longing.** Translated by Coleman Barks. San Francisco: HarperSan Francisco, 2003.

Ryan, Christopher, and Cacilda Jethá. **Sex at Dawn: The Prehistoric Origins of Modern Sexuality.** New York: Harper, 2010.

Sacks, Jonathan. **Faith in the Future.** London: Darton, Longman and Todd, 1995.

_____. **The Great Partnership: Science, Religion, and the Search for Meaning.** New York: Schocken, 2012.

Sanders, Theresa. **Approaching Eden: Adam and Eve in Popular Culture.** Lanham, MD: Rowman & Littlefield, 2009.

Sarna, Nahum M. **Understanding Genesis.** New York: Schocken, 1970.

Schearing, Linda S., and Valarie H. Ziegler. **Enticed by Eden: How Western Culture Uses, Confuses, (and Sometimes Abuses) Adam and Eve.** Waco, TX: Baylor University Press, 2013.

Schwartz, Howard. **Lilith's Cave: Jewish Tales of the Supernatural.** San Francisco: Harper & Row, 1988.

Scruton, Roger. **The Soul of the World.** Princeton, NJ: Princeton University Press, 2014.

Shelley, Mary Wollstonecraft. **Frankenstein.** Edited by J. Paul Hunter. New York: Norton, 2012.

_____. **Frankenstein**. New York: Signet Classic, 2000.

Shevack, Michael. **Adam & Eve: Marriage Secrets from the Garden of Eden**. New York: Paulist Press, 2003.

Shlain, Leonard. **Sex, Time, and Power: How Women's Sexuality Shaped Human Evolution**. New York: Viking, 2003.

Solomon, Andrew. **Far from the Tree: Parents, Children and the Search for Identity**. New York: Scribner, 2012.

Solomon, Robert C. **About Love: Reinventing Romance for Our Times**. Indianapolis, IN: Hackett, 2006.

Solomon, Robert C., and Kathleen Marie Higgins. **The Philosophy of (Erotic) Love**. Lawrence: University of Kansas Press, 1991.

Soloveitchik, Joseph Dov. **The Lonely Man of Faith**. New York: Doubleday, 2006.

Soueif, Ahdaf. **The Map of Love**. New York: Anchor, 2000.

Steinbeck, John. **East of Eden**. New York: Penguin, 2002.

Stendhal. **Love**. Harmondsworth, UK: Penguin, 1975.

Sternberg, Robert J. **Love Is a Story: A New Theory of Relationships**. New York: Oxford University Press, 1998.

Stone, Irving. **The Agony and the Ecstasy: A Biographical Novel of Michelangelo**. New York: New American Library, 2004.

Stone, Merlin. **When God Was a Woman**. New York: Harcourt Brace Jovanovich, 1978.

Stone, Michael E. **A History of the Literature of Adam and Eve**. Atlanta: Scholars, 1992.

Strauch, Dore. **Satan Came to Eden: A Survivor's Account of the "Galápagos Affair."** As told to Walter Brockmann. North Charleston, SC: Troise Publishing, 2015.

Szalavitz, Maia, and Bruce Duncan Perry. **Born for Love: Why Empathy Is Essential— and Endangered**. New York: William Morrow, 2010.

Tennov, Dorothy. **Love and Limerence: The Experience of Being in Love**. Lanham, MD: Scarborough House, 1999.

Trible, Phyllis. **God and the Rhetoric of Sexuality**. Philadelphia: Fortress, 1978.

Trzebiatowska, Marta, and Steve Bruce. **Why Are Women More Religious than Men?** Oxford: Oxford University Press, 2012.

Turgenev, Ivan Sergeevich. **First Love**. Translated by Isaiah Berlin. Harmondsworth, UK: Penguin, 1978.

Twain, Mark. **The Diaries of Adam & Eve**. Edited by Don Roberts. San Francisco: Fair Oaks, 2001.

Twain, Mark. **The Bible According to Mark Twain: Writings on Heaven, Eden, and the Flood**. Edited by Howard G. Baetzhold and Joseph B. McCullough. Athens: University of Georgia Press, 1995.

The Vatican: 100 Masterpieces. London: Scala, 2001.

Visotzky, Burton L. **The Genesis of Ethics.** New York: Three Rivers, 1997.

Watts, Jill. **Mae West: An Icon in Black and White.** New York: Oxford University Press, 2003.

Weiner, Jonathan. **The Beak of the Finch: A Story of Evolution in Our Time.** New York: Knopf, 1994.

Wolkstein, Diane. **The First Love Stories: From Isis and Osiris to Tristan and Iseult.** New York: HarperCollins, 1992.

Wuthnow, Robert. **After the Baby Boomers: How Twenty- and Thirty-somethings Are Shaping the Future of American Religion.** Princeton, NJ: Princeton University Press, 2007.

_____. **The Restructuring of American Religion: Society and Faith since World War II.** Princeton, NJ: Princeton University Press, 1989.

Yalom, Marilyn. **A History of the Wife.** New York: HarperCollins, 2001.

Zevit, Ziony. **What Really Happened in the Garden of Eden?** New Haven, CT: Yale University Press, 2013.

Zornberg, Avivah Gottlieb. **The Beginning of Desire: Reflections on Genesis.** New York: Schocken, 2011.

SOURCES

When quoting from English translations of the Hebrew Bible, I like **Tanakh: The Holy Scriptures** (The New JPS Translation) and **The Torah: A Modern Commentary**, edited by W. Gunther Plaut (Union of American Hebrew Congregations). For the New Testament, **The Holy Bible** (New Revised Standard Version) and, where appropriate, **The Holy Bible: King James Version**. Convenient side-by-side translations are available at BibleGateway.com and BibleHub.com. In keeping with contemporary trends in popular and academic writing, I use the nonsectarian terms B.C.E., Before the Common Era, and C.E., Common Era.

INTRODUCTION—THE FIRST COUPLE: Why Adam and Eve Still Matter

The Thomas Merton quotation used as an epigraph to this book, along with his quotation in the introduction, comes from his collection of essays, **Love and Living**. Augustine's use of "childish" comes from **City of God**. Avraham Biran's quote about Abraham can be found in my book **Abraham: A Journey to the Heart of Three Faiths**.

The statistics about loneliness come from **Loneliness** by John Cacioppo and William Patrick, **Born for Love** by Bruce Duncan Perry and Maia Szalavitz; as well as "Americans Increasingly Likely to Lead Lonely, Loveless Existences, Except in Old Age," by Jordan Weissman, Slate; "A Longtime Proponent of Marriage Wants to Reasses the Institution's Future," by Brigid Schulte, the **Washington Post**; "A Gray Revolution in Living Arrangements," by Jonathan Vespa and Emily Schondelmyer, U.S. Census Bureau; and "Loneliness: A Silent Plague That Is Hurting Young People Most," by Natalie Gil, the **Guardian**.

Erich Fromm's quotes come from **The Art of Loving**; Joseph Campbell's from **The Power of Myth**; Robert Solomon's from **About Love**. Auden's exhortation comes from his poem, "O Tell Me the Truth About Love."

1—FIRST COMES LOVE:
How Adam and Eve Invented Love

A longer, more detailed description of my visit to the confluence of the Tigris and Euphrates, along with other biblical sites in Iraq, can be found in my book

Where God Was Born: A Daring Journey Through the Bible's Greatest Stories.

My discussion of gods and goddesses in the ancient Near East is informed by, and in some cases quotes directly from, **The Creation of Patriarchy** by Gerda Lerner; **In the Wake of the Goddesses** by Tikva Frymer-Kensky; **When God Was a Woman** by Merlin Stone; **Eve** by John Phillips; **Ever Since Adam and Eve** by Malcolm Potts and Roger Short; and **Sapiens** by Yuval Harari.

For more on the relationship between the singular/plural God and the singular/plural humanity, see **The Beginning of Desire** by Avivah Zornberg and **Eternally Eve** by Anne Lapidus Lerner.

The statistics about love across cultures comes from Helen Fisher, **Why We Love** and **Intimacies**, edited by William Jankowiak. My review of the history of love in the West draws heavily from **Love** by Simon May; as well as from **On Romantic Love** by Berit Brogaard; **Love 2.0** by Barbara Frederickson; **In Praise of Love** by Alain Badiou; **The Culture of Love** by Stephen Kerr; and **Love in the Western World** by Denis de Rougemont.

Love in the Hebrew Bible is discussed in Zornberg and May. The interpretation of Genesis 1 as referring to an androgynous creation is discussed in **Adam and Eve in Seventeenth-Century Thought** by Philip Almond; Zornberg and Lerner both quote Rashi on this idea, along with Genesis Rabbah. Robert Alter's writings on Adam and Eve can be found in **Genesis** and

The Art of Biblical Narrative. Robin Waterfield has a helpful introduction to **Symposium** in his Oxford World Classics translation.

The idea of human relation is elegantly explored in Alain de Botton, **On Love**; Martin Buber, **I and Thou**; and Rumi, **The Book of Love**, which contains the unnamed poem quoted here. Freud's "oceanic feeling" comes from **The Future of an Illusion**; Woolf's "two sexes in the mind" comes from **A Room of One's Own**.

2—MEET CUTE:
Who Was Present at the Creation?

The Robert Alter quote is found in **Genesis**. Compilation and analysis of interpretations of the creation story can be found in **Paradise Lost in the Genesis Tradition** by J. M. Evans; **Eve and Adam**, edited by Kristen Kvam, Linda Schearing, and Valarie Ziegler; and **Adam and Eve in Seventeenth-Century Thought**, which contains the John Calvin quote. The analysis of the different uses of **levaddo** and **ezer kenegdo** comes from **Eternally Eve**. Ramban is found in Zornberg; Yeats is found in "Sailing to Byzantium"; and Hobbes in **De Cive**.

Bergson is from **Creative Evolution**; Stevens from "To Henry Church," and Lewis from **The Four Loves**.

The biology of loneliness is covered in fascinating detail in **Loneliness** and **Born for Love**. My quotations from Cacioppo come from our lunch at the University of Chicago. The statistics about the harmful health affects come from his book as well.

The analysis of **tsela'** comes from **What Really Happened in the Garden of Eden?** by Ziony Zevit and **Eternally Eve**. Rashi is found in Evans. Zornberg quotes from **The Beginning of Desire**. **Jane Eyre** quotes from throughout the novel.

On the history of the Sistine Chapel, I relied on **Michelangelo** by Gilbert Creighton; **Michelangelo and the Sistine Chapel** by Andrew Graham-Dixon; **Michelangelo and the Pope's Ceiling** by Ross King; as well as Leo Steinberg, "Who's Who in Michelangelo's **Creation of Adam**"; Maria Rzepinska, "The Divine Wisdom of Michelangelo in **The Creation of Adam**"; and Jane Schulyer, "The Left Side of God."

The joke about Adam and Eve can be found in **What Really Happened in the Garden of Eden?** The history of interpretation is discussed in **Eve; Adam and Eve in Seventeenth-Century Thought; Eternally Eve; Adam, Eve, and the Serpent** by Elaine Pagels; and **Mary Through the Centuries** by Jaroslav Pelikan, as well as elsewhere.

3—THE DEVIL MADE ME DO IT:
What We Do for Love

The line about Milton inventing companionate marriage is inspired by a quotation from Barbara Lewalski in my interview with her at her home. The Solomon quote is from **About Love**. The material about the serpent and the apple is informed by **Adam and Eve in the Protestant Reformation** by Kathleen Crowther; **Approaching Eden** by Theresa Sanders; along with **Eve**, **Adam and Eve in Seventeenth-Century Thought**, and **What Really Happened in the Garden of Eden?**, which also contains the spiritual "Them Bones Will Rise Again."

The historical quotations are found in **What Really Happened**, as well as **Paradise Lost in the Genesis Tradition, Eve's Journey** by Nehama Aschkenasy, **Eve**, and **Adam and Eve in the Protestant Reformation**.

The most helpful biographies of Milton I consulted were **The Life of John Milton** by Lewalski, **John Milton** by Gordon Campbell, and **Anna Beer Milton** by Thomas Corns. My discussion of Milton and women also draws on **Engendering the Fall** by Shannon Miller and **Paradise Lost**, edited by Gordon Tesky, which contains the critical quotations I cite. The details about the Bible's popularity come from **The English Bible and the Seventeenth-Century Revolution** by Christopher Hill.

The material about courtly love comes from **Love** by May; **The Philosophy of (Erotic) Love**, edited by Robert Solomon and Kathleen Marie Higgins; **A History of the Wife** by Marilyn Yalom; and **The Natural History of Love** by Diane Ackerman. The "fortunate fall" is discussed in **Eve**, **Adam and Eve in Seventeenth-Century Thought**, and **Paradise Lost in the Genesis**

Tradition. "O Happy Fall" comes from "A Treatise of Paradise" by John Selked.

Octavio Paz comes from **The Double Flame**; Walt Whitman from "From Pent-up Aching Rivers"; Merton from **Love and Living**; Katha Pollitt from "The Expulsion."

4—CHORE WARS:
Who Needs Love?

The story of Friedrich Ritter and Dore Strauch is memorably told in dueling memoirs: **Satan Came to Eden** by Strauch, with Joseph Troise, editor; and **Floreana** by Margret Wittmer. There's also a thorough documentary called **The Galápagos Affair**, directed by Dan Geller and Dayna Goldfine.

The colorful history of the Garden of Eden is examined in **The History of Paradise** by Jean Delumeau. Similar themes are explored in **Adam and Eve in Seventeenth-Century Thought, Paradise Lost in the Genesis Tradition**, and **What Really Happened in the Garden of Eden?**

For more on the history of marriage see **A History of the Wife, A Natural History of Love**, and **Ever Since Adam and Eve**. The translation of **ezer kenegdo** draws on Alter, Ziony, and Lerner.

The literary history of the Galápagos is captured in **Galápagos** by John Hickman. Ritter's **Atlantic** pieces can be found online at www.Galápagos.to/texts/

atlantic1931.htm. On Darwin's life, I benefited from Janet Browne's two-volume biography, **Voyaging** and **The Power of Place**.

I consulted numerous books on the biological origins of pair bonding, monogamy, and love in humans. These include **Why Is Sex Fun?** by Jared Diamond; **Why We Love** by Helen Fisher; **Born for Love** by Perry and Szalavitz; **The Mating Mind** by Geoffrey Miller; **The Philosophy of (Erotic) Love**, edited by Robert Solomon and Kathleen Marie Higgins; **Intimacies**, edited by William Jankowiak; **The Red Queen** by Matt Ridley; **In Praise of Love** by Alain Badiou, Nicolas Truong, and Peter Bush; and Melvin Konner's **The Evolution of Childhood** and **Women After All**.

The Ben Franklin and Oscar Wilde quotes about love come from **The Jewish Way in Love and Marriage** by Maurice Lamm; the Solomon quotes come from **About Love**; the Egyptian hieroglyph is from **A Natural History of Love**; the James quote comes from **On Vital Reserves**; the **Fiddler on the Roof** lyrics come from the song "Do You Love Me?"

5—THAT LOOK IN THEIR EYES:
How Sex Became Evil, Then Unbecame It

My history of Mae West draws on **Becoming Mae West** by Emily Wortis Leider, **Mae West** by Jill Watts, and **Approaching Eden** by Theresa Sanders. The Adam and Eve incident has been carefully studied by Matthew Murray in "Mae West and the Limits of Radio Censorship," **Colby Quarterly**; Steve Craig in "Out of Eden: The Legion of Decency, the FCC, and Mae West's 1937 Appearance on The Chase & Sanborn Hour," **Journal of Radio Studies**; and Lori Amber Roessner and Matthew Broaddus in "The Sinners and the Scapegoat: Public Reaction in the Press to Mae West's Adam and Eve Skit," **American Journalism**.

My reading of the sexual themes of the biblical story was informed by **Eternally Eve**, **What Really Happened in the Garden of Eden?**, and **Eve's Journey**. The importance of eyes in love is discussed in a wide variety of places, including **Why We Love**, **About Love**, and **The Philosophy of (Erotic) Love**. Zick Rubin's research can be found in "Measurement of Romantic Love," **Journal of Personality and Social Psychology**, among others. For romantic novelists loved using eyes to invoke feelings, see **Madame Bovary**, **Les Misérables**, and **A Pair of Blue Eyes**.

De Botton's "anthropologist of the beloved" is from **On Love**; the detail about orgasm is from **Loneliness**; the etymology of "love" from **Why We Love**. De Botton's "pleasure we take" is from **How to Think More About Sex**.

My discussion about how sex became stigmatized in Western religion draws on **In the Wake of Goddesses**, **Why Is Sex Fun?**, **The Jewish Way of Love and Marriage**, and **Adam, Eve, and the Serpent**, which includes Augustine's comments about parts of shame.

John Mark Comer has written a book called **Love-ology** that draws heavily on the Adam and Eve story. The story of how love came into the open is told thoughtfully in May's **Love**, which contains the quotes from Freud and others.

6—THE OTHER WOMAN:
The Dark Side of Love

The story of Hemingway's **The Garden of Eden** and how it fits into his larger experience of sexual identity has been memorably told in **Hemingway** by Kenneth Lynn and **Hemingway** by James Mellow; as well **Approaching Eden**; "The Garden of Eden and **The Garden of Eden**" by Kelly Fisher Lowe, master's thesis at the University of Tennessee, Knoxville; "Hemingway's Gender Trouble" by J. Gerald Kennedy, **American Literature**; **Hemingway's The Garden of Eden**, by Suzanne del Gizzo and Frederic J. Svoboda; "The Androgynous Papa Hemingway," by James Tuttleton, **The New Criterion**.

The definitive book on the history of Lilith is **Lilith, the First Eve** by Siegmund Hurwitz, edited by Robert Hinshaw. Other works include **Lilith** by George MacDonald, **Lilith's Cave** by Howard Schwartz, and **The Hebrew Goddess** by Raphael Patai. The Christian connection to Lilith is in Pamela Norris, **Eve**; **Adam and Eve in Seventeenth-Century Thought**; and **Adam and Eve in the Protestant Reformation**.

Jill Hammer has written **Sisters at Sinai**, and, with Taya Shere, **The Hebrew Priestesses** and the prayer book **Siddur HaKohanot**.

Judith Plaskow's original story can be found in **The Coming of Lilith**. The history of Lilith in Hollywood, including Lilith Fair, is covered in detail in **Approaching Eden**.

7—FAMILY AFFAIR:
Are We Our Children's Keepers?

The story of **Cain, A Mystery** is told in **Lord Byron's Cain** by Truman Guy Steffan; "Lord Byron in the Wilderness" by Leslie Tannenbaum, **Modern Philology**; and "Byron's Cain" by Leonard Michaels, **Modern Language Association**.

My reading of the banishment draws on **Eternally Eve**, which contains the critique of Genesis 3:16; **The Beginning of Desire**; **Religion and Sexism**, edited by Rosemary Radford Ruether; and three pivotal works by Phyllis Trible: **God and the Rhetoric of Sexuality**, "Eve and Adam: Genesis 2-3 Reread," in **Eve and Adam**, and "Depatriarchalizing in Biblical Interpretation," in **The Jewish Woman**.

Close readings of Cain and Abel can be found in **Cain and Abel in Text and Tradition** by John Byron, and **Eve's Children**, edited by Gerard Luttikhuizen. The Ovid quote comes from **Amores**, Book III, Elegy XI. The statistics on family murders comes from

United States Department of Justice, "Murder in Families," 1994.

Jennifer Senior's **All Joy and No Fun** discusses the impact that children have on their parents, and contains most of the statistics cited here. The Kahneman survey comes from "Toward National Well-Being Accounts," by Daniel Kahneman, Alan Krueger, David Schkade, Norbert Schwarz, and Arthur Stone, **American Economic Review.** The impact of adult children on parents comes from "You Are Such a Disappointment," by Kelly Cichy, Eva Lefkowitz, Eden Davis, and Karen Fingerman, **The Journal of Gerontology Series B.**

Sue Klebold's moving memoir is called **A Mother's Reckoning**; it includes a foreword by Andrew Solomon, who also wrote about the family's story in **Far from the Tree.**

Elaine Stillwell has written a memoir about bereavement called **The Death of a Child.** Statistics on loss of a child come from "A Survey of Bereaved Parents," conducted by NFO Research, June 1999. The quotes from Ephrem the Syrian come from "Imagining What Eve Would Have Said After Cain's Murder of Abel," by Kevin Kalish, **Bridgewater Review.** The story of the raven and dog can be found in **Pirke de Rabbi Eliezer** by Eliezer ben Hyrcanus, translated by Gerald Friedlander.

Shirley Murphy's research appears in "Misconceptions about Parental Bereavement," **Journal of Nursing Scholarship**; "Challenging the Myths About Parents,"

Journal of Nursing Scholarship; and "Finding Meaning in a Child's Violent Death," Death Studies.

Harold Kushner's quote is from When Bad Things Happen to Good People, M. Scott Peck's from The Road Less Traveled; Antoine de Saint-Exupery's from Airman's Odyssey. The Hamilton song mentioned is "It's Quiet Uptown."

8—THE LOVE YOU MAKE:
Bless the Broken Road

Lori Ginzberg has written a helpful biography, Elizabeth Cady Stanton. The story of The Woman's Bible is carefully told in Mrs. Stanton's Bible by Kathi Kern. I benefited from a number of books about the rise of women's influence in religion: The World According to Eve by Cullen Murphy; Womanspirit Rising by Carol Christ and Judith Plaskow; Religion and Sexism by Rosemary Radford Ruether; and Deborah, Golda, and Me by Letty Cottin Pogrebin.

The birth of Seth is analyzed in Lerner, Alter, and others; the idea of love enduring through conflict is discussed in Fromm and May. Dorothy Tennov's work appears in her book Love and Limerence; Helen Fisher's is in Why We Love and others.

My account of the writing of Frankenstein draws heavily on the Norton Critical Edition, edited by J. Paul Hunter, and containing the 1818 text, contexts, and criticism. The theme of love in Romantic literature is explored in **The Culture of Love** by Stephen Kirn. The quote about the invention of modern marriage comes from Yalom; the Austen quote is from **Emma**; the Fromm quote from **The Art of Loving**; Woolf's extended discourse on love as an illusion is in **Night and Day**; the Emma Goldman quote appears in **The Philosophy of (Erotic) Love**; the Daly quote appears in **Approaching Eden**; and the Trible quote in "Eve and Adam." Elizabeth Johnson's signature book of theology is **She Who Is**.

CONCLUSION—AFTERLIFE:
What Adam and Eve Can Teach Us
About Relationships

The life and work of Pope Francis is chronicled in **The Great Reformer** by Austen Ivereigh and **The Francis Miracle** by John Allen.

The Josephus figures come from **Antiquities of the Jews**, Book 1. The story of Eve and Seth returning to the Garden of Eden appears in **Adam and Eve in the Protestant Reformation**.

George Bonanno's research can be found in "Loss, Trauma, and Human Resilience," **American Psychologist**, as well as "The Secret Life of Guilt," by Derek Thompson and "The Space Between Mourning and Grief," by Claire Wilmot, both in **The Atlantic**. Quotes from Shakespeare, Brontë, Didion, Oates, and Díaz are from the sources mentioned. The bell hooks poem is found in her book **A Woman's Mourning Song**.

The idea of covenant is discussed in **Understanding Genesis** by Nahum Sarna, among other places. The Jewish wedding vows are broken down in **The Jewish Way in Love and Marriage**. The Stendhal quote comes from **The Red and the Black**; the Gibran quote from **The Prophet**; the Rilke quote from **Rilke on Love and Other Difficulties**, translated by John Mood; and the Weil quote from **Gravity and Grace**. May discusses **kenosis** in **Love**; Gottman's work appears in **What Makes Love Last?** and **The Seven Principles for Making Marriage Work**, among others.

Zornberg's quote is from **The Beginning of Desire**. The James and Gattis quotes come from **The Philosophy of (Erotic) Love**. Co-narration is discussed in **Conversational Narratives** by Neal Norrick and **Dinner Talk** by Shoshana Blum-Kulka, among others. Fromm on falling in love is from **The Art of Loving**. Piaget is from **The Language and Thought of the Child**. Fisher's research is found in **Why We Love**. Solomon is from **About Love**.

Mark Twain's writings about Adam and Eve appear in **The Diaries of Adam and Eve**, edited by Don Roberts. They are analyzed in **The Bible According to Mark Twain**, by Howard Baetzhold and Joseph McCullough. The story behind Larkin's "An Arundel Tomb," the poem itself, and a recording of the poet reading the work can be found at www.poetryfoundation.org.

INDEX